MASTERING
INTERNATIONAL
SALES LAW

Carolina Academic Press Mastering Series
Russell Weaver, Series Editor

For other titles, please go to caplaw.com.

Mastering Environmental Law
Joel A. Mintz, Tracy D. Hester

Mastering Family Law
Janet Leach Richards

Mastering First Amendment Law
John C. Knechtle

Mastering Income Tax, Second Edition
Gail Levin Richmond, Christopher M. Pietruszkiewicz

Mastering Intellectual Property
George W. Kuney, Donna C. Looper

Mastering International Sales Law
Herbert Lazerow

Mastering Interviewing and Counseling
Kelly M. Feeley, Rebecca C. Morgan

Mastering Labor Law
Paul M. Secunda, Anne Marie Lofaso, Joseph E. Slater, Jeffrey M. Hirsch

Mastering Legal Analysis and Drafting
George W. Kuney, Donna C. Looper

Mastering Legislation, Regulation, and Statutory Interpretation, Third Edition
Linda D. Jellum

Mastering Negotiable Instruments (UCC Articles 3 and 4)
and Other Payment Systems, Second Edition
Michael D. Floyd

Mastering Negotiation
Michael R. Fowler

Mastering Partnership Taxation
Stuart Lazar

Mastering Professional Responsibility, Second Edition
Grace M. Giesel

Mastering Property Law, Revised Printing
Darryl C. Wilson, Cynthia Hawkins DeBose

Mastering Sales
Colin P. Marks, Jeremy Kidd

Mastering Secured Transactions: UCC Article 9, Third Edition
Grace M. Giesel

Mastering Tort Law, Third Edition
Russell L. Weaver, Edward C. Martin, Andrew R. Klein, Paul J. Zwier, II, John H. Bauman

Mastering Trademark and Unfair Competition Law
Lars S. Smith, Llewellyn Joseph Gibbons

Mastering Trusts and Estates
Gail Levin Richmond, Don Castleman

MASTERING INTERNATIONAL SALES LAW

Herbert Lazerow

PROFESSOR OF LAW
UNIVERSITY OF SAN DIEGO SCHOOL OF LAW

CAROLINA ACADEMIC PRESS
Durham, North Carolina

LIBRARY OF CONGRESS CATALOGING-IN-PUBLICATION DATA

Names: Lazerow, Herbert I., author.
Title: Mastering international sales law / Herbert Lazerow.
Description: Durham, North Carolina : Carolina Academic Press,
    2023. | Series: Mastering series | Includes bibliographical
    references and index.
Identifiers: LCCN 2023013796 | ISBN 9781611638998 (paperback) |
    ISBN 9781531008673 (ebook)
Subjects: LCSH: Export sales contracts. | Standardized terms of
    contract. | Sales.
Classification: LCC K1030 .L395 2023 | DDC 343.08/78--dc23/
    eng/20230509
LC record available at https://lccn.loc.gov/2023013796

Carolina Academic Press
700 Kent Street
Durham, North Carolina 27701
(919) 489-7486
www.cap-press.com

Printed in the United States of America

To Jane Frances Lazerow née Goding
wife and best friend,
who sixty years ago accepted my proposal of a lifelong partnership,
and who continually renews and reinvigorates that partnership

Contents

Preface

This book is designed for the law student studying international sales contracts and for the many lawyers who want a quick introduction to the area.

The field is of growing importance. In 1960 and 1970, imports and exports of goods constituted 6% and 8% of U.S. gross domestic product. In 1980 and 1990, that percentage rose to 17% and 15%. In the last three decades, the export + import/gdp has hovered around 20%.

The number of countries adhering to CISG now stands at 95. It includes all of the top seven trading countries (China, United States, Germany, Netherlands, Japan, Hong Kong, and France) measured in total imports and exports, accounting for 44% of all such trade. The major outliers are the UK (#8, 3%), India (#15, 2%), Indonesia (#30, .85%), Ireland (#33, .8%), and South Africa (#37, .5%). Of the top 50 trading countries, accounting for 92% of world trade, only 12% of imports or exports are done by a country that has not ratified CISG.

In the limited number of pages the publisher has allowed me, I discuss the issues important to the study of international sales contracts, as illustrated in the following casebooks:

MARTIN DAVIES & DAVID V. SNYDER, INTERNATIONAL TRANSACTIONS IN GOODS (2014).

GEORGE DAWSON & JEFFREY HARRISON, THE CONVENTION ON CONTRACTS FOR THE INTERNATIONAL SALE OF GOODS (2017)

JOSEPH F. MORRISSEY, INTERNATIONAL SALES LAW AND ARBITRATION (2018).

ELDON H. REILEY, INTERNATIONAL SALES CONTRACTS (2008).

INGEBORG SCHWENZER, CHRISTIANA FOUNTOULAKIS & MARIEL DIMSEY, INTERNATIONAL SALES LAW (3d ed. 2019).

JOHN A. SPANOGLE & PETER WINSHIP, INTERNATIONAL SALES LAW (2d ed. 2012).

Contrary to the civil law tradition, this book focuses on decided cases and the opinions of the CISG Advisory Council. While a civilist would put more emphasis on the writings of distinguished commentators, this book is intended primarily for persons from the common law tradition. In addition, my observation is that the commentators are generally in accord with each other in result (though not always in how they reach the result) and with the weight of the decided cases. This book spends little time on disputes that have neither manifested themselves in decided cases, nor seem likely to do so, despite having stirred scholarly controversy. It also does not try to present a comparative study of CISG and the Uniform Commercial Code, or any of the national legal regimes on sales law.

Readers should understand that a brief book cannot fully cover so large a subject. This book highlights important issues. For more detailed analysis, the volumes below are recommended.

The advent of the United Nations Convention on Contracts for the International Sale of Goods (1980) (called "CISG") and its sister treaty, the United Nations Convention on the Limitation Period in the International Sale of Goods (1974, with its 1980 Protocol) (called "Limitation Treaty") have loosed an avalanche of published works in many languages. For the English speaker, a good work that is more detailed than this is CLAYTON P. GILLETTE & STEVEN D. WALT, THE UN CONVENTION ON CONTRACTS FOR THE INTERNATIONAL SALE OF GOODS (2d. ed. 2016). Those interested in CISG's drafting history should consult JOHN O. HONNOLD & HARRY M. FLECHTNER, UNIFORM LAW FOR INTERNATIONAL SALES UNDER THE 1980 UNITED NATIONS CONVENTION (5th ed. 2021). Comprehensive English-language collections of authorities, including the writings of scholars (more later on why that might be important) are PETER SCHLECHTREIM & INGEBORG SCHWENZER, COMMENTARY ON THE UN CONVENTION ON THE INTERNATIONAL SALE OF GOODS (4th ed. 2016) and CHRISTOPH BRUNNER & BENJAMIN GOTTLIEB, COMMENTARY ON THE UN SALES LAW (CISG) (2019).

Article 7 of CISG calls on courts to be mindful of its international scope when interpreting CISG, and of the need for uniformity in interpretation. This has spurred UNCITRAL with its CLOUT (Case Law On UN Treaties) cases, the University of Bern with CISG-online, and Pace University's Institute of International Commercial Law, to provide many case summaries and translations into English on the internet. I have given short references to cases in the text, with full citations to all three sources, where available, in the table of citations. United States cases are cited in abbreviated fashion in the text, and in Bluebook form in the table of citations. The short references for U.S. cases use the first several words of the plaintiff's name and the level of the court; for non-U.S. cases, the short versions give the goods involved where mentioned, then employ the Distinguishing Signs Used on Vehicles in International Traffic authorized by the Vienna Convention on Road Traffic to designate the country; indicate the level of the court; and show the date of the case as YYYYMMDD.

Acknowledgments

I have been blessed with helpful research associates. Hanna Ahmad, LLM USD 2022 and a student at Eberhard Karls University in Tübingen Germany, helped clarify many questions this non-German-speaker had about the precise meaning of case opinions from Austria, Germany, and the German-speaking part of Switzerland. Allison Harvey, USD JD expected 2024, read the entire text and provided both editorial alternatives and useful substantive suggestions.

The USD law library research librarians, spearheaded by David Isom and Liz Parker, procured everything I asked for, and are responsible for obtaining the precise settings for the new Pace website and the PURLs.

The University of San Diego Law School financed the activities of my research associates and our research librarians, and also provided a generous sabbatical grant that allowed me to complete the first draft of this book. I am also grateful to the UC Law School San Francisco for providing me with work space on my sabbatical.

The number of colleagues at USD, UC Law School SF, and throughout the legal academy whom I have pestered with questions where the subject of this book seems to intersect with their specialties is legion, and all have been generous with their time in responding. More than most, I have relied on the wisdom of David Brennan and the late Bill Lawrence.

Request

No book about law is ever complete. Law is a living organism that evolves. I hope that the readers of this volume will help prepare subsequent editions by e-mailing me their suggestions at lazer@sandiego.edu.

Table of Citations

Cases

United States

Cases from outside the United States

By Goods

Apple juice concentrate, Germany Stuttgart App 12 Mar 2001, no Clout #,
CISG-online 841, https://iicl.law.pace.edu/cisg/case/germany
-oberlandesgericht-hamburg-oberlandesgericht-olg-provincial-court
-appeal-german-131 [https://perma.cc/2334-G5E2], 112, 134, 163, 169
Apple rings, Netherlands App. Hague 22 Apr 2014, Feinbäckerei Otten
GmbH & Co. v. Rhumveld Winter & Konijn B.V., no Clout #, CISG-online
2515, https://iicl.law.pace.edu/cisg/case/netherlands-hague-appellate
-court-feinb%C3%A4ckerei-otten-gmbh-co-kg-v-hdi-gerling-industrie
[https://perma.cc/WK8A-2LQ3], 85
Art books, Switzerland Zurich Trial, 10 Feb 1999, Clout 331, CISG-online
488, https://iicl.law.pace.edu/cisg/case/switzerland-handelsgericht
-commercial-court-aargau-22 [https://perma.cc/ZE2Z-FWAZ], 94, 164
Artframe mouldings, Canada Ontario Trial 31 Aug 1999, La San Giuseppe v.
Forti Moulding Ltd., Clout 341, CISG-online 433, https://iicl.law.pace.edu
/cisg/case/canada-august-31-1999-superior-court-justice-la-san-giuseppe
-v-forti-moulding-ltd [https://perma.cc/HS78-CDVC], 75, 128
Automobile, Germany Naumburg App. 27 Apr 1999, Clout 362, CISG-online
512, https://iicl.law.pace.edu/cisg/case/germany-oberlandesgericht
-hamburg-oberlandesgericht-olg-provincial-court-appeal-german-113
[https://perma.cc/GG5V-D6YQ], 79, 97, 163
Autumn textiles, Germany Oldenburg Trial 24 April 1990, Clout 7, CISG-
online 20, https://iicl.law.pace.edu/cisg/case/germany-ag-alsfeld-ag
-amtsgericht-petty-district-court-german-case-citations-do-not-15
[https://perma.cc/A3CN-J3KG], 163, 205
Bakery freezers, Belgium Ghent App. 14 Nov 2008, Volmari v. Isocab N.V., no
Clout #, CISG-online 1908, perma.cc/E9GR-3VQN, https://iicl.law.pace
.edu/cisg/case/belgium-november-14-2008-hof-van-beroep-appellate
-court-volmari-werner-v-isocab-nv [https://perma.cc/G452-C8JQ], 115
Beer, Germany Brandenburg App. 18 Nov 2008, no Clout #, CISG-online
1734, https://iicl.law.pace.edu/cisg/case/germany-oberlandesgericht
-hamburg-oberlandesgericht-olg-provincial-court-appeal-german-190
[https://perma.cc/7USN-DNN6], 127, 136
Blank CDs, Austria Sup. Ct. 12 Sep 2006, Clout 753, CISG-online 1364,
https://iicl.law.pace.edu/cisg/case/austria-ogh-oberster-gerichtshof
-supreme-court-austrian-case-citations-do-not-generally-12
[https://perma.cc/J863-SKYR], 116
Blouses, France Colmar App. 13 Nov 2002, Clout 491, CISG-online 792, iicl
.law.pace.edu/cisg/case/france-november-13-2002-cour-dappel-court
-appeals-sa-h-ma-et-aktiengesellschaft-t-k-v-sa
[https://perma.cc/ZRY5-LPFR], 117

By Country, Tribunal and Date

(For full citations and page references, see the above arrangement by goods.)

Austria

Courts of Appeal
Graz 7 Mar 2002, Pork
Graz 16 Sep 2002, Garments
Innsbruck 18 Dec 2007, Steel bars

Arbitration
Vienna Arb. Exch. Agr. Prods. 10 Dec 1997, Malting barley

Belgium

Supreme Court
19 Jun 2009, Scafom Int'l BV v. Lorraine Tubes S.A.S., Steel pipes

Courts of Appeal
Antwerp 24 Apr 2006, Gunther Lothringer GmbH v. Fepco Int'l NV,
    Construction materials
Ghent 14 Nov 2008, Volmari v. Isocab N.V., Bakery freezers

Hasselt Trial Court
19 Apr 2006, Bruggen Deuren BVBA v. Top Deuren VOF, Tulip doors

Canada

British Columbia Supreme Court
21 Aug 2003, Mansonville Plastics (B.C,) Ltd. v. Kurtz GmbH, [2003] B.C.J.
    No. 1958, Styrofoam machines

Ontario Trial Court
31 Aug 1999, La San Giuseppe v. Forti Moulding Ltd., Artframe mouldings

Quebec Trial Court
10 Jan 2020, Computer graphic cards

China (P.R.C.)

Supreme Court
7 Jul 2015, ThyssenKrupp Metallurgical Products GmbH v. Sinochem Int'l
    (Overseas) Pte. Ltd, Petroleum coke

Shanghai Court of Appeal
21 Sep 2011, Cleaning machines

Arbitration
14 Mar 1996, Sweet potatoes
18 Sep 1996, Lanthanide metal
18 Aug 1997, Vitamin C
19 Dec 1997, Steel
27 Dec 2002, Medicine packaging machine
Jan 2007, BOSS equipment
11 Mar 2021, Wood flooring

European Court of Justice

C 87/10, 9 Jun 2011, Eurosteel Europe SA v. Edil Centro Spa
C 381/08, 25 Feb 2010, Car Trim GmbH v. KeySafety Systems Srl

Finland

Court of Appeal
Helsinki, 26 Oct 2000, Powerturf carpets

France

Supreme Court
16 Jul 1998, Soc. Les Verreries de Saint Gobain SA c. Soc. Martinswerk
    GmbH, Glassware ingredients
2 Apr 2008, Logicon c. CCT Marketing Ltd., Telephone devices
17 Feb 2015, Dupirè Invicta Ind. c. Gabo Sp. Z o.o., Heating appliances

Courts of Appeal
Colmar 12 Jun 2001, Romay A.G. c. SARL Behr France, Crankcases
Colmar 13 Nov 2002, Blouses.
Grenoble 22 Feb 1995, BRI Production "Bonaventure" S.a.r.l. v. Pan African
    Export, Jeans
Grenoble 26 Apr 1995, Roque c. S.A.R.L. Holding Manin Rivière, Warehouse
Grenoble 13 Sep 1995, Caiato c. Factor France S.A., Parmesan cheese
Grenoble 23 Oct 1996, SCEA GAEC des Beauches Bernard Bruno c. Teso
    Ten Elsen GmbH & Co. KG, Industrial equipment
Grenoble, 21 Oct 1999, Calzados Magnanni c. Shoes General Int'l S.a.r.l,
    Cardin shoes

Germany

Frankfurt/Main 4 Mar 1994, Screws
Frankfurt/Main 23 May 1995, Italian Shoes
Frankfurt/Main 30 Aug 2000, Textile yarn
Hamburg 28 Feb 1997, Iron molybdenum
Karlsruhe 20 Nov 1992, Frozen chicken
Karlsruhe 25 Jun 1997, Adhesive foil
Karlsruhe 10 Dec 2003, Carpets
Karlsruhe 15 Feb 2016, Laser cutter
Koblenz 17 Sep 1993, Computer chip
Koblenz 31 Jan 1997, Acrylic blankets
Koblenz 14 Dec 2006, Wine bottles
Koblenz 21 Nov 2007, Boots
Koblenz 13 Aug 2015, Crown corks
Munich 2 Mar 1994, Coke
Munich 8 Feb 1995, Polypropylene granulate
Munich 8 Mar 1995, Metals
Munich 11 Mar 1998, Cashmere sweaters
Munich 3 Dec 1999, Window-making plant
Munich 13 Nov 2002, Organic barley
Munich 15 Sep 2004, Furniture leather
Munich 5 Mar 2008, Stolen car
Naumburg 27 Apr 1999, Automobile
Rostock 25 Sep 2002, Shrimp
Schleswig-Holstein 29 Oct 2002, Stallion
Stuttgart 12 Mar 2001, Apple juice concentrate
Stuttgart 31 Mar 2008, Repainted car
Stuttgart 21 Dec 2015, Brewing tanks

Trial Courts
Alsfeld 12 May1995, Tiles
Coburg 12 Dec 2006, Plants
Duisburg 13 Apr 2000, Pizza cartons
Frankfurt/Maine 31 Jan 1991, Italian shoes
Frankfurt/Main 11 Apr 2005, Used shoes
Freiburg 22 Aug 2002, VW Golf
Hamburg 17 Jul 2017, Can-liner maker
Hannover 1 Dec 1993, Shoes
Heidelberg 3 Jul 1992, Computer parts
Heidelberg 2 Nov 2005, Natural stone

Koblenz 12 Nov 1996, Italian Shoes
Munich 8 Feb 1995, Graphiplus program
Munich 27 Feb 2002, Rotating globes
Neubrandenburg 3 Aug 2005, Sour Cherries
Oldenburg 24 April 1990, Autumn textiles
Paderborn 25 Jun 1996, PVS granules
Regensburg 24 Sep 1998, Textile sample

Arbitration
Hamburg 21 Mar 1996, Chinese goods

Hungary

Supreme Court
25 Sep 1992, Pratt & Whitney v. Malev Hungarian Airlines, Airplane engines

Budapest Trial Court
24 Mar 1992, Adamfi Video Production GmbH v. Alkotók Studiósa
   Kisszövetkezet, German goods

Budapest Arbitration
5 Dec 1995, Containers

International Chamber of Commerce (ICC) Arbitration
ICC 6281, 26 Aug 1989, Steel bars
ICC 6653, 26 Mar 1993, Maaden Gen. For. Trade Org. for Metal & Bldg.
   Materials v. Thyssen Stahlnion GmbH, Steel bars
ICC Arb 8128/1995, Fertilizer
ICC Arb 8740/1996, Coal
ICC Arb 8786/1997, Clothing
ICC Arb 9117/1998, Mar 1998, Canada-Russia
ICC Arb 9187/1999, Coke
ICC Arb 11849 (2003), Fashion products
ICC Arb 13492/2006, Jul 2006, Iron ore

Italy

Milan Court of Appeal
20 Mar 1998, Italdecor s.a.s. v. Yiu's Ind (H.K.) Ltd., Knitted Goods
11 Dec 1998, Bielloni Castello S.p.A. v. EGO SA, Printing press

Padova Trial Court
11 Jan 2005, Savo v. La Faraona soc. coop. a.r.l., Rabbits

Arbitration
Florence 19 Apr 1994, Leather wear
Milan 4 May 2019, Prada v. Caporicci USA Corp., Alligator hatchlings

Korea, Republic of

Seoul Court of Appeal
19 Jul 2013, Taiwanese goods

Netherlands

Courts of Appeal
Hague 22 Apr 2014, Feinbäckerei Otten GmbH & Co. v. Rhumveld Winter &
    Konijn B.V., Apple rings
's-Hertogenbosch App. 11 Oct 2005, G&G Component Complementaries v.
    Errelle S.r.l., Print boards
's-Hertogenbosch 20 May 2007, Machine
's-Hertogenbosch 22 Sep 2015, Hand cleaner

Trial Courts
Arnhem 17 Jan 2007, Compensators
Gravenhage Trial 23 Apr 2003, Rynpoort Trading & Transport NV v. Meneba
    Meel Wormerveer B.V., Wheat flour
Midden-Nederland Trial 25 Mar 2015, Corporate Web Solutions Ltd. v.
    Vendorlink B.V., Software transfer
Zwolle 5 Mar 1997, CME Cooperative Maritime Etaploise S.A.C.V. v. Bos
    Fishproducts URK BV, Fish
    Arbitration
Arb. Inst. 2319, 15 Oct 2002, Rijn blend

New Zealand

Christchurch Court of Appeal
30 Jul 2010, Smallmon v. Transport Sales Ltd., [2001] NZCA 340, Trucks
    Nelson Trial Court
3 Jun 2015, Nelson Honey & Marketing Ltd. v. William Jacks & Co., Honey

Poland

Supreme Court
11 May 2007, Spoldzielnia Pracy "A" v. GmbH & Co. KG, Shoe leather
22 Oct 2014, Co. K. v. Ins. Co. E, Clothing

Russian Federation

Arbitration
Arb. 309/1993, 3 Mar 1995, Ukrainian goods
Arb. 200/1994 25 Apr 1995, Chocolate
Arb. 340/1999, 10 Feb 2000, Pakistani goods
Arb. 54/1999 24 Jan 2000-US
Arb. 406/1998 6 Jun 2000-England
Arb. 175/2003, 28 May 2004, Egyptian goods

Serbia

Arbitration
23 Jan 2008, White crystal sugar
15 Jul 2008, Milk packager

Spain

Supreme Court
28 Jan 2000, Int'le Jute Maatschappij, BV v. Marín Palomares, SL, Jute

Courts of Appeal
Barcelona 10 Jun 1997, Textile dyes
Cantabria 9 Jul 2013, VSL Middle East LLC v. Trenzas y Cables de Acero PSC
   SL
Murcia 15 Jul 2010, Krane-Maschinen-Service GmbH & Co. Handels-KG v.
   Grúas Andaluza, S.A., Crane, Steel cable
Palencia 16 Sep 2005, Simancas Ediciones S.A. v. Miracle Press Inc., Printing
   press
Pontevedra 19 Dec 2007, Kingfisher Seafoods Ltd. v. Commercial Eloy Rocio
   Mar S.L., Crabs & cockles

Valencia Trial Court
7 Jun 2003, Cherubino Valsangiacomo S.A. v. American Juice Import, Inc.,
   Grape must

Sweden

Stockholm Arbitration
5 Jun 1998, Beijing Light Auto. Co., Ltd. v. Connell Ltd. P'ship, Rail press
5 Apr 2007, Pressure sensors

Switzerland

Supreme Court
28 Oct 1998, Meat
15 Sep 2000, FCF S.A. v. Adriafil Commerciale S.r.l., Egyptian cotton
22 Dec 2000, Textile machine
13 Nov 2003, Laundry machine
17 Jul 2007, Scooters
18 May 2009, Packaging plant
17 Dec 2009, Watches
16 Jul 2012, Spinning mill
2 Apr 2015,Wire rod

Courts of Appeal
Jura 26 Jul 2007, Industrial furnace
Ticino 29 Oct 2003, Wall partitions
Valais 21 Feb 2005, CNC production plant

Trial Courts
Aargau 5 Nov 2002, Inflatable arches
Basel 21 Dec 1992, Textiles
Basel 3 Dec 1997, Urea
St Gallen 3 Jul 1997, Embroidered fabrics
St Gallen 14 Jun 2012, Fruit juice
Schaffhausen 27 Jan 2004, Model locomotives
Valais 27 Apr 2007, Hotel oven
Vaud 28 October 1997, Bulldozer
Zug 21 Oct 1999, PVC
Zurich 26 Apr 1995, Floating center
Zurich 5 Feb 1997, Sunflower oil
Zurich 10 Feb 1999, Art books
Zurich 17 Feb 2000, Software-hardware
Zurich 8 Apr 2013, Aerosol can production line
Zurich 17 Sep 2014, Wire rod

Ukraine

Ukraine Arb. 218y/2011, 23 Jan 2012, Corn

Other Authorities

References to CISG Articles

[Article, Section(s)]

1, 4.11–12, 4.21, 4.54
2, 4.35, 4.41, 4.54
3, 4.46, 4.54
4, 4.54, 4.63–64, 5.05, 6.08, 11.34
5, 4.54, 4.62
6, 2.05, 3.01, 4.52
7, 2.01, 2.04–05, 4.44, 5.06, 7.03, 9.05, 10.48
8, 2.01, 2.12, 2.15, 4.53–54, 5.03, 5.06, 5.08, 6.12, 10.31, 11.27
9, 2.01, 2.13–14, 4.53, 5.03, 5.06, 6.02–03, 6.12, 7.01
10, 4.12
11, 4.64, 5.01, 5.05–06
12, 4.53, 5.06
14, 5.03
15, 5.03–04
16, 4.71, 5.03
18, 5.04, 5.07, 10.31
19, 5.04
23, 5.01
24, 5.03
25, 8.03
26, 10.45
27, 5.04, 6.33, 10.06, 10.31, 10.45
28, 4.53, 11.13–14
29, 2.14, 4.32, 4.64, 5.05, 5.07
30, 4.32, 4.42, 4.63
31, 4.42, 6.02
32, 4.42
33, 4.42
34, 4.42, 10.02
35, 3.02, 6.11–14, 6.16, 6.20, 6.35, 6.43
36, 4.53, 6.01, 6.11
37, 6.11, 6.22, 10.02, 10.04, 10.21
38, 6.11, 6.21, 6.31, 6.34, 9.09, 10.46
39, 3.03, 6.11, 6.21, 6.31, 6.33–35, 9.09, 10.21

Series Editor's Foreword

The Carolina Academic Press Mastering Series is designed to provide you with a tool that will enable you to easily and efficiently "master" the substance and content of law school courses. Throughout the series, the focus is on quality writing that makes legal concepts understandable. As a result, the series is designed to be easy to read and is not unduly cluttered with footnotes or cites to secondary sources.

In order to facilitate student mastery of topics, the Mastering Series includes a number of pedagogical features designed to improve learning and retention. At the beginning of each chapter, you will find a "Roadmap" that tells you about the chapter and provides you with a sense of the material that you will cover. A "Checkpoint" at the end of each chapter encourages you to stop and review the key concepts, reiterating what you have learned. Throughout the book, key terms are explained and emphasized. Finally, a "Master Checklist" at the end of each book reinforces what you have learned and helps you identify any areas that need review or further study. We hope that you will enjoy studying with, and learning from, the Mastering Series.

Russell L. Weaver
PROFESSOR OF LAW & DISTINGUISHED UNIVERSITY SCHOLAR
UNIVERSITY OF LOUISVILLE, LOUIS D. BRANDEIS SCHOOL OF LAW

MASTERING
INTERNATIONAL
SALES LAW

CHAPTER 1

Introduction to International Sales Law

ROADMAP

After reading this chapter, you should understand:

- Enterprises make contracts for future performance to reduce their risks.
- Every risk reduction has a cost and foregoes an opportunity. The contract is evidence that the enterprise values the risk reduction more than the opportunity and believes the cost is reasonable.
- Seller and buyer may have a variety of identities and purposes. They may be individuals, partnerships, corporations, or any type of entity allowed by domestic law. The manufacturer needs to buy raw materials and sell finished goods. Buyer may be a manufacturer who will further change the goods, a wholesaler, a retailer, or a trader who has found an advantageous purchase and hopes to quickly arrange a profitable sale.
- The transaction may be a casual sale, but more frequently will be part of a relationship where the parties have dealt together for years.
- The parties may be dealing at arm's length or they may be companies related to each other by common ownership.
- The contract price may be huge, middling, or small.
- The contract may be a few words spoken by phone, or a book.
- Most contracts consist of standard forms drafted by lawyers for seller and buyer with negotiable terms to be filled in. Standard forms are used for valid business reasons, but are probably more important to seller as a way of controlling seller's sales agents.

- The subject matter of the contract, the goods, may be fungible goods like commodities or unique goods like artwork, but will most frequently be in between—goods that are neither unique nor primary goods.
- International sales present more risks than domestic sales. The parties are less likely to have information about each other. Seller's main risk is that he will deliver the goods but not be paid. Buyer's main risk is that he will pay but not receive the goods ordered. The irrevocable letter of credit requiring an inspection certificate is a way both parties can reduce their main risks.
- If a dispute arises that cannot be resolved by negotiation, the forum in which the dispute will be resolved may significantly affect the results. Wise parties choose a forum for dispute resolution in the contract.
- Different countries apply different choice of law rules, and will also have different substantive law rules. Choosing applicable law may reduce costs and lead to a more favorable outcome.
- One solution has been to promote uniform choice of law rules. A second has been to promote harmonization of domestic law rules for international contracts. A third has been to adopt standard contracts in industries. None has been very successful. The Convention on Contracts for the International Sale of Goods (CISG) is an attempt at an international *lex mercatoria* for the sale of goods.
- A lawyer's duty is to exercise the legal knowledge, skill, thoroughness, and preparation reasonably necessary for the representation. This requires a thorough knowledge of CISG and the ways in which it differs from domestic law.
- CISG is United States law.

A. The International Sale of Goods Transaction

§ 1.01 The Utility of Contracts

People sign contracts calling for future performance to reduce their risks.

Take the simple example of the manufacturer who knows she will need 100 widgets January 3. If she waits until January 2 to procure them, she runs two risks: (1) 100 widgets may not be available then, or (2) The price of widgets may rise substantially. By signing a contract July 1 for the delivery of 100 widgets January 2, she reduces the possibility that either of these two risks will hurt her. The risk is not eliminated. Her seller may not deliver, forcing her to spend money on lawyers to enforce her rights, which will not be reimbursed as damages absent a specific clause in the contract, or her seller may go bankrupt, leaving her with only the hope that enough assets will remain for her to recoup some of her damages in the bankruptcy.

Note that reducing risk has its downside and cost. The price of widgets may plunge between July and January, in which case buyer, having reduced her risk, is not in a position to take advantage of that price change. Every reduction in risk is a reduction in opportunity.

In addition, when approached for future delivery, a wise seller will add something to the sales price to compensate for taking the risk that the price might rise over the next six months unless seller wants the contract to reduce its risk that the price will fall. Our buyer may save the cost of storing the goods for six months, but pay a slightly higher price so that seller will take the risk (and opportunity) of price fluctuation.

Concluding a contract should mean that the person values the reduction in risk more than the loss of opportunity, and believes that the cost of the contract is as reasonable as it can be.

§ 1.02 The Players

The international sales transaction usually moves goods across an international boundary. We think the typical sale is the isolated sale of a gross of widgets from a wholesaler to a retailer. That will sometimes be the case, but not often.

Seller may be the manufacturer, a wholesaler, or a retailer; buyer could be a manufacturer who will use the product to produce another product, a wholesaler who will resell the widgets to retailers or manufacturers, or a retailer who will sell individual widgets to consumers.

Often, seller or buyer is a broker or a trader whose fondest hope is never actually to see the goods. This is especially true if the goods are fungible commodities like corn or crude oil. The broker hopes to resell them before they arrive. She purchased the goods anticipating that their price would rise. Sometimes the purchase is made in a place where buyer knows that the price of the goods is lower than the price where it will be sold. This is called arbitrage. Where the goods are not fungible commodities, the broker may have resold them almost simultaneously with purchasing them. It is likely that she would not have bought the goods without knowing that she had a client who wanted them and was willing to pay her more than her cost to get them.

A second variant is that this sale may not be a casual sale. In most of the decided cases, the parties have dealt with each other before. In real life, most international contracts are between parties who expect to continue to deal with each other. The parties may be linked by a distributorship contract where buyer is the exclusive purchaser for a territory (and so has a strong incentive to promote seller's goods in that territory), by a requirements contract whereby seller has agreed to supply all the widgets buyer needs, or by an exclusive marketing contract, under which buyer has promised to purchase all the widgets seller can produce. Seller may be part of buyer's supply chain, in which case he may be constrained to provide monthly reports to buyer on the most intimate details of his business. He may be further constrained by his position in a network of companies providing parts to major manufacturers where the relationships between the companies are tightly controlled. Alternately, while this sale may be the first between the parties, if the item being sold is complicated, the contract may evolve through a long series of mostly technical discussions between the parties. In this case, though the sale is the first transaction between them, the staffs of buyer and seller may have worked together for a considerable time.

A third variant is that buyer or seller might be individuals, or they might be corporations, partnerships, limited liability companies, associations, trusts, or comparable artificial entities created under foreign laws.

Fourth, an international sale may be a sale to a related party. A related party transaction is one where buyer and seller purport to be different parties and are different legal entities, but they are in fact the same economic interests. This occurs when one party controls the other, such as when a parent corporation sells to its wholly owned subsidiary, or where both parties are controlled by the same economic interest, such as where a holding company owns a controlling interest in both seller and buyer. In 2014, 42% by value of United States international sales of goods were between related parties.

The use of a related party may be dictated by fear of the foreign legal and regulatory system. If a foreign manufacturer sold its goods directly to retailers in the United States, it would have substantial activities here. The foreign manufacturer might be subject to United States labor laws, and within the loving grasp of the Internal Revenue Service. It would not wish to be subject to suit, especially torts suits, in the United States. American tort law has many pro-plaintiff features, such as low filing fees, contingent fee arrangements, the ability to forum shop and sometimes judge shop, extensive discovery, jury trials, strict liability, punitive damages, and a rule that usually each party is responsible for its own legal fees. To avoid these complications, the foreign corporation does no business in the United States. Instead it establishes a United States subsidiary to which it sells its goods. The United States subsidiary is the distributor for the United States (and often for Canada also). The result is that if the U.S. operation fails, it does not drag the foreign parent into bankruptcy with it. Related party sales invoke different income tax considerations than arm's length sales. They also have different risk factors.

Finally, in examining the decided cases, the contract size can vary considerably. Some contracts call for payment in the millions of dollars, while others are so small that you wonder how the aggrieved party ever found a lawyer willing to bring suit. In most decided cases, the amount in controversy is between $100,000 and $1 million, though the addition of interest can substantially raise the stakes in litigation.

§1.03 The Contract

The contract of sale may be almost nonexistent, or it may be a book. Generally, businesses in continental Europe are likely to have short contracts, with the missing details filled in by suppletive law. Americans prefer to insert the details in the contract.

The contract may be concluded in person, by phone or its functional equivalents, by telex, fax, or e-mail, or it may be finalized by completing seller's or buyer's form on their website.

The contract may specify where or when each step in its performance is to take place or not. As with an order placed on Amazon.com, neither buyer nor seller might know before the order is placed from which of seller's many fulfillment centers the order will be sent.

The contract may be individually negotiated and drafted. More likely, seller will have a form contract, with blanks to fill in the details over which there is normally negotiation, such as the items sold, the quantity, the delivery date, and the price. Form contracts usually contain general or standard conditions.

Form contracts probably originated with a common agency problem: the interests of the salespeople are not perfectly aligned with the interests of the firm owners. Most salespeople work either strictly on commission, or on a combination of salary and commission. The more they sell, the more they earn. Many salespeople will promise anything to make the sale. For the owners, the profit is more important than the amount of gross sales. When the salesperson has promised more than the owner is prepared to deliver at the specified price, the owner is faced with the dilemma of whether he will redeem the salesperson's unauthorized promises and keep the customer's goodwill while sacrificing anticipated profit, or whether he will disavow his salesperson's promise. The solution to this is the form contract, which usually states that the salesperson is not authorized to deviate from its terms.

In addition, there are efficiencies in having a uniform contract for all of a firm's sales because that reduces negotiating costs.

Then enters the legal department. As long as legal is drafting a contract to apply to all sales, it will make the terms as favorable to seller as possible. Thus, a device designed to control the owner's salespeople morphs into a device that is decidedly unfair to buyer.

Buyers also have their own forms. While the need to control salespeople is not present and the need to control purchasing agents is less pressing because they usually do not work on commission, buyers have the same desire for cost savings that result from having identical terms applied to all purchases and the same desire to have a contract favorable to them.

Another source of form contracts is the industry association. It is common for companies in the same business to form industry associations to conduct lobbying and engage in other activities benefiting their members. Industry associations will often draft purchase or sales contracts that they recommend to their members.

Whatever the reason, it is common to find a transaction governed by forms generated by both buyer and seller that contain inconsistent terms in their printed versions. Whether the recipients of those forms ever read anything except the terms that are handwritten or typed rather than printed is doubtful.

§ 1.04 The Goods

International sales often concern fungible goods in bulk. Raw materials tend to be graded and sold by volume. Each barrel of West Texas Intermediate crude oil has identical content to every other barrel (we hope), and a typical sale will involve many barrels.

Occasionally, an international sale will involve something unique. When a Chinese art dealer buys a Han Gan (706–783) scroll painting from a New York gallery, there is no equivalent good available.

The sale may be of standard products like cars, but they are not fungible. Each car has its own color and accessories.

Yet another sale might be of products manufactured specifically for the sale, often from designs supplied by buyer.

§ 1.05 The Risks

International sales often present risks not present with domestic sales.

One risk element is that the parties are less likely to know each other. While they may be as close as the few miles separating San Diego from Tijuana, Mexico, one typically deals with longer distances in international sales. Not only are the parties less likely to know each other, they are less likely to have information about each other. There may be no professional gossip about whether the quality of seller's goods is reliable, or whether his deliveries are timely. Foreign laws or practices may make it impossible to obtain a reliable assessment of buyer's creditworthiness.

Seller's main risk is that he will ship the goods but not be paid. Buyer's main risk is that he will pay, but not receive the goods he has ordered. Both risks appear in domestic sales, but they are exacerbated by distance and culture in international sales. International sales usually involve transporting the goods long distances, often by sea and other forms of carriers, so the time between contracting and arrival may be longer than in a domestic sale. International sales often involve the payment of customs duties and the hiring of customs brokers to move goods expeditiously through customs. If buyer defaults, seller may try to retake possession of the goods, but must do so in a foreign legal system where seller is likely to lack any marketing contacts or expertise that would help seller realize significant sums from reselling the goods.

Seller could, in order to make the sale, offer buyer trade credit. Seller ships the goods to buyer with an invoice calling for payment within a fixed time and providing a discount for payment within 30 days. This takes care of buyer's risk because she can examine the goods before paying, but seller remains at risk.

Alternately, seller could demand cash in advance. Today this will usually involve the electronic transfer of funds from buyer's account to seller's. This takes care of seller's risk because he has been paid, but buyer remains at risk and may be unwilling to trust seller.

An intermediate possibility is to require a cash deposit close to seller's cost before seller begins manufacturing or shipping the goods.

One way seller reduces his risk is by negotiating for an irrevocable letter of credit confirmed by seller's bank. The letter of credit is a promise by buyer's bank to pay an agreed sum to seller's bank on the presentation of agreed documents within a fixed period. Seller's bank in turn promises to pay seller that sum on presentation of the same documents. While seller may not know much about buyer, seller has a relationship with and trusts the credit of seller's bank. Seller's bank has an international relationship with buyer's bank, and assumes that buyer's bank values its reputation in international banking circles, so is unlikely to renege on its written promise to pay. Having removed the twin worries of inability to pay and unwillingness to pay, seller is happy with the deal.

The documents required by the letter of credit also satisfy buyer's risk. Requiring a negotiable bill of lading enables buyer to obtain the packages or containers when they arrive, or to transfer the bill of lading to another person while the goods are still at sea. The bill of lading issued by the carrier assures buyer that something has been shipped. Requiring a commercial invoice and a certificate of origin permits buyer to clear the goods through customs when they arrive. However, the bill of lading will probably be stamped "shipper's load and count" or "said to contain" (STC), indicating that the carrier is not certifying the contents of the boxes. Requiring an inspection certificate from a reliable third party assures buyer that the goods are of the quality and quantity required by the contract. Whether the goods will be insured may also be prescribed by contract.

Buyer and seller also face currency risks. Each would like to have the price denominated in its own currency. For seller, that is the currency in which its expenses are likely incurred. For buyer, it is the currency it uses to calculate its likely profit. Seller will normally specify its currency in its offer. Buyer may specify its currency in its acceptance. One party's currency will prevail, usually seller's. If buyer wishes to be protected from the risk of currency fluctuations, it will either buy seller's currency today, or buy a futures contract for delivery of the appropriate amount of currency when it is time to make payment.

While one speaks blithely about eliminating or minimizing risks, neither the letter of credit, the inspection certificate, the insurance policy, or the purchase of foreign currency is free. Each reduction in risk has a cost. Whether that cost will ultimately be borne by seller or buyer will depend on their relative bargaining strengths.

There are other risks of international sales. A country may suddenly introduce a tariff on the import of goods, or prohibit the import altogether. A nation may change its health rules or its product requirements. Countries that were formerly close trading partners may go to war, creating ramifications for enterprises in other countries. A country worried about its diminishing supply of foreign exchange may prohibit payments unless made in the national currency.

B. Uncertainty: The Reason for a Uniform Law on International Sales

§1.11 Different Fora Can Lead to Different Results

Uncertainty is the great enemy of successful business. Parties will spend considerable sums (as illustrated above) to reduce uncertainty.

One of the sources of uncertainty is uncertainty about where any dispute that arises under the contract will be resolved. The uncertainty of the forum can result in uncertainty of time, cost, publicity, and result.

Most international sales disputes are resolved by negotiation between the parties, especially when they involve parties with a continuing relationship. The disputes that go to litigation are a small minority of all disputes. They are the disputes about which lawyers worry and draft contract clauses, and usually occur when the relationship between the parties breaks down. You don't litigate while the marriage is going well; you litigate when divorce is pending. So while the litigated cases may provide an accurate look at international sales relationships on the rocks, they do not convey an accurate picture of smoothly running international sales relationships.

A dispute that cannot be resolved by the parties (even with the aid of mediation) must be resolved by a third party. That third party could be a court or it could be an arbitrator. If the parties do not agree to arbitration in writing, the dispute will be resolved by a court. Every country in the world has a court system, and many countries have multiple systems. Many cities in the world have arbitration facilities, or the parties may establish *ad hoc* arbitration.

Given the choice, most parties to international sales disputes would prefer to litigate or arbitrate the dispute at home, quickly, inexpensively, and in their own language. Litigation at home is often not possible because the local court will not have jurisdiction over the foreign defendant. Jurisdiction over foreign defendants has become more difficult to establish in the United States, due to narrowing constitutional standards for personal jurisdiction, *Daimler*, US Sup. Ct, and constitutional decisions that render quasi-in-rem jurisdiction based solely on the location of property unrelated to the cause of action difficult if not impossible to obtain. *Shaffer*, US Sup. Ct. While plaintiffs are often displeased to need to litigate in defendant's home court, defendants doing business with European Union concerns are often surprised that they can be sued in the place the contract designates for performance even though they have never set foot there. Regulation 1215/2012, arts. 2, 3, 5(1), 23(1). The solution to this uncertainty is to have the contract provide for an exclusive forum in which disputes are to be decided, which constitutes the voluntary submission of the foreign party to the jurisdiction (and venue) of the court or arbitrator.

Since the success of one party in locating dispute resolution at home means that the other party will be operating abroad, it is often not possible to achieve agreement that disputes will be resolved in the jurisdiction of one of the parties. An alternative is to agree on a neutral place, not because it is either party's first choice, but because it is the least uncomfortable choice that the parties can agree on.

Speed in resolution and cost may also be factors. It used to be that arbitration was much faster and much less expensive than litigation. Today, arbitration has become much more complicated, and the time and expense involved have increased. One can restore speed and low cost to arbitration by providing for a sole arbitrator named in advance, no discovery, time limits for the procedure, no written opinion, and the decision a choice between the last offers of the parties. Such a procedure is probably appropriate in a continuous relationship with small disputes, but it sacrifices other interests that the parties may value. Besides, small disputes between businesspeople are likely to be negotiated out rather than resulting in litigation.

The speed with which cases are processed varies from one legal system to another. Likewise, lawyers charge different amounts in different countries.

Most courts require that all documents be translated into the local language. This involves additional expense, and translations do not always capture the exact sense of the original. While some arbitration rules require translation, the parties can set their own language rules for an independent arbitration.

The forum for dispute resolution may significantly affect the outcome. Different fora will have different procedural rules, thereby affecting the willingness of a party to have the dispute resolved there. A jurisdiction with high filing fees requires a significant advanced commitment of capital. A jurisdiction that bans contingent fee arrangements for lawyers means that a losing plaintiff will be required to compensate its lawyers. A jurisdiction that requires that the losing party pay the winning party's legal fees (as well as its own) magnifies the risk of the litigation. A jurisdiction that permits little discovery requires that a plaintiff prove its case without recourse to defendant's records. A jurisdiction that permits class actions may make bringing together plaintiffs who have small claims worthwhile.

None of this is significant for well-advised parties to international sales contracts. Within broad limits, the parties can choose the forum in which their disputes are to be resolved if they can agree on it and if the provisions are carefully drafted. Treaties help smooth the validity of the parties' choices and the enforceability of the results of those choices. *Hague Conf. Conv. Court Choice; UN Conv. Arbitration.*

The important point is that a choice of forum eliminates surprise and reduces costs of resolving the dispute. It also eliminates the possibility, after the dispute has arisen, of the plaintiff choosing the forum that he believes is most advantageous to him.

§ 1.12 Different Countries Have Different Choice of Law and Substantive Legal Provisions

Different countries have different substantive legal provisions. Buyer's law may hold seller liable for his actions, while seller's law provides no liability. Whether the decision-maker will apply buyer's law, seller's law, or the law of some third country is the province of a legal area called choice of law. While choice of law rules used to provide some measure of certainty in some fields, they never provided certainty in contracts. The choice of law for a contract may be buyer's or seller's home country, principal place of business, place of business most closely related to the contract, or the place where the contract was negotiated, the place where the contract was signed, the place of its most significant performance (where is that? the place of manufacture, the place of delivery, the place of ultimate use, the place of payment?), or the place where the breach was alleged to have occurred. If those possible results under traditional choice of law rules were not enough, modern theories have introduced the "most significant relationship" rule and the "governmental interests" rule. Furthermore, a different choice of law might need to be made for each issue in a dispute, raising the indeterminacy of the choice of law exponentially. *Rest. 2d Conflicts § 188.* While choice of law in the European Union is less uncertain because it gives primacy to seller's law, it still provides the opportunity for other law if it is clear that the contract is more closely connected to another country. *Regulation (EC) No. 593/2008, arts.* 4(1)(a), 4(3).

One solution is for the parties to choose governing law in their sales contract. That choice will usually be respected, though some countries require a connection between the law chosen and the transaction. *UCC § 1-301(b)* requires an "appropriate relation" to the state, and some courts have said that it must be "the most appropriate relation." *Boudreau*, US N.C. Sup. Ct. Most rules prohibit the parties from displacing mandatory laws of the jurisdiction (which usually include consumer protection laws) and from the application of laws that violate the public policy of the jurisdiction. *Inter-American Convention* arts. 11 & 18.

Selecting arbitration for dispute resolution does not solve this problem. The arbitrator still needs to decide what law to apply, and most arbitration rules provide no certain answer.

Reaching agreement on governing law may be difficult because neither party wants to designate the other party's law as controlling. In addition, the domestic law chosen may not take appropriate account of the international nature of the international sales transaction.

Specifying a choice of law can be as hazardous as specifying a choice of forum. When the contract is signed, neither party knows whether it will be plaintiff or defendant, or what the subject matter of the dispute will be. Specifying the law has the advantage of eliminating both the argument about which country's choice of law rules to use in determining the choice of law, and the argument about what law would be chosen by those rules. This should reduce the cost of dispute resolution.

§1.13 Alternate Solutions

One solution to this problem might be the adoption by many countries of uniform choice of law rules. This solution has been attempted. It has not been successful. Conventions have been drafted but have not attracted many signatories. The most successful effort has been the imposition of uniform choice of law rules on the Member States of the European Union. *Regulation (EC) No. 593/2008.*

A second potential solution is the unification of the contract law of most of the world. Many eminent scholars have participated in the exercise of drafting perfect contract rules based on the "best" rules in existing systems, but none of these systems have ever been adopted. Countries often see no reason to revise their domestic contract law to accommodate the problems of international contracting.

A third potential solution is the adoption of standard contracts for general use in a particular industry. These contracts tend to be very detailed and very specific to the perceived dispute problems in the industry affected. They operate by providing specific contract rules that displace the necessity for the application of law. Such contracts have had some success in discrete industries, but have no application in industries where they have not been drafted or in cross-industry disputes.

The fourth potential solution, and the one that occupies much of the rest of this book, is the adoption of uniform rules for international sales contracts. This effort began with the theory that there is in fact a "law merchant," or *lex mercatoria*, that has evolved to govern international contracts through the accumulation of international arbitration awards. The work was carried further by drafted conventions, which culminated in the United Nations Vienna Convention on Contracts for the International Sale of Goods (CISG) (1980) and the United Nations Convention on the Limitation Period in the International Sale of Goods (1974).

C. The United States Lawyer's Responsibility for CISG

§1.21 Professional Responsibility and CISG

An American lawyer has a duty to her client to exercise "the legal knowledge, skill, thoroughness and preparation reasonably necessary for the representation" of her client according to ABA Model Rule 1.1. A lawyer who negotiates an international contract, or who attempts to resolve a dispute involving one, needs to be aware of when CISG applies, what its provisions are, how they might affect her client, and what to do about it. A lawyer who advises a client about a purely domestic sale might well advise that client that a different set of rules may apply to an international sale, and that the lawyer should be consulted again should a later sale have international elements.

One of the simplest examples is the fact that CISG is United States law. Contrary to what some courts have suggested, it is not foreign law or international law, nor is its application at the option of one party to a contract, as suggested in *Seven Seas Int'l*, US Trial. It does not invoke Fed. Rul. Civ. Proc. 44.1. Because CISG is United States law, it automatically applies if its scope rules are satisfied, *BP Oil*, US App. Expert testimony about its meaning is not admissible. *Semi-Materials*, US Trial.

The sanction for violation of Rule 1.1 is not trivial. It may result in the suspension or revocation of the lawyer's license to practice law. It may also result in substantial malpractice liability.

CHECKPOINTS

You should have learned that:

- Enterprises make contracts for future performance to reduce their risks.

- Every risk reduction has a cost and foregoes an opportunity. The contract is evidence that the enterprise values the risk reduction more than the opportunity and believes the cost is reasonable.

- Seller and buyer may have a variety of identities and purposes. They may be individuals, partnerships, corporations, or any type of entity allowed by domestic law. The manufacturer needs to buy raw materials and sell finished goods. Buyer may be a manufacturer who will further change the goods, a wholesaler, a retailer, or a trader who has found an advantageous purchase and hopes to quickly arrange a profitable sale.

- The transaction may be a casual sale, but more frequently will be part of a relationship where the parties have dealt together for years.

- The parties may be dealing at arm's length or they may be companies related to each other by common ownership.

- The contract price may be huge, middling, or small.

- The contract may be a few words spoken by phone, or a book.

- Most contracts consist of standard forms drafted by lawyers for seller and buyer with negotiable terms to be filled in. Standard forms are used for valid business reasons, but are probably more important to seller as a way of controlling seller's sales agents.

- The subject matter of the contract, the goods, may be fungible goods like commodities or unique goods like artwork, but will most frequently be in between—goods that are neither unique nor primary goods.

- International sales present more risks than domestic sales. The parties are less likely to have information about each other. Seller's main risk is that he will deliver the goods but not be paid. Buyer's main risk is that he will pay but not receive the goods ordered. The irrevocable letter of credit requiring an inspection certificate is a way both parties can reduce their main risks.

- If a dispute arises that cannot be resolved by negotiation, the forum in which the dispute will be resolved may significantly affect the results. Wise parties choose a forum for dispute resolution in the contract.

- Different countries apply different choice of law rules, and will also have different substantive law rules. Choosing applicable law may reduce costs and lead to a more favorable outcome.

- One solution has been to promote uniform choice of law rules. A second has been to promote harmonization of domestic law rules for international contracts. A third has been to adopt standard contracts in industries. None has been very successful. The Convention on Contracts for the International Sale of Goods (CISG) is an attempt at an international *lex mercatoria* for the sale of goods.

- A lawyer's duty is to exercise the legal knowledge, skill, thoroughness, and preparation reasonably necessary for the representation. This requires a thorough knowledge of CISG and the ways in which it differs from domestic law.

- CISG is United States law.

CHAPTER 2

Interpretation

ROADMAP

After reading this chapter, you should understand:

- In interpreting CISG, it is important to know differences in law drafting and interpretation between common law and civil law countries.

- Civil law statutes are short and general. They leave much room for "the appreciation of the judge."

- In interpreting statutes, civil law states use general principles to supply content for more specific provisions.

- A prime source of law is the writing of distinguished professors in civil law systems.

- Civil law systems do not consider previous judicial opinions to be sources of law.

- If previous judicial opinions are considered, no distinction is made there between holding and dictum.

- CISG specifies that its international character is to be considered in its interpretation. This calls for consideration of different business practices as well as different legal systems.

- CISG calls for uniformity of its interpretation across national boundaries. Difficult because of lack of resources, this nonetheless requires courts to consider interpretations made in other countries.

- CISG asks that in choosing between interpretations of it, consideration be given to whether one interpretation will be more conducive to encouraging good faith in international sales.

- CISG states that where a matter is not specifically dictated by CISG, but is generally covered by it, the matter should be decided by general principles of CISG. There is much disagreement on the substance of those general principles.

- When there is no specific CISG provision and no general principle of CISG can resolve the case, recourse should be had to the domestic law chosen by the parties or by the choice of law principles of the forum.

- CISG also contains rules for determining the intent of the parties to the contract. Intent can be gleaned from the parties' statements or actions, from their prior dealings, or from trade custom.

- The subjective intent of a party's words or conduct will govern if the other party should have understood them.

- If there is no reason for the other party to understand words or conduct, they will be interpreted objectively in accord with what a reasonable person in the position of the other party would have understood, considering all the facts and circumstances surrounding the case.

- This broad scope for evidence of intent means that the U.S. parol evidence rule often cannot be invoked to limit the introduction of evidence of intent. Parties can invoke the parol evidence rule if they make that clear in their contract.

- In the absence of evidence to the contrary, the parties are assumed to incorporate any customs in the international trade in the goods involved into their contract. This requires proof both of the custom and of the fact that it is widely known and observed in the particular international trade.

- Dealings of the parties from prior similar contracts can be used to determine their intent on this contract. The prior dealings must be consistent, relevant to the question at hand, and under similar circumstances.

- Dealings of the parties in administering the contract in dispute may also provide evidence of the contract's meaning.

- In a conflict between trade custom and dealings of the parties, dealings of the parties should prevail as more accurately demonstrating the intent of the parties.

A. Interpretation of CISG

§2.01 Civil Law and Common Law Drafting and Canons of Interpretation

The common law, derived from the law of England, and the civil law, whose origins lie in ancient Rome, have developed different styles of legislation and legislative interpretation, as well as different views of precedent. While it is hazardous to lump together the legal traditions of very different countries, a few generalizations would not be out of line.

In common law countries, statutes tend to be long and detailed. They often follow a protracted, case-by-case, common law development, either to clarify an area or to negate the direction in which a line of cases is moving. There is no expectation that a statute will be consistent with prior law, though one of the canons of construction is that if a statute intends to change existing law, that must be clearly spelled out.

One method of drafting common law statutes whose major impact is on private parties is to assemble representatives of the interested parties and to ask them to agree on a draft law. This has the advantage of assuring that the legislation crafted by the parties is a compromise acceptable to them, though not necessarily philosophically consistent.

One result of this is the rule of construction that the specific parts of the statute prevail over the more general statements.

Sources of law for statutory interpretation tend to include the legislative history, cases previously decided under the law, and often cases decided under analogous laws. The writings of experts are not officially considered sources of law, though courts sometimes cite them in their opinions.

In deciding on the weight to be accorded previous judicial interpretations, a distinction is made between holdings necessary to the result in the case, and dictum, statements of legal principles not necessary to resolve the case. This distinction is justified for the same reason that the opinions of scholars are given little weight—nothing in the real world depends on that opinion.

In civil law countries, statutes tend to be short and general. They will usually be drafted by civil servants in the ministry with jurisdiction over the subject matter of the law. A leading professor in the field will be asked to review the law to assure that it is philosophically consistent with the related body of law.

A principle of interpretation is that the general thrust of the law will be used to interpret the meaning of its specific provisions.

As to sources of the law for interpretation, there is seldom much legislative history in civil law countries, though that may vary. The principal source for interpreting the law is the writing of distinguished academics, such as this book. In some countries, a court would not purport to rely on a previous judicial opinion; in others there may be as many citations to judicial decisions as there are to distinguished writers, especially in CISG cases. No distinction is made between holding and dictum, and courts in civil law countries seem obliged to comment on every aspect of the case, even those that are not in dispute between the parties. It is revelatory that a major treatise on CISG by distinguished continental scholars does not contain a table of cases to direct the reader to the discussion of the many cases it cites. In some countries, there seems to be no distinction between the deference accorded an opinion of a trial court and that of an appellate or supreme court. Civil law judges often recur to the words of the legislation, even though it is clear to a common lawyer that the case is being litigated because the words are not dispositive.

Cases decided in civil law countries tend to present different forms of opinions than those in common law countries. Here there are also national differences, exemplified by the French judicial formula that sets forth premise and conclusion but omits the reasoning that ties premise and conclusion together. Generally, civil law cases provide a much less complete statement of the facts, and in Austria, Germany, and parts of Switzerland, the courts are assiduous in disguising the facts so that the reader cannot guess the identity of the litigants. Common law cases usually focus on the matters in dispute, while civil law cases will comment on matters about which the parties agree. Civil law cases are less likely to provide reasoning, and much more likely to look at legal rules as positive statements rather than as instruments to achieve purposes that need to be considered in interpreting them.

There are other differences between common law and civil law systems. At common law, evidence is presented orally. Civil law evidence is placed into written form by a judicial officer. A civil law court of appeal does not hesitate to correct a fact determination because it has the same opportunity to examine the file as the trial judges had. Fact decisions may be made by juries in common law countries. This necessitates rules of evidence to assure fair decisionmaking. Factfinding in civil law contracts cases will be conducted by a panel of three professional judges.

It is thus clear that lawyers and judges trained in common law are likely to approach interpretation of CISG very differently from lawyers and judges trained in civil law. A common lawyer needs to remember the important role that arts. 7–9, as general provisions, are likely to play in CISG cases.

Despite some of these differences, this book focuses on judicial decisions interpreting CISG, of which there are now many. The scholarly output on CISG has far surpassed industrial strength. While there are some outliers, I find that most thoughtful commentators adhere closely to the cases. It is probably not useful for a transaction planner or a litigator to note that of 13 scholars consulted, eight endorsed one view while five endorsed its opposite.

CISG provides its own interpretive standards. Art. 7 lays down five rules for interpreting CISG. Regard is to be had to: (1) its international character, (2) the need to promote uniformity of application and (3) the need to promote the observance of good faith in international trade. Where questions about matters covered by CISG are not expressly settled, (4) they are to be settled under general principles of CISG. It is only where there are no general principles of CISG applicable that one turns (5) to the law chosen by choice of law doctrine.

§2.02 International Character

In interpreting CISG, it must be borne in mind that its provisions must be applied to contracts between merchants operating in countries where both the background law and business customs are very different. In addition to countries following common law and civil law systems, CISG has been adopted in countries following socialist principles, like Russia and China, and countries whose systems are based on Islamic law, like Egypt or Lebanon. Even within Europe, there are significant differences in business customs between Latin countries and Germanic nations, just as customs differ in the Baltics from those in the Balkans. Add the fact that the treaty has been ratified by countries in South America, Asia, and even a few in Africa, and it is easy to see the variety of business customs that must be accommodated in determining, for instance, what a reasonable time might be.

§2.03 Uniformity

Uniformity of interpretation is a goal, though one not easy to achieve.

The treaty is done in six languages—Arabic, Chinese, English, French, Russian, and Spanish—all of which are official. Those languages do not translate precisely into each other. For working purposes, there are also translations into other languages. In *Laundry machine*, CH Sup. Ct. 20031113, the unofficial German translation gave way to the official languages and, if the official languages conflicted, priority was to be given to the working languages of CISG's drafting, primarily English and secondarily French.

Judgments are rendered in each of the member states in the local language. The text of these judgments may be readily available in some countries, but not in others. Judges in other countries may be unable to read the language in which a judgment is written, and there may no translation available. With all these difficulties, the treaty asks lawyers and judges to do their best to be informed about CISG interpretations worldwide and to seek uniform interpretations of its provisions. Probably because of the common law reliance on precedent, U.S. lawyers and courts have been among the worst in the world in not examining opinions from other countries interpreting CISG. They often recite that a CISG provision is "like" a domestic law provision (even when it is not), and proceed to interpret the CISG provision as though it were domestic law. E.g., *Raw Materials*, US Trial. This is called the "homeward trend," and is to be discouraged. The watchword is that CISG is to be interpreted "autonomously." Terms in CISG should not be interpreted by using provisions of domestic law. That is difficult for courts, especially where CISG uses the same term as domestic law.

This does not mean that domestic law is irrelevant. Finding that a term in domestic law on a question has been interpreted in the same way in a number of different countries when there is scant interpretation of the CISG term may indicate that the agreed-upon interpretation is the most efficient default rule.

Uniformity is particularly difficult to achieve because there is no Supreme Court of CISG to provide authoritative interpretations. Lacking a centralized authority, a group of CISG experts in 2001 formed a voluntary, self-perpetuating association to provide advice on difficult interpretive questions in CISG, called the CISG Advisory Council, at cisgac.com. Courts frequently cite Advisory Council opinions favorably.

No previous decision is considered binding. A case is only as persuasive as its reasoning, and judicial style in some countries omits the reasoning. Nonetheless, foreign cases should be considered and specifically referenced. In the U.S., this is easy because more cases have been translated or abstracted in English than in any other language.

A vexing question has been the allocation of the burden of proof. Many litigants have lost because one party did not prove its case. Courts have generally noted that CISG says little about procedure or burden of proof. They have posited that the party who invokes a right bears the burden of proving he is entitled to that right, while the other party bears the burden of proving non-entitlement. *Egyptian cotton*, CH Sup. Ct. 20000915. This solution is easier to state than to apply in some cases, and is not convincingly authorized by CISG, either specifically or as a general principle. Burden of proof is further discussed in Chapter 12.

§2.04 Good Faith

CISG provides the use of good faith only as a means of interpreting its provisions. While some courts have read the provision as requiring the observance of good faith in all contracts governed by CISG, e.g., *Cleaning machines*, CHN App 20110921; *Wheat flour*, NL Trial 20050119; *Furniture leather*, D App 20040915, this is an incorrect interpretation. Good faith is considered only where there are two possible interpretations of a provision of CISG, one of which is more likely to encourage the observance of good faith than another. For instance, in a case where the question was whether a party would be bound by the other party's standard terms that were never supplied, the court decided that it would better promote good faith to require that standard terms be disclosed in order to be binding. *Sour cherries*, D Trial 20050803. While there is no general requirement of good faith, some aspects of good faith, such as acting reasonably or providing prompt notice, may be general principles of CISG, to be invoked under art. 7(2) where CISG governs the subject but provides no specific rule. The notification requirement could have provided the rationale in *Sour cherries* rather than good faith. The astute litigant will be aware that many courts have said that parties must execute their contracts in good faith, e.g., *Military shoe leather*, PL Sup. Ct. 20070511, but there is no textual support for a pure good faith requirement. Even if a general good faith requirement is imported, there remains the question of what it requires.

§2.05 General Principles of CISG

Where a subject is covered by CISG but a specific resolution does not appear, the matter should be resolved using CISG's general principles. An example is the award of interest on unpaid amounts, which article 78 requires. There is no specification of what constitutes an unpaid amount, when interest begins, whether it is simple or compound, and if compound, how often, and the rate at which it is to be charged. These matters may or may not be resolved using the general principles of CISG.

Considerable disagreement exists about what those general principles might be. It is clear that two such general principles are party autonomy and full compensation for loss resulting from contract breach. The reason for the reference to general principles is to have an autonomous CISG that does not rely on analogies to any local rule for its enunciation. Leaning on national rules will inevitably lead to inconsistent rulings. CISG draftsmen intentionally often chose terms that do not appear in any national law to discourage the use of local law as a tool in interpretation. That tactic has not always been successful, as we shall see when we discuss art. 79.

One problem is that art. 7 is no help when two general principles of CISG collide.

Another problem is that the two general principles mentioned above—party autonomy and full compensation for losses—are mentioned specifically in CISG arts. 6 and 74. Still, it is unclear whether either is supposed to do more work than the text of each of those articles provides. The same is true of many other suggested general principles, such as good faith, mutual cooperation, exchanging information, freedom from form requirements, mitigation of damages, or reasonableness. I believe that general principles of CISG should be used quite sparingly to cabin judicial discretion.

§2.06 Choice of Law

The final rule for interpretation applies when there is no applicable general rule of CISG. There, recourse is to the choice of law embedded in the parties' contract or, if there is none, national law indicated by the forum's choice of law rules. This might lead to forum shopping when there are multiple jurisdictions in which defendant can be sued. The best result occurs when each potential jurisdiction has a choice of law rule that points to the law of the same country. United States choice of law rules for contracts are so uncertain that it is often difficult to predict to which jurisdiction's law the court will turn. European law creates a presumption in favor of seller's law. In *Usinor Industeel*, US Trial, seller had retained title pending payment, but buyer, who thereafter became insolvent, had given a security interest in the property to a bank as security for a loan. The bank first recorded its lien under the UCC. The court failed to find that CISG governed specifically. It did not search for CISG general principles, but looked at U.S. choice of law provisions and found that they favored U.S. law. Seller lost because, not knowing U.S. rules about security interests, it failed to record its interest. The result of such a case is that a seller who is not paid in advance must determine the local law of each jurisdiction to which it ships goods to determine how seller can be protected, as seller did in *Doolim Corp. v. R. Doll*, US Trial. An opposite rule would require a potential lender to determine how a person in possession acquired the goods proposed to be used as security. This would slow the financing processes in a transaction where the lender had no reason to believe that an international transaction was involved.

B. Interpretation of the Contract

§2.11 Intent of the Parties

The primary rule for interpreting the contract is to ascertain and effectuate the intent of the parties. This is entirely consistent with the general CISG principle of the parties' autonomy. Discovering party intent is done by looking at the parties' expressions and actions against the background of their contract. Trade custom and the previous dealings of the parties, if they exist, can supply the presumed intent of the parties.

§2.12 Interpreting Words or Action

CISG provides that the subjective intent of a party's words or actions govern if the other party understands them. Normally, a contract to sell a Rolls-Royce requires the delivery of a Rolls-Royce. If the speaker has a special meaning that the listener understands, that special meaning will govern. Where the speaker owns a Volkswagen that he calls his Rolls-Royce and the listener knows this, a statement that he will sell his Rolls-Royce to the listener for a price more appropriate to a Volkswagen will be interpreted to mean the sale of the Volkswagen. Art. 8(1). Evidence of the speaker's meaning and the listener's understanding may even trump a subsequent writing if sufficiently persuasive. In *MCC-Marble Ceramic*, US App, the lower court should have considered the testimony of parties that the contract was formed orally and the writing was intended to memorialize it, but not intended to include seller's general conditions on the form used. Such cases do not arise frequently, whether because speakers seldom have special meanings, or because listeners usually have no reason to know them. Art. 8(1) will also apply where the term to be construed has only one possible meaning and there is no evidence of any special meaning used by the speaker. However, in that case, the same result is secured by art. 8(2) because that sole meaning can only be the objective meaning.

In most cases, the words or actions of the parties are interpreted according to the meaning an objective observer would give to them. Art. 8(2); *MCC-Marble Ceramic*, US App. This method of interpretation looks to the understanding a reasonable person in the situation of the hearer would have. Where seller of bowling alleys was obligated to repurchase them except where buyer has "otherwise disposed of them," the question was whether a lease of the alleys otherwise disposed of the alleys. The court held that because the phrase could have a number of different meanings, the court could not be sure that seller understood the phrase in the same way that buyer meant it. Consequently, art. 8(1) could not be used. Looking to art. 8(2)'s objective meaning, the court should have asked what the phrase should have meant to someone in the position of the reader. Instead it employed the technique of construing the phrase most strictly against the draftsman after finding that putting the alleys in the hands of a third person by a lease might cause the alleys to deteriorate more rapidly than if they remained subject to buyer's control. *Bowling alleys*, D Sup. Ct. 20140528.

Sometimes the parties themselves provide evidence of their objective intent. In *Hanwha*, US Trial, each party wrote to the other that there would be no contract unless the other agreed to its choice of law by a signed writing. The court had no difficulty in finding that since they never agreed in writing (and because neither side performed), there was no contract. Where a contract depended on a company insuring buyer's payment, there was no contract when the insurance was denied. *Pork*, A App 20020307.

Art. 8(3) specifies a broad field of evidence, including the negotiations and the subsequent conduct of the parties. In *Embroidered Fabrics*, CH Trial 19970703, the court determined that buyer, in making her offer, intended to be bound if the offeree accepted. The evidence was the fact that after delivery of the fabric to the embroiderer, buyer both requested an invoice and complained about the quality of the fabric, showing that buyer thought she was bound by the contract.

Major conflict has arisen over whether CISG destroys the parol evidence rule. The parol evidence rule states that when parties have integrated their agreement into a writing, no evidence other than the writing can be considered in construing it. Arguments against application of the parol evidence rule cite the statement that evidence of negotiation and subsequent conduct can be considered. Arguments for the parol evidence rule are based on the same language, but point out that the court is seeking the parties' intent, and where it can be established that the intent of the parties was to confine their agreement to the written page, that should prevail. They argue that art. 8(3) only requires that "due consideration" be given to parol evidence, and that when the parties have integrated their agreement, no consideration is due.

In seeking the parties' intent, all evidence is admissible, including evidence about how the contract was negotiated. *Pork*, A App 20020307. This is true despite the U.S. parol evidence rule holding that where there is an integrated contract, no other evidence of its meaning is admissible. *MCC-Marble Ceramic*, US App; *ECEM European Chemical*, US Trial.

A good example involved the sale of a stallion who died in transit from seller to buyer with a 30,000DM down payment. Buyer was to train the stallion for up to three months before selling it. Seller argued that risk of loss passed on delivery to the first carrier and the requirement of resale of the horse was a condition subsequent. In contrast, buyer argued that it was trade custom in the sale of horses that the sale did not take place until buyer approved of the horse, and the resale of the horse was a condition precedent to the contract. Examining the communications between the parties, the court held that the eventual sale of the horse was a condition precedent to paying the full purchase price, but the payment of the 30,000DM deposit was not subject to any precondition. *Stallion*, D App 20021029.

A sale of jeans did not mention any resale limitations in the contract, but the parties talked in negotiations about sales to Africa and Latin America because seller had already granted exclusive territories in Europe and the U.S. Considering all this evidence, the court concluded that the intent of the parties was to limit resales to Africa and Latin America. *Jeans*, F App 19950222.

Sometimes courts go too far in their use of evidence to find intent. Normally, when a letter of credit is called for in the sales contract, it is to assure that seller will be paid. The contract obligates buyer to furnish seller with a letter of credit providing that seller will be paid if seller furnishes specified documents before a set date. The letter of credit is likely to be phrased similarly: seller will be paid when seller furnishes certain documents by a date. One court used the letter of credit to imply an obligation in the sales contract on the part of seller to furnish the documents by the specified date. *Wire rod*, CH Sup. Ct. 2015. No harm was done, as this was dictum. Seller prevailed because buyer tried to avoid the contract without justification, but the court's use of a conditional requirement of the letter of credit to construct an obligation was inappropriate.

One should not read *MCC-Marble Ceramic*, US App too expansively. The case could have been decided on grounds that the proffered affidavit was tendered to prove that the writing was not intended to be an integration of the contract. Indeed, it was not even intended to be part of the contract, which had previously been concluded orally. Had it done so, the court would not have needed to decide whether CISG repeals the parole evidence rule. What CISG should not do is permit the introduction of evidence that directly contradicts the parties' written agreement.

Parties might be able to confine their contract to an integrated writing, but they need to make the intent to exclude evidence from negotiation or representations of agents specific in the contract. *MCC-Marble Ceramic*, US App. They should also specify in the contract that they intend to derogate from art. 8(3). While that may have a better chance, a court might still use art. 8(3) to determine what the exclusion clause means.

MCC-Marble should be read as eliminating the automatic and wholesale application of the parole evidence rule, not making evidence controlling. "Due consideration" requires weighing.

§2.13 Trade Usage

In the absence of agreement to the contrary, the parties incorporate into their contract any applicable trade usage that is widely known and regularly observed. Art. 9(2). The trade usage must be a usage in the international trade in the goods involved in the contract. It will seldom be binding. There may be disputes about whether the custom actually exists; whether the goods sold are subject to the custom; whether the custom is widely known and regularly observed; or whether the custom, which is simply a domestic custom, extends to international trade. The party who is alleging the trade custom must prove what the custom is, and that it generally applies to the international trade in this product. This requires the proof of facts. *Wood*, A Sup. Ct. 20000321.

Unlike the careless holdings in a number of U.S. cases, it cannot be assumed that the enactment of CISG has incorporated international customs such as Incoterms. E.g., *St Paul Guardian*, US Trial. That is a matter that must be proven. Art. 9(2); *Laser devices*, A Sup. Ct. 20041214. One reason Incoterms are not incorporated is that there are many Incoterms with differing features. The party alleging the Incoterm must prove that it is a custom in this trade to use a particular Incoterm.

Trade usage can be established on the basis of common domestic law. Austria and Switzerland both provide that a commercial confirmation that is not disputed forms a contract according to its terms. The court said that it was not to be presumed that other rules applied to international contracts between merchants in the two countries. *Textiles*, CH Trial 19921221. Consequently, a party opposed to the trade custom should be prepared to prove that the alleged custom is either not widely known or not widely practiced in the international trade. Some courts have even suggested that sets of rules, such as the Unidroit Principles of International Commercial Contracts or the Principles of European Contract Law, should be the basis of trade custom and displace the rules of CISG, but no court has so held. *Heating appliances*, F Sup. Ct. 20150217. This case is a good example of why using law as a springboard for custom may not be appropriate. Seller was arguing to be excused from performance based on hardship. CISG has several provisions excusing parties from damages or entirely for defective performance, such as art. 79, but none based on hardship.

Whether the party should have known of the custom is another question. A party should know of it if the party's place of business is in the geographic region and business where the custom applies. It likewise should be aware when it continuously does business in that region. *Wood*, A Sup. Ct. 20000321. A newbie to the trade might claim that he had no reason to know of the custom, but if contracting with someone who knows it, that person will think it applies in the absence of a declaration of newness to the trade. That declaration should call forth information about the custom from the experienced trader, or else the custom should not apply.

The reason trade usage helps interpret the meaning of the contract is that in the absence of evidence to the contrary, it is presumed that the parties, who are engaged in the trade, knew about the usage and would have countermanded it if they did not wish it applied to their contract. Using trade custom relieves the parties of the expense of drafting the custom into their contract.

§2.14 Dealings of the Parties

Dealings of the parties operate in two directions.

Prior dealings of the parties in prior similar contracts control interpretation unless countermanded because it is assumed that those dealings constitute an interpretation of their previous contracts by the parties. Art. 9(1). If there is no agreement to the contrary, it is reasonable to expect their new agreement to follow the meaning of the old. The principle here is that there is no better way to ascertain what the parties meant than to see what they in fact did.

Opinions differ about how many instances of the interpretation must exist to constitute "practices which they have established between themselves." Parties who have dealt with each other for some time have opportunities to create practices. The parties in more than 20 previous contracts had not considered the contract concluded until it was embodied in an integrated writing.

The court concluded that this was a practice that they had established so that no contract existed without agreement on an integrated writing, which was absent in this case. *Hanwha*, US Trial. Where seller allowed buyer credit for pizza boxes delivered damaged in the only two previous cases of damage, the court held that credit in two instances was insufficient to establish a usage. *Pizza cartons*, D Trial 20000413. Another court stated that two instances were not enough to establish prior practices, though the force of that case is weakened by the fact that there was no indication that buyer ever acquiesced in the practice. *Urea*, CH Trial 19971203. Another court said that previous practices could be in the same contract, but only if it was clear that both parties followed those practices. *Propane*, A Sup. Ct. 19960206.

A practice should be considered even if it only occurred once. The reason behind incorporating practices into the contract is to effectuate the parties' intent. Nothing states intent more clearly than what the parties have done by agreement, even if they have only done it once. Where the contract provided that a test of the phenol before it was loaded was conclusive, but the parties continued to test it after loading and upon arriving at the destination, the court found that the early test was not intended to be conclusive of conformity at the crucial point of delivery to the first carrier. *Cedar Petrochemicals*, US Trial.

In order to be a prior practice, the practice must have been followed consistently. Intermittent practices are not evidence of contract interpretation. Where seller accepted buyer's offer by using confirmations to indicate the place of delivery in only three of the eleven prior contracts, this did not establish a practice of the parties. *Laser devices*, A Sup. Ct. 20041214.

Practice after contracting may or may not be reliable evidence of what the parties intended when they concluded the contract. Alternatively, practices may be evidence that the parties have amended their contract by conduct, which only requires their agreement. It does not require either new consideration or a writing (in the absence of a contractual requirement). That agreement can be manifested by conduct. Art. 29.

Some care needs to be exercised in finding that the parties' practices, either in previous contracts or in the administration of the present contract, represent their interpretation of the contract. Where one party breaches, the other party may not contest it because the amount is too small to be worth fighting about, because the facts are unclear, or because the continued relationship is worth more than the contract damages. Not every practice represents an interpretation of the contract.

§2.15 Conflicts Between Trade Usage and Prior Dealings

Sometimes the parties prove that there is a trade usage in the relevant sector, and that the parties had established practices of their own that conflicted. Which prevails? In one case, the contract specified that tantalum carbide would be sold "on consignment." Buyer proved that "consignment" in the trade means that the sale is not made until buyer either sells or uses the goods. Buyer claimed that while a larger amount was delivered according to the contract, he was only obliged to pay for what he used. Seller pointed out that the practice between the parties had been for buyer to use all the material delivered, but to make a usage report to seller, following which buyer was billed for the usage. Without more, this might not have been enough to establish that the parties' past practices required payment for all that was contracted, payment due as they were used. But seller also documented an incident where buyer wanted to return part of an order, seller refused, and buyer acquiesced. The court rightly held that practices of the parties overruled trade custom because it demonstrates the parties' actual intent. *Treibacher Ind.*, US App. While this is certainly the correct result, it must be leavened with the cautions mentioned above that it is often much more difficult to determine the practices of the parties that represent contract interpretation than it is to determine trade custom. One should also note that buyer could have claimed that use of the word "consignment" could be regarded as an express part of the contract, but seller might have responded that the meaning of any express term is subject to the intent search dictated by art. 8 that might defeat a dictionary definition. Here, the previous practice of the parties bolstered that special meaning.

CHECKPOINTS

You should have learned that:

- In interpreting CISG, it is important to know differences in law drafting and interpretation between common law and civil law countries.
- Civil law statutes are short and general. They leave much room for "the appreciation of the judge."
- In interpreting statutes, civil law states use general principles to supply content for more specific provisions.

- A prime source of law is the writing of distinguished professors in civil law systems.

- Civil law systems do not consider previous judicial opinions sources of law.

- If previous judicial opinions are considered, no distinction is made there between holding and dictum.

- CISG specifies that its international character is to be considered in its interpretation. This calls for consideration of different business practices as well as different legal systems.

- CISG calls for uniformity of its interpretation across national boundaries. Difficult because of lack of resources, this nonetheless requires courts to consider interpretations made in other countries.

- CISG asks that in choosing between interpretations of it, consideration be given to whether one interpretation will be more conducive to encouraging good faith in international sales.

- CISG states that where a matter is not specifically dictated by CISG, but is generally covered by it, the matter should be decided by general principles of CISG. There is much disagreement on the substance of those general principles.

- When there is no specific CISG provision and no general principle of CISG can resolve the case, recourse should be had to the domestic law chosen by the parties or by the choice of law principles of the forum.

- CISG also contains rules for determining the intent of the parties to the contract. Intent can be gleaned from the parties' statements or actions, from their prior dealings, or from trade custom.

- The subjective intent of a party's words or conduct will govern if the other party should have understood them.

- If there is no reason for the other party to understand words or conduct, they will be interpreted objectively in accord with what a reasonable person in the position of the other party would have understood, considering all the facts and circumstances surrounding the case.

- This broad scope for evidence of intent means that the U.S. parol evidence rule often cannot be invoked to limit the introduction of evidence of intent. Parties can invoke the parol evidence rule if they make that clear in their contract.

- In the absence of evidence to the contrary, the parties are assumed to incorporate any customs in the international trade in the goods involved into their contract. This requires proof both of the custom and of the fact that it is widely known and observed in the particular international trade.

- Dealings of the parties from prior similar contracts can be used to determine their intent on this contract. The prior dealings must be consistent, relevant to the question at hand, and under similar circumstances.

- Dealings of the parties in administering the contract in dispute may also provide evidence of the contract's meaning.

- In a conflict between trade custom and dealings of the parties, dealings of the parties should prevail as more accurately demonstrating the intent of the parties.

CHAPTER 3

Policies Behind CISG

ROADMAP

After reading this chapter, you should understand:

- CISG establishes default rules. Those rules are most successful when they anticipate the rules that the parties would have written for themselves had they possessed perfect foresight, enough time, and unlimited resources.
- The parties, with a few exceptions, can change these rules.
- The rules the parties would have negotiated usually involved keeping costs low, reducing the opportunity for strategic behavior, and fundamental fairness.
- Costs can be kept low by assigning responsibility to the person in the best position to fulfill those responsibilities. That will usually be either the person in possession, the person with the greater knowledge, or the person who can do what is required at the least cost.
- Requiring prompt notice of matters amiss in the relationship is one way in which strategic behavior is reduced.

---

§3.01 Introduction

The most important characteristic of CISG is that, with few exceptions, it provides default rules. Those rules are applied unless the parties change those rules. Art. 6 makes it clear that the parties have broad authority to contract for most rules they agree upon.

Parties to international sales contracts are mostly profit-seeking enterprises. Profit tends to be maximized when costs are minimized.

This party autonomy indicates that the default rules of CISG should be those rules that most parties would have reached by independent bargaining. If they are not, parties will need to spend resources negotiating and drafting contracts to change CISG's rules that could be better spent on other things.

One characteristic of rules that the parties are likely to reach in independent bargaining is reduced cost. Parties can allocate costs between them by the pricing mechanism. If a rule produces more cost than another rule, that cost can be reallocated, but it continues to burden one or both of the contracting parties.

Second, CISG tries to avoid misunderstandings between contracting parties.

A third characteristic that CISG's rules should seek is fundamental fairness. Parties aware of the rules will often seek to change them if they are not perceived as being fair.

§ 3.02 Reducing Cost

Many provisions illustrate the proposition that CISG tries to keep costs down.

Costs are generally reduced if duties are placed on the party best placed to perform them. The party who can at the least cost assure the security of the goods is usually the party in possession of them. The CISG default rule is that risk of loss is on seller as long as the goods are in seller's possession. When seller delivers the goods, risk of loss passes to buyer. Arts. 66–70. This is a perfectly symmetrical rule if seller delivers the goods to buyer, who immediately takes possession. That is seldom the case for international sales. Usually, the goods are delivered to a carrier, who will eventually deliver them to buyer. Sometimes the chain is much longer. Seller delivers the goods to a trucker, who delivers them to an ocean carrier, who delivers them to a railroad, who delivers them to a trucker, who delivers them to buyer. In that case, risk of loss passes to buyer long before she obtains possession of the goods. The principle that risk of loss follows possession seems to be violated, and it is. For the period when neither seller nor buyer has physical possession of the goods because they are in the hands of a carrier, buyer has the risk of loss. In that situation, either buyer or seller must have the risk of loss, as the carrier is somewhat protected from liability because of national or international limits. There is no clear reason to suppose that either seller or buyer could do anything to prevent loss while the goods are possessed by the carrier. However, buyer is better placed to determine whether the loss occurred while the goods were in the hands of the carrier or after they were delivered to buyer.

Sometimes liability is assigned based on which party is likely to have superior knowledge. For goods, seller is more likely to know their properties than buyer, so seller is obligated to provide goods that are fit for their ordinary uses. Art. 35(2)(a). If buyer intends to use the goods for a purpose that is unusual, seller is not liable to make the goods suitable to that use unless buyer tells seller of the intended use. Art. 35(2)(b). When notified, seller's superior knowledge of the product's characteristics enable seller to advise on whether the goods are suitable, unless buyer has superior expertise. Art. 35(3).

§3.03 Avoiding Misunderstandings

CISG generally requires that parties notify each other of what would otherwise be unexpected changes in the relationship. Buyer who receives goods that do not conform to the contract must notify seller of the defect. This permits seller to quickly cure the defect, rather than having the parties engage in costly litigation about it. Art. 39. Seller who is worried that buyer will be unable to pay the purchase price is required to give buyer notice and time to provide assurances before avoiding the contract. Arts. 71–72. There are a variety of reasons CISG requires these notifications, but one is to avoid misunderstandings between the contracting parties by requiring a party preparing to act to notify the other party of the reasons for the action.

§3.04 Fundamental Fairness

If a rule is perceived as fundamentally unfair, parties will spend resources trying to change it. Whether they will succeed will depend on the relative bargaining strength of the parties.

One example of the influence of fundamental fairness on CISG interpretations is the question of the inclusion of one party's standard terms in the contract. In some domestic law systems, seller can include standard terms with the delivery of the product, and they become part of the contract. CISG provides much less scope for the imposition of standard terms. Those terms need to be available to the other party before the contract is concluded, and in a form likely to signal the other party that they are part of the contract. Standard terms on the back of an invoice are not part of the contract because they are not provided before the contract is concluded. Even if this is the tenth contract between the parties and the same standard terms were provided on invoices after the previous nine contracts, the standard terms still do not become part of the contract because in none of the previous contracts was it drawn to the other party's attention that the invoice was intended to modify the contract already negotiated.

§3.05 Reducing Opportunities for Strategic Behavior

A subset of both reducing costs and fundamental fairness is CISG's attempt to reduce opportunities for strategic behavior.

In the real world of contracts, most contracts are performed, or performed as modified by the agreement of the parties. The litigated contract cases usually involve situations where the market in which the contract is to be performed is far different from the market in which it was concluded. The market price of the goods to be delivered has changed substantially, or the currency in which payment is to be made has risen or fallen substantially compared to the currency in which the other party deals. In those situations, the real reason that the disadvantaged party wants to rid himself of the contractual obligations is that the contract has turned from a profit-generator to a loss-maker. Many CISG provisions are designed to restrain parties from behaving opportunistically.

Perhaps the clearest example of that is limiting the remedy of contract avoidance largely to fundamental breaches. The domestic law of many countries permits contract avoidance for any deviation from the contract's terms. CISG prevents avoidance unless the breach is truly serious. It mandates performance of the contract as closely as possible, and limits remedies for non-fundamental breach to those that are likely to be less costly.

Another example is the absence from CISG of indeterminate doctrines like *force majeure*, hardship, or impracticality of performance and the substitution of a doctrine with more fixed parameters. Instead of terminating the contract, complying with the parameters only affects liability for damages, and performance is expected when the obstacle no longer exists or can be overcome.

A third example is the requirement that prompt notice be given specifying any nonconformities in the goods. Failure to give prompt notice results in loss of buyer's right to contest the conformity of the goods. While the notice requirement has many purposes, one of them is surely to reduce opportunistic behavior (and lawyer creativity) by limiting conformity disputes to those set forth in the notice of nonconformity.

CHECKPOINTS

You should have learned that:

- CISG establishes default rules. Those rules are most successful when they anticipate the rules that the parties would have written for themselves had they possessed perfect foresight, enough time, and unlimited resources.

- The parties, with a few exceptions, can change these rules.

- The rules the parties would have negotiated usually involved keeping costs low, reducing the opportunity for strategic behavior, and fundamental fairness.

- Costs can be kept low by assigning responsibility to the person in the best position to fulfill those responsibilities. That will usually be either the person in possession, the person with the greater knowledge, or the person who can do what is required at the least cost.

- Requiring prompt notice of matters amiss in the relationship is one way in which strategic behavior is reduced.

CHAPTER 4

Scope

ROADMAP

After reading this chapter, you should understand:

- CISG applies to some, but not all, international contracts for the sale of goods. CISG's terms are used to determine whether it applies.
- Technically, CISG is a contract between states, obliging the courts of signatory states to apply it when appropriate. In fact, it is often applied when appropriate by non-signatory states and by arbitral tribunals.
- CISG applies to contracts for the sale of goods between parties who have their places of business in different states, and either: (1) those states are both contracting states or (2) the applicable choice of law rule points to the law of a contracting state, and the forum state has not opted out of that provision.
- CISG does not apply if the actual internationality of the contract is not apparent to both parties by the time the contract is concluded.
- An agent for an undisclosed principal should be considered a party.
- Where a party has more than one place of business, the place of business that has the closest connection to the contract and its performance is the place used.
- A party must do business at a place for more than a limited time to qualify it as a place of business.
- A place of business may be a branch, or may be separately organized.
- An agent may or may not be a place of business of the principal.
- A sale obligates seller to deliver and transfer property in goods or documents and buyer must pay the price and take delivery. Whether

a sale has taken place depends on the substance of the transaction, not its form.

- A sale includes a barter.

- In the absence of other evidence, there is no sale between a consignor and his consignee.

- A sale may take place within a framework agreement such as a distribution, exclusive supply, or requirements contract if the goods and quantity are identifiable. A framework agreement without such specification is not governed by CISG.

- CISG does not define goods. Anything that is physically deliverable may qualify as goods. Land or buildings do not qualify unless the contract calls for the buildings to be delivered.

- Some goods are not governed by CISG. They include investment securities, negotiable instruments, money, ships, aircraft, or electricity.

- The provision of services is not the sale of goods, but the sale of goods often involves ancillary services. A contract is governed by CISG unless the value of the services provided exceeds the value of the goods, considering that the cost of labor and other services required to produce goods are not counted as services.

- A contract is not governed by CISG if buyer provides a substantial part of the value of materials used to make the goods.

- CISG does not govern contracts for goods bought for "personal, family or household use" unless seller neither knew nor ought to have known of that purpose.

- Parties may exclude CISG or any of its elements. They may also choose to be governed by CISG even though in the absence of the election, they would not be.

- CISG does not govern torts suits, though tort damages may be recovered if they result from breach of contract.

- CISG does not determine title to property, though it does allocate the risk of loss.

- CISG does not apply to determine the validity of a contract or any of its clauses unless it applies by its terms. This certainly applies to capacity and duress. Whether it applies to other questions of validity, voidability, or enforceability is unclear.

- CISG does not govern set-offs against the contract of other responsibilities between the parties resulting from other transactions.
- Where CISG applies in the U.S., it preempts comparable state contract law and tort issues that are essentially breach of contract. The federal courts have federal question jurisdiction without regard to the amount in controversy.

§4.01 Introduction: Rules for Determining Scope

At the outset, one is met with a conundrum. If CISG applies, its rules apply to all applicable aspects of the matter covered by CISG except where the parties exclude it. But by what rules do we determine whether CISG applies? CISG has scope rules, but those rules do not automatically apply themselves. The situation often needs to be interpreted and will often depend on the intent of the parties. It seems illogical to apply CISG's rules before we know that CISG applies, but that is exactly what we do—perhaps by default, because there are no other obvious rules to apply.

CISG is a contract between states. When applicable, it is a choice of law rule telling the courts of the country to apply CISG. It places no obligation on courts of states that have not adhered, or on arbitral tribunals. Nonetheless, arbitrators and courts of non-adherent states tend to apply CISG when CISG calls for its application.

CISG applies to international contracts for the sale of goods, but it does not apply to all such contracts. To apply, CISG must meet some positive criteria, and avoid some exclusions.

A. Scope Based on Parties

§4.11 Internationality

CISG applies to contracts for the sale of goods where the parties' places of business are in different countries that belong to the treaty. Art. 1(1)(a).

There is no requirement that goods move across national boundaries. If a buyer with a place of business in Paris purchases widgets from a New York seller and has them delivered to the French buyer's purchaser in the U.S., CISG applies because buyer and seller have places of business in different adherent countries.

Likewise, the nationalities of buyer and seller are irrelevant, so CISG also applies if both buyer and seller in the widget case are American citizens. It is the place of business that measures the internationality. Art. 1(3). In *Pizza cartons*, D Trial 20000413, CISG applied to a sale between two Italian citizens because one had his sole place of business in Italy and the other in Germany. This provision should be easy to apply, but it has snared several courts.

One problem has been in identifying the parties to the contract. Normally, the parties to the contract are its signatories if a written contract, or the two parties in conversation if it is oral. Where it is clear to both parties that each is acting as an agent, the parties to the contract should be their principals because the agents are not engaging on their own behalf, but for the accounts of their principals.

Sometimes a party argues that it is not liable because it was acting as an undisclosed agent for buyer or seller. This argument is more likely to succeed when buyer instructs seller to deliver the goods to a third party who is in fact the undisclosed principal and seller has some reason to know that buyer is acting as an agent. Persons claiming to be only agents have been found to be parties, at least where the contract did not specify that they were acting as agents. *BOSS equipment*, CHN Arb 200701. This is appropriate. If a party did not know that its contracting opposite was an agent, it probably relied on the creditworthiness or reputation of the counterparty. That reliance should not be disregarded.

The time at which the applicability of CISG is determined is when the contract is concluded. CISG did not apply to a dispute between a German and a Syrian because Germany had not become a party to CISG when the contract was concluded. Instead, CISG applied because the parties had chosen French law as governing, and France was a CISG adherent when the contract was concluded. *Steel bars*, ICC 6653, 19930326. Likewise, a contract between a non-CISG party is not governed by CISG even though the non-CISG party later assigns the contract to a CISG party. *Impuls I.D.*, US Trial. The date of conclusion of the contract also applies when the contract is between persons with places of business in different countries, but plaintiff's claim is later assigned to a person whose place of business is in the same country as defendant's. *Attorneys Trust*, US App. This contrasts with the U.S. rule for determining diversity of citizenship jurisdiction, which requires parties from different states when the complaint is filed. *28 U.S.C. §1332(d)(7)*.

Actual internationality, the fact that the parties have their places of business in different countries, is indispensable to the application of CISG. Even if actual internationality exists, CISG does not apply if internationality is not apparent to both parties by the time the contract is concluded. Art. 1(3). An online auction is not governed by CISG because neither party knows where the place of business of the other is located, and because auctions are specifically excluded. *Ford pickup F150*, D App 20160408.

Occasionally, the question of the country in which a place of business exists is raised. This has been true of Taiwan, Macao. and Hong Kong. The U.S. State Department does not recognize any of them as a separate country, but views them as part of the People's Republic of China. CISG permits a country to exclude certain self-governing areas from CISG, art. 93, but China has not done so. Instead, China has submitted a list of treaties that it considers applicable to Macao and Hong Kong on which CISG does not appear. Some courts say that CISG does not apply to these territories, *Telephone devices*, F Sup. Ct. 20080402; others say it does. *CNA Int'l*, US Trial. The court in *Attorneys Trust*, US App, did not understand the question doubly, incorrectly thinking that Taiwan signed CISG, and equally incorrectly holding that CISG is foreign law. China has now declared that CISG applies to Hong Kong for contracts concluded from December 2022. That raises the question of whether CISG applies to contracts concluded previously.

§4.12 Party with Multiple Places of Business

Where a party has more than one place of business, the place of business that has the closest connection to the contract and its performance is the place to use.

In *McDowell Valley Vineyards*, it is unclear whether there was a written contract. Buyer submitted an invoice from Sabate USA as evidence of the contract when it sued Sabate USA, its French parent, and two related corporations, in a California state court. Sabate France tried to remove the case to federal court on grounds that CISG, federal law, applied. The court found that Sabate USA was the contracting party, thereby negating the application of CISG (and federal question jurisdiction). The court's rationale is unclear. It seems to be a vague substance-over-form reasoning throwing the entire matter into uncertainty.

The proper way to decide the case is to start with the parties to the contract—those who signed the written contract, if one exists, or those who assented to the oral contract. In the absence of anything further, those are the parties to the contract. Assuming that Sabate France signed the contract and Sabate USA did not (the court provides insufficient detail to be certain), without more, Sabate USA would not be a party to the contract. The question would need to be whether Sabate USA was a place of business of Sabate France.

There were two ways to decide that the contract in *McDowell* was not international, but it required a bit more analysis. Art. 10 provides that where a party has more than one place of business, you count the place with the closest relationship to the contract and its performance. To invoke art. 10, the court first needs to find that a party to the contract has more than one place of business. It appeared that Sabate France did not have a place of business in the U.S. It had a California subsidiary. The court might have pierced the corporate veil by finding that Sabate USA did not exist, in which case the Sabate USA office is part of Sabate France. Piercing the corporate veil is usually done when the corporation has engaged in serious misconduct and is in fact the alter ego of its shareholder. The court could then find that the U.S. office had the closest relationship to the contract. Piercing the corporate veil would have been difficult in this case, as it appeared that Sabate USA had too much substance and too much separate identity to be disregarded as a separate corporate entity, and there appears to be little serious misconduct to permit veil-piercing.

Alternatively, the court might have found that Sabate USA acted as so much of an agent of its parent as to be a separate place of business of the parent, and the place of business with the closest relationship to the contract and its performance. CISG has no rules relating to agency, so some might argue that a choice of law decision must be made to determine whether French or California law is to be used to determine whether Sabate USA is an agent of Sabate France. I believe that is unnecessary because all one need find is whether a particular place is a place of business of a party. That should be decided under CISG to have a uniform interpretation of the term. Whether USA is technically an agent of France under either law is not relevant.

There are really two questions here. The first is whether the alleged place of business is a place of business. If it is, the second question is whether it is a place of business of the party.

To be a place of business, the business must have more than a transitory relationship with the place. The French and Spanish terms translate as "establishment," and the underlying reasoning of the provision seems to require some long-term connection. The hotel room where seller stays for a week while negotiating the contract should not be a place of business, even though seller uses it for business, as well as living space. A place of business need not be owned; it can be leased.

While different commentators have postulated (largely on the basis of domestic law) that a place of business must have different degrees of authority, the authority of the place of business should not matter in determining whether it is a place of business. An information office is just as much a place of business as a sales office. This is because the other party will not know how much authority each place of business of his contracting partner possesses. It would thus be impossible for the other party to determine when he signs the contract whether CISG applies or not, and that is untenable. This is consistent with art. 1(2)'s disqualification of CISG if a party does not know that the parties have their places of business in different countries. However, an information office is much less likely to have the closest connection to the contract and its performance than an office with more authority would. It is also unlikely that the other party will know whether the place has independent contracting authority, so the other party would not know whether CISG applied or not.

Contrary to a French decision where a French buyer dealt with a German seller through its French branch, there is no requirement that a place of business have independent legal personality in order to be counted. *Electronic components*, F App 19920422. In fact, art. 10 seems premised on the proposition that the place of business will often not have independent legal personality and simply be a branch of the party. A branch does not have independent legal personality; it is the enterprise that has legal personality.

A different entity may be alleged to be a place of business. This is likely to be a common problem, as standard procedure for international sales is for an enterprise of one country to avoid having an office in the other country, for jurisdiction, tort liability, bankruptcy, and tax reasons. Instead, a wholly owned or partially owned subsidiary or sister company is established. If it does substantial business, it should be a place of business. A branch or a controlled subsidiary that sells the party's products exclusively is clearly the party's place of business. Sometimes an enterprise operates through an independent agent who handles the products of many sellers or buyers, usually because the party lacks marketing expertise or contacts in the country. Such an independent agent may be a place of business, but is probably not the party's place of business; I have found no cases on the question.

Then the court analyzes the transactions between buyer and seller, and the likely performance. In *Vision Sys.*, US Trial, the court noted that all contact between buyer and seller was through seller's U.S. subsidiary, so found insufficient internationality to invoke CISG. The court made no mention of the millions of dollars of research and development, as well as the manufacturing, provided by the contract that would take place in Australia, the home country of the parent. In other words, the court analyzed the relation of seller's places of business to formation of the contract, but not to its performance.

To return to *McDowell*, if Sabate USA is a place of business of Sabate France, it is not clear that the U.S. office had the closest relationship to the contract to sell cork manufactured in France to a U.S. vintner. The cause of the complaint was that the cork was represented as not giving an odor to the wine. In fact, the cork made the wine smell bad. The odor representations were made in California by Sabate USA, while the cork that breached those representations was made in France, and delivered to buyer in California by Sabate France. The court recites the activities of the U.S. subsidiary, but does not recite the activities of the French parent.

A similar case with the opposite result was *Asanti Technologies*, US Trial. There, at least, it was clear who the contracting parties were. Defendant had places of business in both Canada and the U.S., as well as a U.S. agent that appears to be an independent company to whom buyer was directed to place purchase orders. The court considered whether the Canadian or the U.S. office was more closely connected, disregarding the U.S. agent. Since the allegation was breach of warranty, the court held that the more closely connected office was the office from which the representation was made. The court pointed out that the electronic components were developed and engineered at the U.S. office with which plaintiff was in daily contact, but noted that the products were manufactured in Canada. It did not set forth why it thought the Canadian connections were closer than the U.S. connections.

One notes that a parallel case to *McDowell* with the same facts, except that buyer was a Canadian vintner, remained in federal court. *Chateau des Charmes*, US App. There was no point in arguing that Sabate USA was the appropriate place of business because CISG would have applied whether the place of business was France or the U.S.

Some cases are clearer. A Swiss company with a branch in Serbia sold a milk processing system and packaging to a Serbian. The arbitrator found that the Swiss headquarters had the closest connection because it negotiated the contract, signed it, delivered the machine, and received payment, while its Serbian subsidiary was only involved in attempts to resolve the dispute that arose. *Milk packager*, SRB Arb 20080715.

The closest relationship rule may cause significant difficulties because it enumerates several factors to be considered: where the contract is negotiated, where it is concluded, and where it is performed. The place of performance should generally be preferred because that is likely to be the country of manufacture, delivery, and payment. The place of negotiation is likely to be more than one place if negotiations continue for any length of time or are over the internet. The place of negotiation shares with the place where the contract is concluded the problem that it is of little substantive significance.

The "closest relationship" rule only applies to the extent of the knowledge of the parties when they conclude the contract, a fact that the cases often overlook. If buyer does not know that seller has a second location, that location is not counted; or if buyer knows of the second location but is unaware that the second location will be primarily responsible for performance of the contract, the second location may not be closest to the contract's performance. For example, when buying goods on Amazon.com, buyer does not know (and probably does not care) from which fulfillment center Amazon will ship those goods. Seller may not know either before checking its computerized inventory.

B. Scope Based on Choice of Law

§4.21 Choice of Law

Art. 1(1)(b) provides that CISG applies when there is internationality and "when the rules of private international law lead to the application of the law of a Contracting State." There are no internationally agreed rules of private international law, nor is there any indication that CISG intended to establish such rules for CISG cases. Each country has its rules, which the U.S. calls choice of law rules. The closest one comes to internationally agreed rules are those of the European Union, codified in the Regulation 1215/2012, where art. 3 permits the parties to choose their law and, in the absence of party choice, art. 4 chooses the law of seller's habitual residence except in unusual cases.

Most frequently, art. 1(1)(b) will be invoked when seller is in a CISG state (like Germany), and buyer is not (like England), *Iron molybdenum*, D App 19970228, or when one of the parties is in a nation that ratified CISG after the contract was concluded. *Frozen chicken*, D App 19921120. It can also occur when the parties choose the law of a Member State, even though the state of one of the parties has not adhered to CISG, as in *Taiwanese goods*, ROK App 20130719, or where neither of the parties is in a CISG state, but the contract is to be performed in a Member State.

Art. 95 permits countries to reserve to art. 1(1)(b), and the United States has done so, citing the uncertainty of choice of law rules and the unfairness of having U.S. law preempted while the law of the other country would not be. Controversy has arisen over the meaning of the reservation because art. 95 only says that the reserving state "will not be bound" by art. 1(1)(b). This could constitute a forum-restraining rule, meaning that U.S. courts are not obligated to apply CISG. United States courts seem to have adopted this interpretation, though never with a full discussion of the question. In *Prime Start*, US Trial, the court so ruled in a paragraph without considering the alternate interpretation, which has been endorsed in Germany. *Veneer cutter*, D App 19930702. That alternate is that the reservation means that when U.S. law is selected, U.S. law does not include CISG. This might be termed the selected law approach. *CISG-AC 15* at least impliedly chooses between these approaches. It comes down partially on the side of the forum-restraining approach by saying that a reserving state has no public international law obligation to force its courts to apply CISG, but a court may apply it. It clearly rejects the selected law approach by saying that a forum state that has not reserved to art. 1(1)(b) must apply it even if the law selected is that of a country that has reserved to it.

The forum-restraining interpretation has the clear practical problem of encouraging forum shopping if plaintiff wishes to apply or to avoid CISG, and *Prime Start* presents a good example. A British Virgin Islands (not a CISG country) buyer sued a U.S. seller for delivering nonconforming specialty lumber. The lumber was manufactured in Canada and delivered to the construction site of buyer's client in Russia. CISG might have applied to a dispute between buyer and his client, which may explain why buyer wanted CISG applied here. Neither Russia nor Canada had reserved to CISG, so a suit brought in either country would, if the choice of law provision pointed to either country or the U.S., have resulted in the application of CISG.

Technically, the U.S. reservation only restrains U.S. courts, so one would expect that a U.S. arbitration might or might not find CISG applicable under art. 1(1)(b).

C. Scope Based on the Transaction

§4.31 General

CISG applies to contracts "... of sale of goods ..." The treaty defines neither the term "sale" nor the term "goods." Courts have not been equally shy.

§4.32 Sale

Extrapolating from arts. 30 and 53, courts have concluded that a sale obligates seller to deliver and transfer property in goods or documents and buyer must pay the price and take delivery. *Rabbits*, I Trial 2005011.

Courts look to the substance of the transaction, not its form, so a lease or a mortgage can turn out to be a sale. *Software transfer*, NL Trial 20150325. In a contract called a lease, the fact that the full price was due in two installments and buyer would become owner when the second installment was paid made the transaction a sale. *Milk packager*, SRB Arb 20080715. Where seller paid duties and transportation costs without being reimbursed by buyer, and buyer did not return the oven to the place where it was when the contract was concluded, the court decided that the transaction was not a rental, but a sale. *Hotel oven*, CH Trial 20070427. If the purchaser must continue paying a substantial amount as long as he continues to use the goods, or buyer's use is otherwise limited in time, the transaction is probably a lease or a license. *Software transfer*, NL Trial 20150325.

Withholding the transfer of title until full payment is made as a security device does not make the transaction less of a sale. *St Paul Guardian*, US Trial.

A sale is still a sale, even if it is conditioned on the happening of a future event. In *Stallion*, D App 20021029, the court held that a deposit toward a sale was unconditional, but the final sale was conditional on resale of the horse, and both aspects of the transaction were governed by CISG. Similarly, CISG applied to a contract to sell frozen pork that was conditional on approval by seller's insurance company, which was not forthcoming. *Pork*, A App 20020307.

Resale agreements are sales, even if embedded in leases. *Bowling alleys*, D Sup. Ct. 20140528. The lease part of the transaction is not governed by CISG.

Modifications of international sales agreements are governed by CISG, as are agreements to terminate such contracts, which are also modifications. Art. 29. They are regarded as part of the sales contract because they affect the rights of the parties.

Sometimes transactions that are really sales are characterized as leases for income tax purposes in order to assure (and sometimes to accelerate) their deductibility.

Many international sales agreements were cast in the form of barter, where the purchase price was expressed in goods rather than in a currency. The usual reason for these exchanges was that governments, short on hard currency, forbade or regulated the use of foreign exchange. The solution was to export goods, which buyer would sell abroad. Exchanges are also frequently used in the art world, both because there were significant tax benefits until 2018 and to avoid the banking system. For whatever reason it is used, there is a difference of opinion about whether CISG applies to barters. Some point out that CISG is phrased as buyer paying for goods, while others state that payment may be in currency or in other goods. I believe that an exchange of goods is a sale of goods. Some suggest that it is two sales of goods if there are goods on both sides of the exchange. In an ordinary sale, there is a buyer and a seller. In an exchange, there are two buyers and two sellers. Whether one conceives of it as one or two sales, each party undertakes seller's and buyer's responsibilities for the goods it gives up and receives.

§4.33 Consignments

Technically, a consignment exists when goods are shipped to an agent with sales instruction. The agent holds the goods as a bailee. When the agent makes a sale, property in the goods transfers to buyer. Where plaintiff shipped kiwis to defendant for sale, in one case specifying a sales price and in the other not doing so, and plaintiff forwarded the amount received for selling the kiwis less his expenses and commission, the court held that there was no sale of kiwi fruit from plaintiff to defendant, so defendant did not owe plaintiff the purchase price for the unsold kiwis. *Martini & Ricci*, US Trial. Indeed, it seems that defendant was hired as an agent, to perform a service (selling) for plaintiff.

When the term "consignment" appears in an international sales contract, it may not have its technical meaning. In a case called a consignment where tantalum carbide was delivered to buyer with the understanding that buyer would report the usage and would be billed as used, but buyer could not return unsold product, the court held the parties' usage indicated that a sale had taken place, and the word "consignment" had an unusual meaning for their contract. *Treibacher Ind.*, US App.

§4.34 Framework Agreements

International framework agreements can be distributorships, requirements contracts, output contracts, joint ventures, franchise agreements, or other contracts that set the relationship of the parties. To the extent that such an agreement involves a sale of goods, it is governed by CISG; otherwise, CISG does not apply.

It is common in sales to appoint someone as the manufacturer's exclusive distributor for a territory. The agreement sometimes fixes the price at which goods will be sold to the distributor. Sometimes it fixes the price at which the distributor will sell the goods to third parties. Other times, especially where there is active competition regulation, it does not. For international sales, the manufacturer is likely to have little knowledge of effective marketing in the territory. Granting the distributor exclusive rights there encourages the distributor to develop a market for the product, secure that no one else can cash in on the market he has carefully developed. This is called a framework agreement. If it does not specify a quantity of goods, it is not a sale and CISG does not apply. *AMCO Ukservice*, US Trial; *Viva Vino*, US Trial.

The same is true if the framework agreement requires the purchase of a minimum quantity or price of goods, but does not specify what goods must be bought. *Helen Kaminsky*, US Trial.

However, an order of a specific quantity of goods within the context of the framework agreement would be a sale, and CISG would apply to that order. If the framework agreement includes a commitment to buy a minimum number of specified items, it is a sale of that number of items, and CISG applies. *Crankcases*, F App 20010612. It is not a sale of a greater number.

In one case where there had been a definitive order pursuant to a distribution contract, the court wrongly refused to apply CISG to the sale, which certainly incorporated provisions of the distributorship contract, rather than confront the question of whether CISG overrides the automatic stay in bankruptcy. *Helen Kaminsky*, US Trial.

Perhaps CISG should apply to the sales part of the contract, but not to the distribution part of it. That raises the disturbing thought that two different legal systems might be applied to different parts of a contract that is unified and interdependent. That will always be the case where there are sales pursuant to a distributorship contract because CISG does not cover all aspects of the contract—only those related to the sales relationship between buyer and seller.

A contract calling for seller to supply buyer's needs of a commodity will be covered by CISG as long as the commodity can be identified and a price determined. While the number to be supplied cannot be specified in advance, it can be calculated as buyer's needs develop.

Whether franchise agreements are sales of goods will depend on the agreement. If the franchise agreement requires purchase of goods the identity, quantity, and price of which can be identified, CISG applies. If it only involves the license of trademarks, copyrights, and know-how, CISG does not apply.

§4.35 Auctions

CISG does not apply to auction sales. Auctions are heavily regulated by domestic law. Art. 2(b); *Ford pickup F150*, D App 20160408.

D. Scope Based on the Goods

§4.41 Excluded goods

Sales of certain goods are excluded from CISG.

In some cases, it is because those items are not usually considered goods, like corporate stock or other investment securities, negotiable instruments, or money. Art. 2(d). However, when those items are functioning in other ways, such as Spanish doubloons that are no longer recognized as legal tender, or negotiable instruments that are historical collectibles, CISG should apply.

Sales of ships, aircraft, and electricity are not subject to CISG, either because countries do not agree about whether they are goods, or because many countries heavily regulate their transfer. Art. 2(e), (f). Petroleum products such as gas or crude oil that can be used to generate electricity are not excluded. *Rijn blend*, NL Arb 2319, 20021015.

§4.42 Immovables as Goods

CISG does not define "goods," but there are several provisions that try to distinguish between goods and services. One definition of goods is that they must generally be movable in the physical sense because they must be delivered. One should not confuse this requirement with either the legal definition of real property in common law jurisdictions or immovables in civil law jurisdictions. The sale of land is clearly not the sale of goods, but items to be affixed to the land are goods until they are attached. *Prefabricated house*, CH App 20090303. One might think that something that was an immovable when the contract was concluded and would again be an immovable after the contract was performed would not be "goods," but that is not the case. The sale of a used warehouse to be dismantled and delivered to buyer was held to be "*marchandise*" without significant discussion. *Warehouse*, F App 19950426. Where the sale was of a spinning mill to be reconstructed on buyer's property, the court applied CISG without believing it necessary to explore the problem of whether what was being sold was an immovable both when the contract was concluded and after it was performed. *Spinning mill*, CH Sup. Ct. 20120716. The goods need only be movable at the time of delivery.

This test is perhaps implied by CISG's requirement that goods be delivered. Arts. 30–34. However, goods need not have a physical manifestation at all. Mass-produced computer programs have been held to be goods. *Software-hardware*, CH Trial 20000217.

§4.43 Things Attached to Land—Minerals, Timber, Growing Crops

Commentators have wondered whether minerals, timber, or growing crops were goods, primarily because distinctions are drawn in national laws. The problem does not seem to be of practical importance because no reported court cases have involved these items. Commentators often distinguish contracts that call for seller to sever the items from contracts where buyers will sever and deliver them. Either way, the business world treats them as goods, and so should CISG.

§4.44 Services as Goods

Goods are not services, but goods often include services. Many goods are manufactured. Manufacturing usually involves the combination of materials and labor. In addition, it is not unusual for the sale of machinery to include obligations on seller to set up the machinery at buyer's place, to assure that it is working properly, and to train buyer's staff to operate and maintain the machinery. E.g., *Floating center*, CH Trial 19950426. All that labor constitutes services. CISG was not designed to govern contracts for the provision of services. It is entirely possible that some issues will not be resolved by CISG. Nonetheless, CISG applies to the entire contract unless it is predominantly services. *Wall partitions*, CH App 20031029. That may result in CISG being applied to some issues, and domestic law being applied to others that are not covered by CISG, under art. 7(2), in the same contract.

§4.45 Preponderantly Services

CISG does not apply if the preponderant part of the obligations of the person who supplies the goods is the supply of services. What is the preponderant part is determined by value, as shown in the warehouse case, where the cost of the warehouse was more than three times the cost of taking it apart and delivering it. *Warehouse*, F App 19950426. A court stated that even when the services supplied were of equal value to the goods supplied, the predominant part was not services. *Window-making plant*, D App 19991203. The comment was true, but gratuitous, as the services of several mechanics for six weeks to assemble the plant and make it operative were trivial compared to the cost of making the plant. One court (and the Advisory Council) suggested in dicta that qualitative factors need to be considered, but provided no guidance about what those factors might be or how they might be measured quantitatively. *Steel bars*, A App 20071218. Generally, one proceeds on the basis of value.

Occasionally, a contract is too specific. Where Prada contracted to pay $100 each for live alligator hatchlings one year old, Prada also specified services of seller to procure eggs from trappers, transport them, incubate and hatch them, and care for the alligators for a year, and the arbitrators found (without specifying the evidence or quantifying the value of the services provided) that the value of the services exceeded the value of the alligators, so CISG did not apply. *Alligator hatchlings*, I Arb 20190504. Had the contract only specified the delivery of year-old alligators in good health, CISG would have applied.

The reason for this is that labor needed to produce a product is not counted as services. Detailed cost accounting is not required. Indeed, while such information would be available to seller, it would not be available to buyer when the contract was concluded. If it were counted as services, buyer would never know whether CISG applied to the contract. *CISG-AC 4*. Thus, where seller makes and serves food and drink at buyer's wedding, the labor required for the preparation of the food and drink (and perhaps to transport it) is not counted as services, while the labor required to set up, serve it, and clean up afterward, is services.

§4.46 Contract Processing

Where buyer undertakes to supply a substantial part of the materials used to manufacture the goods, the contract is not for goods. Art. 3(1). This provision envisages a situation where the raw materials, such as shoe soles and uppers, are shipped to seller to be stitched together. Seller is actually providing a service.

What is clear from the provision is that it is the contemplation of the contract that is important, not what actually happens, though what actually happens may reflect an amendment to the contract. Consequently, materials supplied by buyer by way of repairs after the goods are delivered should not be considered unless their provision constitutes modification of the contract. *Injection-moulding tools*, D Sup. Ct. 20140924.

The provision is not specific about what it means for buyer to supply materials in the context of international sales. Does buyer supply materials if they are supplied by a party related to buyer such as a subsidiary corporation? Does buyer supply materials if buyer guarantees seller's contract to purchase the material? Does it depend on whether the guarantee is called? If buyer loans seller the money to buy the materials? If buyer's deposit is used to buy the materials?

It appears that "materials" include only goods incorporated in the final product, or used in making it. Drawings, plans, and machines used in making the final product are not materials. *Injection-moulding tools*, D Sup. Ct. 20140924.

How much is a substantial part of the materials? That is determined based on value, though the French term is *essentielle*, which seems to call for qualitative, rather than quantitative analysis. *CISG-AC 4*. One court hedged its bets by finding that supplying a few tools was neither essential nor substantial, but failed to explain why. *Window maker*, D App 19991203 Essential is not a workable standard. In order to have the finished product, every ingredient is essential because incorporating every ingredient is a cost that would have been avoided if not essential. So the measure must be quantitative, not qualitative. It is clearly less than a majority of the materials, as the drafters used "predominant" in art. 3(2) to signify more than the other. A Hungarian arbitration opined that providing materials worth less than 10% of the average value of the final product was not substantial. *Containers*, H Arb 19951205. One would tend to agree that 10% is not normally substantial, but the tribunal got the measurement wrong. The question is whether it is a substantial part of the total materials used, not whether it is a substantial part of the value of the finished product.

§4.47 Software and Reports

Standardized computer software has been correctly held to be goods. *Software-hardware*, CH Trial 20000217; *Graphiplus program*, D Trial 19950208. An implication is that custom-crafted software, and other custom-made items such as market reports, are not goods. That analysis is mistaken. Distinguishing software based on whether it is delivered physically or online disregards the fact that the important part of the transaction is the usability of the software by buyer. Distinguishing custom-crafted software from mass-produced software would be inappropriate given that other custom-crafted products are clearly goods. The same is true of e-books, games, apps, or replayable music or movies distributed online.

What is important is to distinguish sales from leases. The fact that seller may call the transaction a license is not determinative. If buyer needs to pay a periodic fee to keep using the software, it is probably a license rather than a sale

On the other hand, the question has been raised as to whether information or data can be goods if committed to paper. Just as the software delivery system should not determine whether software is goods, so the fact that it is written down should not make information into goods. *Market analysis*, D App 19940826.

E. Scope Based on the Parties' Intent

§4.51 Personal Use

CISG does not apply to goods bought for "personal, family or household use" unless seller neither knew nor ought to have known of that purpose. The exclusion has two requirements: (1) the purpose of the purchase must be for personal, family, or household use, and (2) the reasonably attentive seller must be aware of that purpose. The reason for the rule is that most countries have consumer protection provisions that are far from uniform. CISG is not designed to protect the consumer. The central notion of CISG is party autonomy, which means that the party with the better bargaining power can take advantage of the other party. The drafters meant to keep consumer protection laws in place. However, as consumer protection laws are quite various about their definitional inclusions, it is still possible for a national consumer protection law to conflict with the application of CISG.

A good example was the purchase by the Chinese collector Michael Xufu Huang of a Cecily Brown painting from the Paula Cooper Gallery at Art Basel in Miami Beach in December 2019. The contract provided that it would be governed by "U.S. law." This appeared to be an international sale excluded from CISG by the personal use exception and subject to the UCC because Huang appeared to be buying for his own collection. In fact, he was buying for resale to a Monaco-based Argentine collector, so the purchase was not for personal use, and CISG should apply, even though it appeared to the Gallery that this was a sale for personal use. *The Art Newspaper*, 1/13/2021.

Whether buyers tell sellers why they are buying the goods will vary with the relationship, but often they do not. Buyer's purpose often needs to be deduced from surrounding circumstances. The purchase of a single item is often for personal use, but not when it is commercial grade that is usually used in businesses. The purchase of multiple identical items is likely to be for inventory unless it is common for consumers to use those multiple items together, or to use them up so quickly that they often buy multiples of them.

If buyer pays with a personal check, that may be evidence of a personal purpose, but it is usually not probative of what seller should have known when the contract was concluded because payment usually occurs after the contract was entered into.

The exclusion from CISG for personal use raises a difficulty for a retailer. One system of law, CISG, applies to his purchases; a different system, a domestic law, applies to his sales. He may find himself liable to a customer but unable to collect from his seller. Despite party autonomy, the retailer and his customer cannot opt into CISG because most consumer protection statutes are mandatory law. The retailer can attempt to apply his consumer protection law to his purchases, but that will require the accord of his seller, which may be difficult to obtain.

This provision raises problems when the goods are used for both personal and business purposes. That is the case for the computer on which this book was written. While courts may apply a principal purpose test, it has no support in CISG and would probably be difficult to prove either way without looking to percentage of use after the purchase.

§4.52 Excluding CISG

The parties can decide that CISG will not apply to their contract. Art. 6 states that the parties may exclude CISG.

The difficulty arises in effectuating that intent. CISG must be excluded in a way that is clear and agreed to by the parties. Most attempts at exclusion do so by referring to the law of a state that has ratified CISG, so CISG is part of that state's law. If all the contract says is that the law of Germany applies, it is ambiguous whether the parties intend only the domestic law of Germany, or German law including CISG. Without more, courts are likely to say that CISG is the law of Germany, so CISG applies. *Repainted car*, D App 20080331; *Asante Techs*, US Trial; *Cucumbers*, D App 19930108. Cases to the contrary are few and early. *Leather wear*, I Arb 19940419. The parties could exclude CISG by a statement specifically excluding it. They could implicitly exclude it by choosing the law of a jurisdiction where CISG is not in force, or by choosing a specific code or statute.

Exclusion of CISG should not be inferred from the parties' choice of a court to handle their disputes. *Repainted car*, D App 20080331. Nor should choice of an arbitral seat imply a choice of law, as the court suggested in *Chinese goods*, D Arb 19960321. *CISG-AC Op 16* argues that failure to argue CISG at trial, or domestic law provisions on waiver, should not be regarded as excluding CISG. True, as exemplified in *Vulcanized rubber*, I Trial 20000712, where the court recognized the parties' error and applied CISG even though the parties arguments were based on Italian law. The court found this the result of mistake, not of choice. On the other hand, one doubts the fairness of asking an appellate court to remand a case for retrial at significant expense on a legal theory that neither party raised at trial. In the U.S., an argument that federal law, such as CISG, preempts state law must be made at trial, or is waived, unless it goes to the court's jurisdiction. *Colo. Tire*, US App.

In most cases, however, the argument for excluding CISG seems to result from the unthinking use by parties of standard conditions that do not seem to take CISG into consideration at all.

In one case, a court held reference to "law of the International Chamber of Commerce of Paris" insufficient to exclude CISG because it could not determine any such law relevant to the dispute at hand. *Rabbits*, I Trial 20050111.

The parties must agree in order to exclude CISG. Where one party's standard conditions chose Latvian law and the other's chose German law and neither specifically excluded CISG, which was the law of both countries, CISG applied. *Repainted car*, D App 20080331.

§4.53 Excluding Provisions of CISG

Parties can also select specific provisions of CISG to exclude. They may do so specifically, though their contracts seldom say they are excluding a specific article. Usually they exclude an article or parts of it by implication. A CISG provision is excluded by implication when the contract provides rules that, if implemented, would negate the CISG provision.

Selection of a trade term may be viewed as displacing CISG provisions on delivery and risk of loss, but it can also be viewed as consistent with CISG's invitation to the parties to write their own terms. The result is the same—the trade term applies. A clause that provides that the contract reflects the entire agreement of the parties does not displace art. 8 and 9's instructions on finding the intent of the parties. A clause that a third-party inspection is binding on the parties does not displace art. 36(1)'s insistence that a nonconformity existing when the risk of loss passes is to be taken into account even if its existence is not discovered until later. *Cedar Petrochemicals*, US Trial. It is obvious that parties who wish to exclude CISG provisions should do so specifically.

It is not uncommon for parties to modify CISG provisions on what constitutes conformity of the goods, when notice of nonconformity needs to be given, or that consequential damages will not be paid. E.g., *Ajax Tool*, US Trial.

In *Wood flooring*, CHN Arb 20210311, the parties provided that late payment would incur liquidated damages of .05% per day of late payment. While the court did not discuss whether this supplanted art. 78 on interest, its opinion made that decision because it ordered no interest.

One provision that cannot be excluded by the parties is art. 12, which permits countries that ratify CISG to opt out of its provision that does not require a written contract. The parties also cannot exclude any of the few provisions of CISG that are addressed to states. For instance, parties probably cannot opt out of art. 28, which does not require a court to order specific performance if it would not do so in a comparable domestic sales case.

§4.54 Opting in to CISG

Some controversy, mostly theoretical, has erupted over whether parties could opt in to CISG if their contract did not otherwise qualify as CISG-applicable. There is no prohibition on opting in, and it is entirely within the spirit of CISG, because one of its general principles is party autonomy. The arbitrator applied CISG to the extent possible to a distribution framework agreement because the parties had designated it as governing. *Fashion products*, ICC Arb 11849 (2003) The United States, in reserving to art. 1(1)(b), explicitly stated that parties could opt in. *U.S. State Dept., Legal Analysis.*

A more difficult problem is raised by arts. 2–5, which provide either that "this convention shall not apply" or "is not concerned with" certain contracts or legal issues. At least in theory, if the parties to a contract to which CISG says it does not apply elect CISG, that includes the statements from arts. 2–5 that CISG does not apply. A decision-maker faced with this situation should seek the intent of the parties and find that CISG does apply, but a careful drafter would provide for the application of CISG except for the disqualifying article. If a court is faced with the question of an opt-in for a contract that CISG specifically excludes, it should look for the intent of the parties, guided by art. 8. For instance, if the parties wish to elect CISG to apply to the sale of a vessel, there seems to be no reason why that should not operate to waive art. 2(e).

The careful drafter will remember that CISG will not replace mandatory law because mandatory law is a matter of validity that is governed by domestic law. Even a specific clause choosing CISG will not be effective to oust a mandatory domestic consumer protection law.

It must be noted that parties that opt in to CISG are saving resources by using shorthand to write the text of CISG into its contract—it is not really making CISG its law because CISG is only law when ratified by a particular country. For that reason, where the parties opt in to CISG but do not have diversity of citizenship, the U.S. federal courts lack jurisdiction over the case because there is no federal question.

F. Scope Based on the Nature of the Suit

§4.61 CISG Suit Exclusions

CISG specifies that a number of causes of action or issues are covered or are not governed by CISG. We will see that this is only partly true.

§4.62 Torts

CISG says it is not applicable to liability of seller for death or personal injury caused by the goods. Art. 5. Courts have expanded "death or personal injury" to include all torts. Sometimes disappointed buyers want to sue in tort because of the availability of enhanced damages. Plaintiff may frame a breach of contract as interference with business relations. Courts have declined to decide those cases under CISG. *Viva Vino*, US Trial. One French court, however, has seemed to permit a breach of contract action under CISG and an abuse of process tort claim under French law for basically the same facts plus defendant's conduct in the litigation to proceed in the same litigation with separate damage awards. *Jeans*, F App 19950222. What is at work here is perhaps comparable to the doctrine of preemption. In U.S. law, where a federal statute exhaustively covers the same activity as state law, state law does not apply because it has been preempted by federal law. Likewise, where CISG provides remedies for a fact situation, a party should not be permitted to reduce or enhance them by characterizing his cause of action as one for tort.

On the other hand, it is clear that where buyer pays a third party who suffered death or personal injury as a result of seller's defective product, buyer's damages include the payment she made for death or personal injury. *CISG-AC*

*12.*That seems to be the assumption of the court where buyer sued seller for property damage and personal injury caused by a defective machine. *Veneer cutter*, D App 19930702. CISG is not being used to determine the tort liability; that has already been fixed under domestic law. It is being used to measure the damages for breach of contract.

The reason for the rule is clear. CISG's provisions are not appropriate to adjudicate torts suits. They are designed for contract disputes between buyer and seller. To the extent that the dispute is in essence a contracts dispute, CISG will govern. To the extent that it is broader, recourse must be had to domestic law in addition.

§4.63 Title to Property

CISG says that "except as expressly provided," it is not concerned with the effect the contract has on property in the goods. Art. 4(b). This exclusion is quite limited, as arts. 66–70 govern the passage of the risk of loss, art. 30 requires seller to transfer title, and arts. 41–42 require that the goods not be subject to title or intellectual property claims. Failure to comply with any of these sections may subject seller to liability for breach of contract. Those sections may also determine who has significant aspects of ownership as between buyer and seller. CISG does not determine who owns the property in a dispute between either seller or buyer and a third party, such as a lender, the trustee in bankruptcy, or a purchaser. *Usinor Industeel*, US Trial.

§4.64 Validity

Most difficult is the issue of validity. CISG says that it applies to formation of the contract and the rights of the contract parties under it, but it does not apply to determine the validity of the contract or of any of its provisions or of any usage "except as otherwise expressly provided." Art. 4(a). Most commentators and courts forget the "except" clause, but it can be very important. A first question might determine how expressly is "expressly provided." For example, CISG expressly provides that no writing is required for a contract. Its prohibition on formal requirements is a bit less express because there is no definition or example of other formal requirements. Even less expressly, CISG says nothing about contracts entered into as a result of a mistake, but it has numerous articles expressly about the formation of contracts that say nothing about mistake. Is mistake "otherwise expressly provided?" The case has yet to arise.

There is general agreement that validity includes allegations of lack of capacity to enter into the contract, such as minority, insanity, duress, or illegality.

After that, agreement tends to disappear. For instance, art. 78 provides for interest on overdue amounts, but the payment of interest would be illegal in some countries that adhere. Does art. 4 or art. 78 prevail?

A penalty clause for breach of contract is invalid in some countries, unenforceable in others, and modifiable by the judge in yet others; but a general principle of CISG is party autonomy. What prevails?

In some countries, a contract that is not signed is invalid; in other countries, it is only unenforceable against a party that did not sign; in still others, it is perfectly valid. Arts. 11 and 29 state that neither a contract nor its amendment need be in writing. Is the writing requirement a matter of validity only in those countries that so state, or is it also validity in countries where the contract is unenforceable, or is it overridden by the specific language of CISG?

What about that peculiarly Anglo-Saxon concept of consideration, where there is no specific language in CISG—just the statement that a contract has no form requirements, and the omission of consideration from the requirements to form a contract? Is consideration a matter of form, enforceability, or validity, and whose law determines that? *Geneva Pharmaceuticals*, US Trial, in a summary and unsatisfactory opinion unsupported by reasoning, held that a validity question is raised whenever local law might declare a contract void, voidable, or unenforceable.

The more questions that are excluded because of validity by national laws, the less uniform CISG is, and the more likely forum shopping will be encouraged. Like the other terms of CISG, validity should be interpreted autonomously and without reference to national laws. CISG does not seem to provide much guidance about how that interpretation is to be made.

A starting point would ask whether CISG otherwise provides. CISG clearly provides that unless a country has reserved to art. 11, writing is not required for a contract. It is less clear that CISG expressly provides rules about consideration when it says nothing on the subject in its discussion of contract formation. CISG clearly otherwise provides that interest must be paid.

A court might do a comparative law survey to determine if a large number of CISG signatories believe that the issue is a matter of validity.

Presumably, parties could specifically state that article 4(a) does not apply, but I have not found such a case. Usually they are arguing that some clause implies that CISG will govern the question of validity, a more difficult case to make.

§4.65 Set-off and Recoupment

Set-off allows a party owing payment to another party the ability to offset the debt against the contract price. Since CISG only applies to the relationship of the parties with respect to the contract, set-off is not governed by CISG but by domestic law. *Cashmere sweaters*, D App 19980311. However, where set-off is permitted under local law, seller who demands full purchase price without allowing the set-off as a condition to delivery has breached the contract by demanding more than his entitlement. *Grinding machines*, CH Sup. Ct. 20061220.

Recoupment, on the other hand, is the ability to even out various breaches of the contract by both parties, and is governed by CISG, because all elements necessary derive from the contract.

G. U.S. Consequences of Scope

§4.71 Preemption and Jurisdiction

It is not unusual for a plaintiff to bring a mixed cause of action that alleges breach of contract as well as a tort. In *Electrocraft Arkansas*, US Trial, the complaint included counts for negligence, strict liability, and tortious interference with business expectancy. The court's first task is to determine the causes of action to which CISG applies and the facts necessary to support them. Because CISG is federal law, it preempts comparable state law, but only to the extent that the same facts are required for the cause of action. Because the alleged negligence and strict liability were done in performance of the contract and simply alleged that defendant was negligent or strictly liable for failure of contract performance, the court held that those state law claims were preempted by CISG. By contrast, the court found that the cause of action for intentional interference was not preempted by CISG, even though based on the same failure to supply adequate motors, because of the additional state law requirement to prove willful and malicious conduct. Likewise, an allegation of fraud in inducing the other party to enter into the contract is not preempted by CISG, though a breach of contract action would be preempted. *Geneva Pharmaceuticals*, US Trial.

One open question is whether art. 16(2)(b), providing that an offer cannot be revoked if the offeree reasonably relied on it being irrevocable, is sufficiently similar to state law promissory estoppel that it would displace the state law.

There would still be jurisdiction in the federal court because of the federal questions on the breach of contract action. The court would retain pendent jurisdiction of the state law fraud claim.

CHECKPOINTS

After reading this chapter, you should understand:

- CISG applies to some, but not all, international contracts for the sale of goods. CISG's terms are used to determine whether it applies.
- Technically, CISG is a contract between states, obliging the courts of signatory states to apply it when appropriate. In fact, it is often applied when appropriate by non-signatory states and by arbitral tribunals.
- CISG applies to contracts for the sale of goods between parties who have their places of business in different states, and either: (1) those states are both contracting states or (2) the applicable choice of law rule points to the law of a contracting state, and the forum state has not opted out of that provision.
- CISG does not apply if the actual internationality of the contract is not apparent to both parties by the time the contract is concluded.
- An agent for an undisclosed principal should be considered a party.
- Where a party has more than one place of business, the place of business that has the closest connection to the contract and its performance is the place used.
- A party must do business at a place for more than a limited time to qualify it as a place of business.
- A place of business may be a branch, or may be separately organized.
- An agent may or may not be a place of business of the principal.
- A sale obligates seller to deliver and transfer property in goods or documents and buyer must pay the price and take delivery. Whether a sale has taken place depends on the substance of the transaction, not its form.
- A sale includes a barter.
- In the absence of other evidence, there is no sale between a consignor and his consignee.

- A sale may take place within a framework agreement such as a distribution, exclusive supply, or requirements contract if the goods and quantity are identifiable. A framework agreement without such specification is not governed by CISG.

- CISG does not define goods. Anything that is physically deliverable may qualify as goods. Land or buildings do not qualify unless the contract calls for the buildings to be delivered.

- Some goods are not governed by CISG. They include investment securities, negotiable instruments, money, ships, aircraft, or electricity.

- The provision of services is not the sale of goods, but the sale of goods often involves ancillary services. A contract is governed by CISG unless the value of the services provided exceeds the value of the goods, considering that the cost of labor and other services required to produce goods are not counted as services.

- A contract is not governed by CISG if buyer provides a substantial part of the value of materials used to make the goods.

- CISG does not govern contracts for goods bought for "personal, family or household use" unless seller neither knew nor ought to have known of that purpose.

- Parties may exclude CISG or any of its elements. They may also choose to be governed by CISG even though in the absence of the election, they would not be.

- CISG does not govern torts suits, though tort damages may be recovered if they result from breach of contract.

- CISG does not determine title to property, though it does allocate the risk of loss.

- CISG does not apply to determine the validity of a contract or any of its clauses unless it applies by its terms. This certainly applies to capacity and duress. Whether it applies to other questions of validity, voidability, or enforceability is unclear.

- CISG does not govern set-offs against the contract of other responsibilities between the parties resulting from other transactions.

- Where CISG applies in the U.S., it preempts comparable state contract law and tort issues that are essentially breach of contract. The federal courts have federal question jurisdiction without regard to the amount in controversy.

CHAPTER 5

Formation and Re-formation

ROADMAP

After reading this chapter, you should understand:

- CISG specifically says a contract is formed by offer and acceptance. Contracts can also be formed by mutual consent even though identifying an offer and an acceptance would be artificial.

- CISG does not result in liability for failure to negotiate a sales contract. The laws of some member states prescribe liability for failure to negotiate in good faith.

- An offer is a definable proposal to specific persons indicating an intent to be bound in case of acceptance. The identity of the goods and quantity to be sold must be determinable. The price if not specified or determinable is fair market value if one can be ascertained.

- An advertisement is not normally an offer, but it may be an offer if the quantity to be sold is stated to be limited to the first number of people who respond with credit cards.

- The dealings of the parties may indicate that one or both parties do not intend to be bound until all points are resolved or until the contract is integrated into a formal writing.

- An offer is effective when it reaches the offeree.

- An offer is revocable unless it indicates that it is not, or unless the offeree reasonably thinks it is irrevocable and acts to his detriment in reliance on irrevocability.

- Express rejection terminates an offer.

- Acceptance is effective when received.

- Silence does not normally accept an offer, but it may be acceptance of new terms proposed in a confirmation or other communication to which the recipient does not object.

- Acceptance can be by conduct, but tribunals should be careful to assure that the conduct unambiguously indicates consent.

- Normally, acceptance must be of all the terms of the contract.

- Where the contract is executory, a purported acceptance proposing differing terms rejects the original offer and is itself a new offer.

- Where the contract has been partially performed, some courts count the performance as acceptance of the last written offer, while others find that the contract consists only of those clauses on which the parties have agreed.

- After a contract has been concluded, later communications can only be proposals to amend the contract.

- Neither consideration nor a writing is required for most contracts, but a writing may be required when one of the parties has a place of business in a state that has reserved to art. 11.

- A contract can be amended by mere agreement in words or conduct unless the contract specifies that it must be amended in writing. Even then, it can be amended by conduct.

- Where a contract is amended either orally or by conduct, it may be clear that the amendment has taken place, but unclear what the terms of the amendment might be.

- The terms of a contract are the terms to which the parties have agreed.

- Terms communicated after the contract has been concluded are not terms of the contract, but proposals to amend the contract.

- To be a term of the contract, the non-proposing party needs to know that the term is part of the contract, and what the term is. That person also needs to have a reasonable opportunity to consider the term before being bound.

- Standard terms printed on invoices are not part of the contract.

- Where parties exchange forms with contradictory standard terms, courts sometimes find that the contract was concluded orally so it does not contain the standard terms of either party.

§5.01 Introduction

CISG has chosen an offer-acceptance paradigm for the formation of a contract by stating that a contract is formed when the acceptance of an offer becomes effective. Art. 23. However, a contract for sale may exist (even when it is impossible to identify an offer and an acceptance) where the parties show from their intent that they have reached agreement, *Graphiplus program*, D Trial 19950208; *Metals*, D App 19950308, though some courts have stated that no contract can exist without offer and acceptance. *Propane*, A Sup. Ct. 19960206. Courts should not strain to find an artificial offer and acceptance when there has been agreement. A contract need not be in writing unless a state has reserved to that provision. Arts. 11, 96.

§5.02 Pre-contractual Liability

United States law is clear that, in the absence of misrepresentation, a party to a negotiation is not liable for failure to reach contractual agreement, even if the other party has spent substantial resources in preparing for and engaging in the negotiation. That is not true of the law of some of our European trading partners.

Any such liability will not result from CISG because CISG only deals with contracts for the sale of goods. The liability would be under domestic law. For instance, in *Screws*, D App 19940304, the court seriously considered imposing pre-contractual liability but did not do so because buyer did not prove that seller had created legitimate confidence that the contract would be concluded, either by representations or by inducing buyer to render advanced performance.

However, that does not mean that CISG is irrelevant. Most pre-contractual liability relates to the arbitrary termination of negotiations before agreement on a contract is reached. If the contract, if reached, would clearly have been governed by CISG, CISG may have provisions that would preempt local law. Most offers are revocable. Revoking a revocable offer does not result in injury. Some offers are irrevocable. Revoking an irrevocable offer does not prevent the offeree from accepting it and thereby forming a contract. CISG provides remedies for breach of such a contract.

In a legal environment that requires neither consideration nor a writing for a contract to exist, it might be argued that the act of negotiating a contract is a contract to negotiate in good faith. While local law may or may not endorse that view, a contract to negotiate is not a contract for the sale of goods.

It is thus useful before negotiations begin to enter into a pre-contract contract that provides, perhaps among other things, for whatever formalities the parties wish to impose for having a contract, and that also provides that neither party will be liable to the other for any action taken during the negotiation.

It is also wise when entering a negotiation to be clear about the resources you are willing to commit to reach a contract. In custom manufacturing, especially at the forefront of technological development, substantial technical difficulties may need to be hammered out before a contract can be concluded. This may involve considerable expense on both sides, as in *Airplane engines*, H Sup. Ct. 19920925. Parties should give some advanced thought to how much they are willing to invest before having contractual assurances.

§ 5.03 Offer

An offer is a definite proposal to specific persons indicating an intent to be bound in case of acceptance.

A proposal is definite if it specifies the price, the quantity, and the nature of the goods. It may also be definite if there is a way of ascertaining these items. Art. 14. This should be regarded as a safe harbor saying that the proposal is definite if all three items are set forth, but one should not read from it that failure to meet the terms means that there is no offer. A previous contract between the parties that specified a price may determine the price in the new offer. Art. 9(1); *German goods*, HU Trial 19920324. A trade custom may make the terms sufficiently definite. Art. 9(2); *Geneva Pharmaceuticals*, US Trial. When seller has a published catalogue and buyer mentions no price, the price will be the catalogue price. If no price is otherwise specified, it will be the market price at the time of contracting if there is one. Art. 55; *Electronic components*, F App 19920422.

Some have perceived an inconsistency between art. 14 and art. 55, the former demanding that a price be fixable for an offer, and the latter fixing the price where the parties neglect to do so. But there is no inconsistency. Art. 14 only says that a proposal is an offer if it sets forth a way to fix the price; it does not make that the exclusive route to an offer, and art. 55 supplements it by providing a way to fix the price.

An alternative analysis would hold that where the parties clearly intended to have a contract, that implicitly excludes the price requirement of art. 14 and substitutes art. 55.

Where the parties agreed to negotiate the price of a variable agricultural commodity "to be fixed during the season," one court held that the price would be what seller charged to other independent buyers at the time of sale to buyer where the parties in fact never reached agreement on the price. The theory of the case must have been that "to be fixed during the season" meant the market price at the season, which does not require art. 55. *Sour cherries*, D Trial 20050803. However, in another case where the parties had agreed that they would fix the price in a later negotiation that did not succeed, it was held that the market price could not be used because the parties, by agreeing to fix the price by negotiation, did not fall within art. 55 and derogated from it. *Ukrainian goods*, RUS Arb 19950303. Both cases might have been correctly decided if it is understood that it depends on the intent of the parties as to whether there was a contract with the price fixed as the market price, or whether the parties intended to have a contract only if they agreed on the price in their later negotiation. In neither case is art. 55 appropriate because art. 55 refers to the market price at the time the contract is concluded, and both cases assumed that it was the market price at some other time.

Art. 55 provides that if no price is fixed, the parties mean to choose the market price at the time of contracting. Where seller invoiced a price and buyer did not object to the price, the court held the invoiced price to be the market price, presumably because buyer did not protest that it was not the market price in a timely fashion. *Embroidered Fabrics*, CH Trial 19970703. The insertion of art. 55 into CISG signals that the price should be the market price unless the objecting party proves that it was the parties' intent not to have a contract unless they could agree on a price.

One court determined the quality of the goods from the price charged for them on the assumption that parties acting at arm's length normally conclude contracts where the performance of both parties is of equal value. *Chinchilla pelts*, A Sup. Ct. 19941110. There is no textual support for this, but it is presumably an application of art. 8 in determining the intent of the parties.

While quantity is not usually a problem, it can be. If 100 widgets are ordered, the delivery of 90 or 110 may be conforming if there is an industry custom or prior dealing to indicate that quantity deviations of up to 10% are acceptable. *Artframe mouldings*, CDN Trial 19990831.

An offer can be sufficiently definite even if it is one of several alternative offers. *Airplane engines*, H Sup. Ct. 19920925. It is not unusual for a seller to provide different prices depending on whether the goods are to be shipped f.o.b. or c.i.f., and buyer chooses between them.

A proposal offered to a number of people may be an offer if it has limits. The purpose of requiring specific persons is to prevent general advertisements from becoming offers, thereby making sellers uncertain about how much inventory to carry or buyers uncertain about how many goods they are purchasing. An advertisement that seller has 100 shovels for sale at $10 each to the first people who claim them by providing valid credit card numbers would be a valid offer, even though seller has no idea who will buy the shovels.

Most offers meeting the above standard will not be troubled by the "intent to be bound" standard. Some contracts, especially those that are complicated, show evidence that the parties do not intend to be bound even when price, quantity, and quality are fixed. This may be the case where there is a long period of negotiation about many subsidiary matters, or it may be because the parties in their past dealings with each other have not acted as though they thought they had a binding contract until all the details were worked out. *Hanwha*, US Trial. There may also be lack of intention to be bound when the speaker invites the recipient to make an offer. *Screws*, D App 19940304. But unless there are disagreements about specific issues, the fact that the parties agree that they will memorialize their agreement in a formal contract at a later time does not prevent the formation of a contract, especially when the goods have been delivered. *Graphiplus program*, D Trial 19950208.

Whether an offeror intends to be bound is determined by the interpretive rules of art. 8. The fact that the offer is made to only one person is evidence that the offeror intends to be bound. The fact that the offer is "subject to prior sale" does not negate the intention to be bound if the offeree is the first to accept. *Ship spare parts*, D Sup. Ct. 20150325. One court has held that intention to be bound is not enough unless combined in the same document with the definite items required, even though those items were well-known to both parties because a contract had previously been reached with seller's parent. *Textile yarn*, D App 20000830. That case seems excessively formalistic. In *Embroidered Fabrics*, CH Trial 19970703, the court determined that the offeror-buyer intended to be bound based on her subsequent actions of requesting an invoice and complaining about the quality of the goods, both indicating she thought that a contract existed.

An offer is effective when it reaches the offeree. If the offeror's valid revocation of the offer reaches the offeree before the offer does, there is no offer to accept. Arts. 15, 24.

Offers are revocable unless the offer indicates that it is irrevocable. Arts. 15, 16. This would be the case where the offeror gives the offeree a fixed time within which to respond. *Crane*, E App 20100715. One question raised by this case, but not answered, is whether an offer with a fixed date that is expressly communicated to be subject to prior sale is an offer that indicates that it is irrevocable. It is perhaps only revocable by prior sale.

The words "it indicates" may be intended to suspend the search for intent and to focus solely on objective meaning. No case has tackled this question, and it is probably best not to see these two words as modifying art. 8's test for meaning.

An offer may also be irrevocable where the offeree reasonably thinks the offer is irrevocable and acts in reliance on it. This sounds very much like the U.S. doctrine of promissory estoppel, though it does not specifically rely on foreseeability to offeror of offeree's reliance, nor does it require that offeree's reliance be detrimental, though courts might well read both of those requirements in *Geneva Pharmaceuticals*, US Trial. Acting on the offer may involve obtaining materials or personnel, or beginning production, or rejecting competing offers, though the offeree will need to prove that these actions were specific to the offer and not in the ordinary course of its business.

An express rejection terminates the offer. For a reply that purports to be an acceptance but contains materially different terms, see below.

§5.04 Acceptance

An acceptance is effective when received by the offeror or his computer. *CISG-AC Op. 1*. This is a little unusual, because generally communications are effective when dispatched, even if they are never received, but it is consistent with the rules on offers. Arts. 15, 27. This can raise a problem for acceptance by conduct, because the acceptance is not effective until the conduct comes to the attention of the offeror. *Pasta Zara*, US Trial.

An acceptance is also presumably effective where received, though in an era where many contracts are made by phone or internet, locating the contract at a particular place seems artificial. Artificial or not, it may be necessary. *Honey*, NZ Trial 20150603. Silence without more does not accept an offer, *Compensators, NL Trial* 20070117, but failure to object at crucial points may provide evidence of a party's intent or state of mind at the time. For instance, where buyer objected to the price of an invoice but not to the quantity, she was deemed to have agreed to the quantity invoiced. *Embroidered Fabrics*, CH Trial 19970703. A buyer who accepted lobster tails and signed an attached invoice without objection accepted the sales contract. *Congelados*, US Trial.

Silence will constitute acceptance where, in previous dealings, a shoe manufacturer shipped orders without first formally accepting them. *Cardin shoes*, F. App 19991021.

Cobalt sulfate, D Sup. Ct. 19960403, suggests that one party can make silence into acceptance by specifying just that in the offer. Seller's offer stated: "Without return of a signed copy by mail within 2x24 hours (after you received originals) we consider this contract accepted." Absent trade custom or prior dealings of the parties, that seems questionable.

Unless the offer specifies otherwise, acceptance could be by an act such as shipping the goods, using them, or paying the purchase price. *Insulating materials*, A Sup. Ct. 20121213; *Congelados*, US Trial. A buyer who had not signed a proposed contract amendment was held to have accepted it by making two payments in accord with the amendment. *Wood flooring*, CHN Arb 20210311. In *Golden Valley Grape Juice*, US Trial, the court talks about acceptance by conduct, but there was formal acceptance of seller's standard conditions by accepting the offering e-mail to which they were attached. A court is unlikely to find acceptance from doing an act the person was already obligated to perform. In *C9 Ventures* (not a CISG case), where the lessee of helium tanks received an invoice with the tank, paying the invoice was not consent to the standard terms on the invoice. But acceptance was found where the party took the benefits of the contract, even though protesting five months later (after receiving a letter of credit) an unwillingness to be bound by certain clauses of it. *Filanto v. Chilewich*, US Trial. The key here seemed to be that seller knew that buyer intended all the provisions of his contract with his sub-buyer to apply to the contract with his supplier and unreasonably delayed protesting. Acceptance by an act may be effective by doing the act without communication to the offeror if that is the term of the offer or the practice of the parties. Art. 18(3). However, the party alleging such an acceptance must be prepared to prove the practice or the term of the offer. *Pasta Zara*, US Trial.

Acceptance by act that is not specified in the offer runs the risk that the act will not come to the attention of the offeror before the offeror revokes the offer, or before it is revoked by expiration of a reasonable time.

Acceptance by act is insufficient to authorize arbitration in the U.S. United States law requires either a contract signed by both parties, or an exchange of letters where each party has signed. A contract where buyer promises to pay a certain amount by specified dates and does in fact make the first two payments is insufficient for a U.S. court to confirm an arbitration award. *Jiangsu Beier*, US Trial. Countries that adhere to the New York Convention impose the same requirement, *Metals*, D App 19950308, and art. 90 specifies that CISG provisions yield to other treaties.

Acceptance by conduct can be taken to unwarranted extremes. In one case where buyer claimed that the order was 540 pairs of shoes short, the court said that the reduced delivery was a rejection of buyer's offer and a counteroffer, which was accepted when buyer accepted the smaller delivery. *Italian Shoes*, D App 19950523. This makes a mockery of the original contract and deprives buyer of what he was entitled to expect.

Acceptance in theory must be of all terms in the offer. Where fewer than all the terms are agreed upon, it is possible that a contract might be formed on those terms where the parties intended that to be a contract, but the party urging the contract will seldom be able to prove that limited intent. *Screws*, D App 19940304.

Frequently, offerees send back papers that purport to be acceptances, but contain additional or different terms. Art. 19 says that if the differences are material, the purported acceptance is a rejection and a new offer. If the differences are not material a contract is formed, including the differences unless the original offeror objects. There follows a list of things that are material that includes everything of significance about a contract: price, payment, quality, quantity, place of delivery, time of delivery, extent of liability, and dispute settlement mechanisms. One court has held that where seller proposed changing the place of delivery (and therefore the place of payment) from seller's factory to seller's airport, the change is so minor as to not be material, even though CISG says that all matters related to payment and delivery are material. *Taiwanese goods*, ROK App 20130719. In a similar vein, where the offer to buy a car was for delivery no later than March 15 and seller responded "deliver April, time of delivery remains reserved," the court held the variance minor and accepted by buyer for lack of objection. *Automobile*, D App 19990427. Such interpretations are to be discouraged because they make CISG less certain, thereby making it difficult for clients to predict outcomes. Yet in the Korean case, the change not only appeared to be trivial, but advantageous to the party challenging it, and in the German case the court, in finding what a reasonable time for delivery might be, fell back on the intent expressed by buyer, and held that a reasonable time was no later than March 15. The message of these cases is that whether a proposed change is material or not may depend on all the facts and circumstances, despite CISG's enumeration of things that are material. One might suggest that they are only presumptively material, and not an exclusive list of all things that might be material under the facts of the case.

An important point to reiterate is that offering new terms rejects the original offer. Where the original offer contained an arbitration clause, but a subsequent offer from the same party did not include it and failed to incorporate the previous documents, no arbitration clause was in the contract because the contract was formed by acceptance of the later offer. *Meduri Farms*, US Trial.

The problem here is that if each time a different term is mentioned and one insists on a mirror image acceptance of an offer, no exchange of paper can form a contract because seller and buyer will inevitably have different standard terms. The traditional "last shot" rule—which finds that the last paper is the only remaining offer—which is accepted by the other side performing, has been much criticized as arbitrary, but it is the logical extension of CISG's emphasis on offer and acceptance. Much more rational is the "knock-out" rule, where the contract is formed by all the agreed-upon terms, and the terms of the parties that are inconsistent with each other are knocked out and replaced by CISG's supplemental rules.

After the contract has been concluded, later changes communicated by one party are proposals to amend the contract. They do not change the contract unless accepted by the other party. *Jute*, E Sup. Ct. 20000128.

§ 5.05 Consideration

There is no mention of a requirement of consideration in CISG. There is no such requirement. It can be argued that this is a matter of validity of the contract in U.S. law and so governed by domestic law under art. 4(a), and *Geneva Pharmaceuticals*, US Trial, so stated, though it appears that there was adequate consideration in that case. On the other hand, art. 4 provides that CISG applies to the formation of the contract. It seems clear that CISG was intended to do away with the requirement of consideration for the formation of a contract because it was not mentioned. That textual argument is weakened because CISG was not intended to do away with the requirement of capacity, a key requirement for contract formation. In an equally unsatisfactory opinion where there was clearly consideration, *Shuttle Packaging*, US Trial, stated that consideration is not required under CISG. Art. 11 states that a contract of sale is not subject to any form requirement, but that raises the question of whether consideration is a matter of form or substance. Consideration is not usually a practical problem in contract formation for sales contracts. Few contracts for the international sale of goods are concluded without both parties providing consideration. Where the issue is more likely to arise is in the amendment of a sales contract. Amendment is often done without new consideration being provided. Art. 29(1) provides "A contract may be modified or terminated by the mere agreement of the parties." That seems to state that nothing is required other than the parties' agreement, so consideration should not be required.

§5.06 Writing

A contract need not be in writing unless a state has reserved to that provision. Arts. 11, 96. This means that many contracts will be concluded over the phone for substantial amounts of money. Where that is the case, the court is left with the difficult job of determining whether a contract exists, and what its terms might be. This is a matter of interpretation of the contract to be pursued under arts. 8 and 9. *Embroidered Fabrics*, CH Trial 19970703; *Pork*, A App 20020307. When a contract is made orally, it is always a good idea to follow as quickly as possible with a written communication confirming the important terms of it, as was done in *Sour cherries*, D Trial 20050803.

Where a Member State has reserved to art. 11, art. 11 does not apply. The question then becomes, what does apply? One view is that a writing is required whenever there is a contracting party whose place of business is in the reserving state. A second view is that a writing is only required when the case is brought before a court in a reserving state. The preferable view is that a choice of law analysis is required, and a writing is mandated only if that analysis leads to the law of a state whose domestic law requires a writing and has reserved to art. 11. This is certainly a situation not specifically dealt with by CISG, so art. 7(2) calls on the court to apply general principles of CISG and, in default thereof, the law of the state selected by private international law principles, presumably of the forum state. However, art. 7(1)'s call to consider the international nature of CISG might require consideration of the choice of law principles of all states involved and, if they differ, choosing the one with the greatest salience to the issue involved. In one case, that awful choice was avoided when the arbitrator found that the choice of law rules of all three states pointed to Yugoslav law—one because the contract was signed there, a second because it was the principal office of seller, and a third because it was seller's habitual residence. *Steel bars*, ICC 6281. *Forestal Guarani*, US App, was a case where the court considered only the choice of law rules of the forum, and sent the case back to the district court for a decision on that. Interestingly, it was not the U.S. that had reserved to art. 11, but the seller's country, Argentina, and the purchase price had been substantially paid by the U.S. buyer. In fact, most courts and commentators have considered only the choice of law rules of the forum state.

Regardless of how many choice of law rules are consulted, a result that points to the law of a country such as the United States that has not reserved to article 11 is problematic because the law of that country with respect to international sales contracts is CISG. However, art. 12 says that CISG does not apply to this issue. It is even more of an anomaly if the domestic law of the country requires a writing, because by not reserving to art. 11, the country has in effect declared that while the writing requirement applies to domestic contracts, it need not apply to international contracts.

The prior question is whether there is any general principle of CISG that might resolve the case under art. 7(2). One is effectuating the intent of the parties, but that general principle would seem to entirely negate the ability of countries to reserve to art. 11 because that principle would always result in the enforcement of the contract. The same is true of preserving as much of the contract as possible. It seems that there are no general principles of CISG that will sensibly resolve these cases, so recourse must be had to choice of law.

Laws change, but diplomacy grinds slowly. Suppose a country that has validly reserved to art. 11 changes its domestic law so that contracts no longer need be in writing, but that country has not withdrawn its reservation to art. 11 as permitted by art. 97(4). The country no longer qualifies to make a declaration reserving to art. 11, but it did qualify when the declaration was filed.

§5.07 Amendment

While the lack of a writing requirement in the making of a contract has been problematic, the lack of either a writing or a consideration requirement has made it very easy for courts to find that the parties have amended or terminated the contract. Art. 29(1) provides that a contract may be modified or terminated by "mere agreement," which argues that neither consideration nor a writing is required. The result is that a party may be completely deprived of a remedy when trying to be accommodating and work out a solution in a post-breach situation. A German court found that the parties had terminated a contract for wood when buyer complained about its nonconformity, then seller announced that he would market the wood himself. Neither party expressly disclaimed the contract. *Wood*, D App 19940222. One wonders whether the court would have made the same ruling had it been buyer suing for nonconformity of the goods, rather than seller's assignee claiming the purchase price.

See also *Valero*, US App, where the court found that the parties had amended their original contract under questionable circumstances.

While the court in *Wood* found agreement by implication, the general rule is that silence does not constitute acceptance. Art. 18(1). Where an oral contract was followed by seller's invoice making a choice of court, the invoice was properly held to be a proposal to amend the oral contract that was not accepted by buyer, even though invoices were sent 11 times with no response from buyer. It was not proven that buyer ever read seller's invoices. *Chateau des Charmes*, US App Acceptance or rejection of a party's proposal to amend or terminate a contract can be found by implication of its statements. Where a party talked about curing past defects and being prepared for future performance, the other party could not have interpreted that as assent to terminating the contract. *Hand cleaner*, NL App 20150922.

The other problem with contract changes not in writing is that it may be obvious that the contract has been changed, but quite ambiguous on what the new contract provides. Take a contract to sell property for $1 million, payable at $20,000 a month for 50 months. After month 10, buyer tenders and seller accepts $10,000 per month for five months. The contract has been changed to a payment of $10,000 per month, but for how long? Has the principal amount been changed, the payment period elongated, or both?

Many of these amendment and termination problems can be avoided by accepting the invitation of art. 29(2) and inserting in the original written contract a provision that it can only be amended or terminated in writing, which will be upheld. *Canada-Russia*, ICC Arb 9117/1998. One must doubt the accuracy of the arbitrator's statement that such an agreement makes the court less likely to consider the practices of the parties. Art. 29(2) specifically states that a party may be precluded from invoking such a clause where the other party has relied on conduct indicating either amendment or termination.

In one case, the writing agreement was overridden by trade custom. Buyer and seller contracted that modifications required the written consent of both parties. The court held that Austrian standard B2110 was part of the contract, presumably by trade custom. That standard provides that a writing requirement is satisfied if it is transmitted by one party and not objected to by the other party within a reasonable time. While there appears to be a conflict between the two provisions, the court harmonized it by using standard B2110 to define what the parties meant by written consent. There was no discussion of the application of article 8 to determine intent, or the fact that actual intent should trump trade custom. *Steel bars*, A App 20071218.

A more appropriate decision applied CISG when the parties specified law of Ukraine, even though the contract also incorporated the Grain and Feed Trade Association form contract, which excluded CISG. *Corn*, Ukraine Arb 218y/2011, 20120123. The direct expression of the parties for Ukraine law, which is CISG, should trump an indirect expression of the parties through adoption of a form trade contract.

Conduct can include words. Where the contract called for payment by letter of credit but seller wrote buyer that he had a credit and payment by bank guarantee would do, and buyer obtained the bank guarantee, the court held that this amended the contract and failure to obtain the letter of credit was not a breach. *Steel cable*, E App 20130709.

The CISG Advisory Council has tried to rein in the tendency to find contract amendment easily, particularly when the result is exclusion of CISG. *CISG-AC 16*.

§5.08 Terms of the Contract

Assuming that a contract exists, what are the terms of that contract? This question often arises when part of the contract is alleged to be the form of one or both parties. In a perfect world, the offeree simply accepts the offer. In the real world, it does not occur so neatly.

In order to be a term of the contract, the non-proposing party needs to know that the term is part of the contract and what the term is. That person also needs to have a reasonable opportunity to consider it before being bound. *CISG-AC Op. 13*. This follows from art. 8's command that "statements made by and other conduct of a party are to be interpreted according to the understanding that a reasonable person of the same kind as the other party would have had in the same circumstances."

The easiest case is where the standard terms are part of the offer. They are seldom on the same page as the offer because they are usually too long. If the offer is made by e-mail with the standard terms attached, the standard terms are part of the contract. In *Golden Valley Grape Juice*, US Trial, standard terms specifically agreed to (and even translated by the agreeing party) were an accepted part of the offer even though never supplied. The court made no point of this, but it should be noted that they were not standard terms of the individual party, but ORGALIME terms used industry-wide and readily available online so they need not have been supplied. *Brewing tanks*, D App 20151221. The terms need not be provided so long as they can be easily referenced by the other party, such as by a clause providing the URL in reasonably conspicuous type. In *Venison*, D App 19991028, seller's standard terms were used by the parties in earlier transactions and were made accessible to buyer.

Where seller's acceptance referred to seller's standard conditions, which were not attached to the acceptance, the court held that those standard conditions were not part of the contract. *Gear-cutting machine*, D Sup. Ct. 20011031. Placing the offeree's standard terms on the back of the acceptance is not enough because that does not indicate assent of the offeror. *Compensators*, NL App 20070529. While the case seems unexceptional on the facts given above, the parties had completed a number of previous similar transactions, always with the same standard terms on the back, so this was not the first time that buyer had received these terms. Under those circumstances, it would appear more likely to hold that buyer had received ample opportunity to decide whether he was willing to abide by those terms, but not in a format that would draw attention to the fact that this was part of the contract.

The question is whether the parties intended to incorporate the standard terms into their contract, a fact question, that the jury in *ECEM European Chemical 2*, US Trial, answered in the negative. Where the standard terms were in fact easily accessible on the internet, but seller never stated that or provided a URL for them, the court held them not part of the contract. *Apple rings*, NL App 20140422. In *Can-liner maker*, D Trial 20170717, providing the specific URL was insufficient to incorporate the terms, though it is unclear whether the vice was that the contract was negotiated by letter rather than by e-mail, or that seller failed to prove that the standard terms were in fact on that website at the crucial time.

It is not uncommon for standard terms to be in the language of the person propounding those terms, which in an international sale will often not be the language of the other party. A U.S. court has the most extreme dicta on this. It said in a footnote: "We find it nothing short of astounding that an individual, purportedly experienced in commercial matters, would sign a contract in a foreign language and expect not to be bound simply because he could not comprehend its terms." *MCC-Marble Ceramic*, US App Some courts have held that where the language can be easily translated in the other party's country, the terms become part of the contract. *Tantal powder*, A Sup. Ct. 20031217. Others have suggested that the terms should be in the language of the other party or in the language in which the contract was negotiated, which is endorsed by *CISG-AC Op. 13*, on grounds that art. 8 requires that statements be interpreted as the reasonable hearer would understand them.

Translation can be an inherently tricky business, epitomized by the Italian expression *tradurre é tradire*: translation is treason. A Chinese seller provided English and Chinese versions of a contract to supply KN-95 masks. Both purported to be the prevailing version and identical in meaning. In fact, they differed on whether CISG was excluded and whether and where arbitration was required. The court held that that none of the variant clauses were part of the contract because they were not agreed to. It implied that there was a contract with respect to clauses that were identical in both languages. *Matter of New York*, US Trial.

Standard terms provided in an invoice accompanying the goods that arrive after the offer has been accepted are not part of the contract. They are proposals to amend the contract, which will fail absent assent by the other party. *VLM Food Trading*, US App; *Urea*, CH Trial 19971203, *Chicago Prime Packers*, US Trial; *Fruit juice*, CH Trial 20120614; *Machine*, NL App 20070529. On the other hand, signing and returning the invoice, even when the signer neither read the invoice nor understood the significance of it, was consent to the choice of court clause it contained, according to one court. *BTC-USA*, US Trial.

§5.09 Finding a Contract after Performance

As a matter of practicality, courts will sometimes hold that no contract exists when the contract is entirely executory because the parties have not agreed by offer and acceptance, and they do not appear to have reached consensus. When there has been partial performance, the courts strive to find that the contract exists because of the practical difficulties of unwinding an international sale that has been at least partially performed. One of the impediments to this is where the court cannot find an offer and acceptance, as where parties have put forth standard terms that are contradictory, or where neither party appears to have accepted everything that the other set forth. *Orica Australia*, US Trial.

One way in which courts sometimes avoid the offer-acceptance problem is by holding that the contract was concluded orally, thus excluding both parties' standard terms, and leaving the matter that the parties contest to suppletive law. *MCC-Marble Ceramic*, US App; *Chateau des Charmes*, US App. This will not always work, especially with courts that are tied to the Statute of Frauds or other domestic law. In *Barbara Berry*, US Trial, the court granted summary judgment without considering whether the contract was oral or formed by the parties' later exchange of forms, and whether seller's general conditions, conveyed with its acceptance and printed on the packaging, were part of the contract under CISG. The Ninth Circuit reversed, instructing the court to consider both questions under CISG. *Barbara Berry*, US App. The trial court again granted summary judgment without considering those issues, this time on grounds that even if CISG applied, there was no proof of nonconformity because buyer used the raspberry stock to generate more stock, which is not a normal use. *Barbara Berry II*, US Trial. The principle is what I call *stare decisis*.

Another device, where the parties have conflicting standard terms, is to find that the contract is made by the last written proposal, and acceptance by performance. *Glassware ingredients*, F Sup. Ct. 19980716. This is a solution that is transparently artificial, as the party accepting the goods had no intention of accepting the other party's terms. An extreme example of this (where there were no general terms involved) involved a hotel that asked seller whether seller could furnish an oven, which seller delivered and installed. The court correctly held that buyer's letter was not an offer but an invitation to make an offer, then in desperation held that seller's delivery of the oven was an offer that was accepted by buyer permitting its installation. *Hotel oven*, CH Trial 20070427.

A third possible move is preferable: to hold that where the parties clearly intended an agreement, the terms of the agreement are those to which the parties agreed, and the terms about which there is disagreement are not part of the contract. *Powdered milk*, D Sup. Ct. 20020109.

In all cases, the emphasis should not be on the mechanical, but on trying to determine the parties' intent—did they think they had a contract, and what did they think its terms were? The court in *Orica Australia*, US Trial, properly denied a motion for summary judgment because those facts were deeply and reasonably disputed by the parties.

CHECKPOINTS

You should have learned that:

- CISG specifically says a contract is formed by offer and acceptance. Contracts can also be formed by mutual consent even though identifying an offer and an acceptance would be artificial.

- CISG does not result in liability for failure to negotiate a sales contract. The laws of some member states prescribe liability for failure to negotiate in good faith.

- An offer is a definable proposal to specific persons indicating an intent to be bound in case of acceptance. The identity of the goods and quantity to be sold must be determinable. The price if not specified or determinable is fair market value if one can be ascertained.

- An advertisement is not normally an offer, but it may be an offer if the quantity to be sold is stated to be limited to the first number of people who respond with credit cards.

- The dealings of the parties may indicate that one or both parties do not intend to be bound until all points are resolved or until the contract is integrated into a formal writing.

- An offer is effective when it reaches the offeree.

- An offer is revocable unless it indicates that it is not, or unless the offeree reasonably thinks it is irrevocable and acts to his detriment in reliance on irrevocability.

- Express rejection terminates an offer.

- Acceptance is effective when received.

- Silence does not normally accept an offer, but it may be acceptance of new terms proposed in a confirmation or other communication to which the recipient does not object.

- Acceptance can be by conduct, but tribunals should be careful to assure that the conduct unambiguously indicates consent.

- Normally, acceptance must be of all the terms of the contract.

- Where the contract is executory, a purported acceptance proposing differing terms rejects the original offer and is itself a new offer.

- Where the contract has been partially performed, some courts count the performance as acceptance of the last written offer, while others find that the contract consists only of those clauses on which the parties have agreed.

- After a contract has been concluded, later communications can only be proposals to amend the contract.

- Neither consideration nor a writing is required for most contracts, but a writing may be required when one of the parties has a place of business in a state that has reserved to art. 11.

- A contract can be amended by mere agreement in words or conduct unless the contract specifies that it must be amended in writing. Even then, it can be amended by conduct.

- Where a contract is amended either orally or by conduct, it may be clear that the amendment has taken place, but unclear what the terms of the amendment might be.

- The terms of a contract are the terms to which the parties have agreed.

- Terms communicated after the contract has been concluded are not terms of the contract, but proposals to amend the contract.

- To be a term of the contract, the non-proposing party needs to know that the term is part of the contract, and what the term is. That person also needs to have a reasonable opportunity to consider the term before being bound.

- Standard terms printed on invoices are not part of the contract.

- Where parties exchange forms with contradictory standard terms, courts sometimes find that the contract was concluded orally so it does not contain the standard terms of either party.

CHAPTER 6

Seller Delivers, Risk of Loss, Conformity of Goods & Third-Party Claims

---

ROADMAP

After reading this chapter, you should understand:

- Seller's main obligation is to deliver physical possession and ownership of the goods or documents agreed upon free from known intellectual property claims.

- The time and place of delivery are crucial to many aspects of seller's performance. They determine where and when the goods or documents must conform, where and when seller must fulfill other obligations, and where and when buyer must pay.

- Seller must deliver the goods or documents where and when the contract provides. Usually, parties will provide the place of delivery and passage of risk of loss by using a recognized trade term.

- When the contract does not provide and if carriage of goods is involved, seller delivers by handing the goods to the first carrier. The first carrier is someone other than seller or buyer.

- Passage of risk of loss from seller to buyer generally occurs on delivery.

- Delivery is often made by delivering documents conferring the right to eventual possession of goods.

- Trade terms usually do not include a time for delivery. CISG provides that delivery must be within a reasonable time unless the parties have otherwise provided.

- Where trade terms that can be derived from more than one source are used, it is important to specify the source.

- Students should know the different responsibilities that go with trade terms fob, cif, and the d terms.

- In the European Union, there is generally adjudicatory jurisdiction at the place of performance of a sales contract.

- Goods must normally conform to the contract. This means that they must comply with the quantity and quality called for by the contract, and be accompanied by any required documents.

- Goods must be fit for the purposes for which such goods are ordinarily used.

- In the absence of other specifications, the goods must be marketable.

- Seller is liable for failure of the goods to be fit for any unusual purpose known to seller before conclusion of the contract, except where it was unreasonable for buyer to rely on seller's skill.

- Where seller provides buyer with a model or sample of the goods sufficient to discover any nonconformity, seller is not liable for failure of the goods to conform in ways that should have been discovered from the model or sample.

- Seller is not liable for nonconformity of which buyer was aware when the contract was concluded.

- Seller is not liable for nonconformity where it was unreasonable for buyer to rely on seller's skill.

- Seller is liable for failure to package the goods adequately for their anticipated transport.

- Conformity requirements can be disclaimed by mutual agreement.

- Goods must conform at the time and place where risk of loss passes.

- Seller is responsible for complying with legal regulations in buyer's country except when the rules are difficult to ascertain and seller has no good commercial reasons for discovering them.

- Buyer is obligated to examine the goods in a reasonable manner as soon as practicable and to give specific notice to seller of nonconformity within a reasonable time.

- Prompt and specific notice is required in order to give seller the opportunity to cure, to provide reliable evidence of the nonconformity and when it occurred, and to limit disputes about conformity to the nonconformities listed in the notice.

- The timeliness of the notice depends on the nature of the goods, whether the defect is obvious or hidden, the examination required to discover it, and the status of buyer. Less time is allowed for perishable or seasonal goods. Hidden defects should be reported as soon as a reasonable buyer would have discovered them. A person who does not regularly deal in the goods concerned has longer to report nonconformities than a person in the business.

- The notice of nonconformity must relate the symptoms, but does not require buyer to divine the ultimate cause.

- Buyer who does not give timely and specific notice of nonconformity cannot rely on any remedies provided for nonconformity unless excused. Buyer is excused if seller could not have been unaware of the defect and did not inform buyer of it. If buyer can show reasonable excuse for failure to give timely and specific notice, buyer retains the remedies of price reduction and damages (but not for lost profits), but not the remedies of specific performance or avoidance.

- Seller must deliver the goods free from any unexcepted non-IP right or claim of a third party.

- Seller must also deliver goods free from any unexpected right or claim based on intellectual property in buyer's state, or a state where the parties contemplated that the goods would be resold or used, but only if seller could not have been unaware of the right or claim, there was no reason for buyer to be aware of the claim, and the claim did not result from following buyer's instructions.

A. Delivery Obligations and Trade Terms

§6.01 Seller's Obligation

Seller's main obligation is to deliver physical possession and the ownership of the goods or documents agreed upon free from known intellectual property claims. The time and place of delivery are crucial to many aspects of seller's performance. They determine where and when the goods or documents must conform; where and when seller must fulfill other obligations; and where and when buyer must pay. I use the term "nonconformity" to include any deviation from seller's obligations, even though technically nonconformity only refers to shortfalls in the goods. In most cases, the time and place where delivery must be made is also the time and place where the risk of loss passes. Art. 67. Whether the nonconformity is known at the time is not relevant; what is important is the existence of the nonconformity at the time. Art. 36. *Frozen pork*, D Sup. Ct. 20050302. The place of delivery may have less obvious consequences. In countries of the European Union, a court at the place of performance will have judicial jurisdiction to determine breach of contract actions in the absence of a clause siting exclusive jurisdiction elsewhere. *Brussels reg*, art. 4, 5, 6, 7(1), 25.

§6.02 Delivery and Passage of Risk of Loss

Seller must deliver the goods or documents where and when the contract provides. In the vast majority of cases, parties will provide the place of delivery and passage of risk of loss by using a recognized trade term, the most popular of which are *fob* and *cif*. Under CISG, when the contract does not provide and if carriage of goods is involved (as it usually is), seller delivers by handing the goods to the first carrier, which is where the risk of loss passes. Art. 67(1).

The first carrier is someone other than seller. Art. 31(a). It can be the trucker who picks up goods from seller's warehouse, the ship to which seller delivers the goods, or a freight forwarder engaged to arrange the carriage. If seller is delivering the goods itself, that is a delivery provided by the contract and does not involve the carriage of goods. This usually means that seller will deliver to buyer's place of business. *Art books*, CH Trial 19990210. Otherwise, goods are to be delivered where they are or where they are to be made or, if none of the above applies, where seller has his place of business on contracting. Art. 31. Note that the above rules (including the first carrier rule) give way to the specifics of the trade term if the parties use a trade term.

Carriage of goods need not be specified; it may be implied from the fact that seller and buyer have places of business in different countries and no provision for delivery is found in the contract. In *Pizza cartons*, D Trial 20000413, the contract was held to involve carriage of goods by the fact of the distance from Italy to Duisberg, Germany.

Passage of the risk of loss is generally consistent with delivery. Arts. 66–70. This is even true where seller has retained title until he is paid. Title retention is usually a security device that does not affect either delivery requirements or passage of risk of loss. While no court has specifically discussed the question, it appears assumed that such a reservation of title is not sufficiently inconsistent with CISG to constitute an implied rejection of a CISG term involving passage of the risk of loss. *St. Paul Guardian*, US Trial.

There is no magic about using recognized trade terms except that the use saves the cost of negotiating and interpreting variants. Occasionally, parties use a term in the contract that is not a recognized trade term, but that alters default rules. The designations "free buyer's address," "franco domicile," "duty paid," and "non taxed" led the court to rule that the parties had designated delivery to buyer's residence. *Frozen chicken*, D App 19921120. But it should be noted that in cif destination incoterms, seller pays to get the goods to the destination, but risk of loss passes and delivery is made when the goods are placed on board the vessel at seller's arrangement.

We normally think that delivery is the physical handing over of goods, but delivery is often made by the delivery of documents enabling buyer to obtain the goods at a future time. While this is most frequently done with goods being shipped, in *Cobalt sulfate*, D Sup. Ct. 19960403, seller deposited goods in a warehouse and provided buyer with documents allowing buyer to access the goods. Where delivery is by means of documents, it would be unusual if the contract did not specify where and within what period the documents are to be delivered.

A problem for which I have found no cases is the situation where goods are sold while in transit, which is surprising, because sales in transit are common. Such sales are usually effectuated by the transfer of documents permitting the goods to be claimed at their destination. Perhaps the reason for the paucity of litigation is that the usual purpose of that litigation is to assign the risk of loss, and art. 68 generally fixes the risk of loss at the moment the contract selling the goods in transit is concluded.

A distinction must be made between documents of title, such as bills of lading or warehouse receipts, and documents related to conformity of the goods, such as instructions or certificates of origin. Failure to deliver documents of title is a breach by failure of delivery; failure to deliver conformity documents is not a failure to deliver, but a nonconforming delivery. The notice requirements and remedies differ.

However, the risk of loss does not pass until the goods are specified to the contract. A seller who ships goods for a dozen customers to his foreign agent to be parceled out does not pass the risk of loss until the shipment is divided, either by marking the goods, designation in the shipping documents, or notice to the buyer. Art. 67(2).

When goods are transferred while in transit, CISG is not specific about when or where delivery occurs. The general rule is that risk of loss passes when the contract is concluded. However, where the initial seller provides insurance, as in a cif trade term, risk of loss will normally pass from the initial loading, even though technically this sub-buyer had no rights in these goods at that time. That will not be the case if buyer (who is now seller) knows that there is something wrong with the goods. Art. 68.

In the rare case not covered by the previous rules, risk of loss passes when identified goods are made available to buyer and buyer has been notified of it. Art. 69.

These default rules make economic sense. Putting the risk of loss on the person who can reduce the risk of loss at the lowest cost makes sense for everyone because it reduces the overall cost of the sale. Alternatively, the risk should be with the person who can most easily insure the goods and prove any damages. While seller controls the goods, seller can reduce loss most economically. While buyer has the goods, it is buyer. Once goods are delivered to the carrier, it is really the carrier who is in the best position to prevent loss, but carriers are usually protected by limitations of liability. Buyer is in a better position to verify the loss and to try to determine where the loss occurred, though that is sometimes difficult. Where several carriers are likely to be involved, passing risk of loss from seller to buyer at the first or after the last carrier eliminates the duty to determine exactly where the loss occurred.

Where seller agrees to arrange transport, as in a cfr or cif contract, seller must arrange reasonable transport. *Citgo Petroleum*, US Trial.

Time of delivery is a different matter. Trade terms generally do not govern the time of delivery. Wise parties will incorporate a time in their contract in order to reduce disputes, but they frequently do not do so. Lacking a fixed date for delivery, it is within a reasonable time. Art. 33(c). One court suggested that the statement "we will shoot for January 15th" is probably not dispensing with CISG and setting a specific delivery time. *Norfolk Southern*, US Trial.

Computing a reasonable time is often disputable. One court stated that the fact that goods intended for the Christmas season were delivered in January should not be taken into account, *Textile dyes*, E App 19970620, while another indicated that the statements of buyer about the importance of delivery by a certain date should be considered despite the fact that seller did not agree to them and reserved the right to choose a delivery date, and despite seller's proof that it was trade usage to have delivery delays of two to four weeks. *Automobile*, D App 19990427. Both cases seem misguided. The length of a reasonable time should be decided based on all the facts and circumstances, especially what others in similar situations habitually do. That includes the expressed or understood needs of the parties, such as the time seller will need to prepare the goods, and buyer's use requirements. *Alpha Prime*, US Trial.

More time is reasonable if seller must specially manufacture the goods than if seller already has them in inventory. While the seasonal nature of goods is not determinative, it is certainly a factor to be considered. The same is true of the expressed desires of both buyer and seller. If there is a trade custom, it will become part of the contract under art. 9(2) and will control, so there would be no need to determine what a reasonable time for delivery might be. In most cases, there will be sufficient evidence presented by the parties as to the length of a reasonable time that summary judgment will not be granted. *Alpha Prime*, US Trial.

§6.03 Trade Terms

Trade terms are shorthand expressions that parties can use in their contracts to specify the rights and obligations of the parties. The International Chamber of Commerce publishes trade terms called Incoterms®. The Uniform Commercial Code contains trade terms. §§2-319 to 2-325. The most popular trade terms, fob and cif, are used in both Incoterms® and the UCC. They have somewhat different incidents, so it is important to know whether the parties intended to incorporate UCC or Incoterm trade terms. The absence of designation may require a court to determine whether the parties intended the UCC or Incoterm trade term. If the parties have specified in prior dealings, or if there is a usage in the international trade of the goods involved, the court is likely to rule for the parties' prior use or the trade usage. Art. 9. While courts state the rule correctly, some courts do not require the party urging Incoterms to prove either its past use, or that it is a well-known and frequently used custom in this trade. E.g., *St. Paul*, US Trial; *BP Oil*, US App. If the parties specify either Incoterms or UCC, the trade term becomes part of the contract without regard to whether there is prior usage or trade custom.

The advantage of trade terms is that by using a few words, the parties can incorporate pages of provisions into their contract, thereby producing negotiating and drafting savings.

Trade terms generally provide the place of delivery and therefore the transfer of the risk of loss, who is responsible for freight, insurance, export clearance, import customs duties, loading, and unloading.

Trade terms can be loosely grouped into four categories. Terms beginning with "e," like ex-works, normally impose the least obligation on seller. Seller need only place the goods at buyer's disposal and notify buyer. Terms beginning with "f," like fca, fas, or fob, all require at least that seller clear the goods for export, and some require that seller move the goods or load them. Terms beginning with "c," like cfr, cif, cpt, and cip, require more of seller. Seller must arrange and pay for shipping in all cases, and insurance in most. Terms beginning with "d," like dap, dpu, and ddp, make delivery occur in buyer's country, and impose more responsibility on seller.

§6.04 FOB

FOB is a trade term meaning "free on board." FOB Incoterms means that seller delivers by causing the goods to be placed on board a ship. UCC FOB is the same where followed by the shipping port. Where followed by the destination port, it requires seller to pay for the transport of the goods to the destination port. UCC FOB can be used for any means of transport, whereas FOB Incoterms can only be used for ocean carriage. As a result, if it is clear from the contract that the goods are to go by rail, road, or air, a court is likely to hold that the parties did not intend FOB Incoterms. Where FOB is used, buyer must designate the ship to be used and pay for freight and insurance (if wanted); seller must deliver the goods on board the designated ship.

§6.05 CIF

CIF is a trade term meaning "cost, insurance, freight." The seller delivers by causing the goods to be placed on board, with freight and insurance paid to the designated destination. Insurance is for 110% of the invoice price on grounds that there might be some value fluctuation while the goods are in transit. UCC C&F and Incoterms CFR are the same as CIF, except that they do not require the seller to procure insurance. They are usually used when the volume buyer has a blanket insurance policy on imports, which is much less expensive than individually insuring each shipment.

§6.06 D Terms

Incoterms beginning with the letter "D" require the seller to deliver goods at the named destination. In *McDowell Valley Vineyards*, the parties provided for DDP (Delivered Duty Paid). Risk of loss does not pass until the goods arrive at that destination and customs duties have been paid. Where a Polish seller and a Ukrainian buyer agreed to DDU (Delivered Duty Unpaid) buyer's place of business, the truck carrying the goods reached the destination city but was hijacked before reaching the destination address. The Poland Supreme Court held risk of loss had not yet passed to buyer, so seller's insurance company was liable to seller for the loss. *Clothing*, Poland Sup. Ct. 20141022. Selecting a D incoterm provides contractually a place of delivery when the risk of loss passes that is more advantageous to buyer. *Glass fibre cables*, D Sup. Ct., 20121107. The fact that the goods do not arrive at that place until a later time also benefits buyer.

§6.07 Jurisdiction Based on Place of Performance

Unless a contract has an exclusive choice of forum clause, one can always sue a defendant at its principal place of business. An unusual provision of European Union law grants additional permissible jurisdiction to adjudicate disputes over sales contracts at the place the contract is to be performed. Regulation 1215/2012, art. 4, 5, 6, 7(1), 25. The place of performance may be dictated by the parties' contract, including the use of trade terms. If the contract specifies a place of delivery, that is the place of performance. The result is that use of incoterms beginning with C, E, or F will subject buyer to suit in seller's country because delivery occurs there and use of incoterms beginning with D will subject seller to suit in buyer's country, all provided that the country of performance is within the European Union. However, if the contract does not provide for a place of delivery, CISG cannot be used to specify it for purposes of jurisdiction. If the parties do not provide by contract, jurisdiction to sue is located where the purchaser obtained "actual power of disposal over those goods at the final destination." *Car Trim*, ECJ 20100225; *Electrosteel*, ECJ 20110609. This will be buyer's country because that will be the first place at which buyer will have physical control of the goods where the contract does not specify a place of delivery.

§6.08 Delivery of Title

CISG does not provide rules for the delivery of ownership. Art. 4(b). Those rules must be derived from domestic law. Those rules are not uniform.

In countries following the consensual model, domestic law provides that title passes from seller to buyer as soon as the agreement is reached and the goods are identified to the contract.

Other countries follow the delivery model. There, transfer of ownership depends on the transfer of possession with intent to convey title.

Under either model, the parties may delay the transfer of ownership by a retention of title clause. This occurs frequently when the sale is at least partially on credit, and seller retains ownership until the purchase price is paid in full. While such a clause is valid between the parties (though it does not affect the passage of the risk of loss, *St. Paul Guardian*, US Trial), whether third parties will be bound by it will depend on domestic law. *Usinor Industeel*, US Trial.

B. Conformity

§6.11 Conformity of the Goods in General

Conformity of the goods has several components. The goods must conform in nature and quality to the contract; they must be in the quantity called for by the contract; they must be accompanied by required documents, such as certificates of origin or test results, or instruction manuals; they cannot be subject to claims against seller's title; and they cannot be subject to intellectual property claims of which seller is aware at the time of contracting. In order to exercise remedies for nonconformity, buyer must normally give prompt and specific notice of the nonconformity. Arts. 35–44. The requirement of conformity is an implicit judgment that the seller is better able, because of increased familiarity with the goods, to determine their conformity than is the buyer. In addition, since sellers in general are more likely to sell multiple exemplars of the goods, sellers can spread the loss of individual defects by slightly raising the price for everyone. For those reasons, sellers are better positioned to assure conformity of the goods and to remedy any nonconformity than buyers would be.

§6.12 Quality Conformity with Specific Requirements

Goods must conform to the specific requirements of the contract, no matter what they might be. Art. 35(1). Because the interpretation of the contract under CISG may call for more than the words of the contract, there is frequent litigation about what the contract's specific requirements might mean that call upon the interpretive rules of arts. 8 and 9. *Textile machine*, CH Sup Ct 20001222. Where the contract called for Christmas trees U.S.D.A. graded #1, trees "just as good" do not conform, as the buyer may resell them representing that they have been so graded, and be liable to her purchaser. *Siskyou Evergreen*, US bankruptcy. Likewise, where the contract calls for goods conforming to a regulation that requires organic certification, the fact that the goods may be organic is not enough; it must be accompanied by the required certification. *Organic barley*, D App 20021113; *Fruit juice*, CH Trial 20120614; accord, *Cobalt sulfate*, D Sup. Ct. 19960403.

Specific requirements in the contract may relate to more than the quality of the goods. In *Valero Marketing*, US Trial, the parties agreed that the naphtha would be shipped on a boat approved by Valero, which approval would not be unreasonably withheld. The court found that Valero had unreasonably withheld approval of the Bear G, but that was not significant because seller used the rejected boat nonetheless. As a result, buyer, rather than seller, was in breach.

The goods delivered may even be worth more than the goods promised. They are still nonconforming, but the value of what was delivered may enter into the computation of damages.

§6.13 Quality Conformity with Implied Requirements; Normal Use

Goods must be fit for the purposes for which such goods are ordinarily used. Art. 35(2)(a). An automobile must transport people from one place to another, in addition to looking like a car.

Disagreements can exist about what the ordinary use of goods might be. The ordinary use of a horse might vary depending on whether it is the type of horse that children ride, that pulls heavy loads, that races, or that is used primarily for stud services.

The ordinary use may also depend on seller's knowledge of buyer's business. A seller of ground clay who knows that buyer will use it to separate potatoes into human and animal food must provide clay that is not laced with a pesticide like dioxin, which would make the potatoes unfit for both humans and animals. Even if the defect can be corrected relatively simply, the product is still nonconforming. *Kaolinite*, D Sup. Ct. 20120926.

Where a nursery sold raspberry stock that was normally planted, using the stock to propagate other stock was held not to be an ordinary use. *Barbara Berry II*, US Trial.

The question of ordinary use is sometimes tied to the question of what the contract calls for. Shipments of a crude oil mix can be used for a variety of purposes, but are mostly used for refining, so that is an ordinary use. An excess of mercury prevents further refining. Where the contract did not provide the quality, the tribunal was faced with deciding whether the quality was average, merchantable, reasonable, or superior. The arbitrator looked to the contract price, and determined that the price specified would buy crude oil of reasonable quality, but then defined reasonable quality as that which would be bought in the market at the price specified. That certainly sounds like marketable quality; it also sounds like circular reasoning. The tribunal also found that further processing was an ordinary use of this quality of crude. *Rijn blend*, NL Arb 2319, 20021015.

Each of these definitions has its problems. "Reasonable" is always something that lawyers can argue about because it requires consideration of all facts and circumstances; "average" is difficult for the parties to determine because neither of them handles all the transactions in the particular goods, and because it seems to call for elimination of all below-average goods, which would raise the average over time; "superior" seems an unlikely interpretation of the contract in the absence of more evidence. While "marketable" may not always be easy to prove, experts in the field will testify about whether this shipment would be one that would be easily resalable in the market in which the transaction took place at roughly the contract price.

While there are no cases on this point, it would seem that an ordinary use might include any of a number of uses to which the product is ordinarily put.

§6.14 Quality Conformity with Implied Requirements: Unusual Use

Seller is liable for failure of the goods to be fit for any unusual purpose known to seller before conclusion of the contract, except where it was unreasonable for buyer to rely on seller's skill. Art. 35(2)(b). It matters not whether seller acquires the knowledge from buyer, a third person, or general research. This provision is designed to deal with information problems. It encourages buyers to reveal unusual, intended uses for the goods. It also encourages sellers, who usually have superior knowledge of the properties of the goods, to tell buyers whether the goods are suitable for buyer's use.

It is suggested that a contract provision calling for delivery of plants to a specific place is enough notice that the plants are to be used there and that seller knows that the use might be there, despite the fact that it is not rare in international sales to trans-ship goods. *Plants*, D Trial 20061212. This indicates that seller need not be certain of the unusual use; seller need only be aware that it is a possibility.

One might ask whether the provision on unusual use displaces the requirement that the goods be fit for an ordinary purpose simply because buyer has made another intended purpose known to seller. That assumes that there are two exclusive categories. For ordinary use, art. 35(2)(a) governs, whether seller knows that the goods will be used for ordinary purposes or not. A particular purpose must always be a purpose that is not ordinary, and that must always be known to seller. However, where a used warehouse was sold to buyer, the court assumed without discussion that reassembling it as a warehouse was a particular use. *Warehouse*, F App 19950426. It is not clear that reassembling it as a warehouse is not an ordinary use. Indeed, it is hard to think of other uses that would be more ordinary. Perhaps building material? Scrap?

The ordinary purpose of an inflatable triumphal arch is for advertising and decoration, and it is important that the arch stay inflated. Buyer made known to seller that these arches would be used on an auto racing track. As a result of a test, additional safety measures were taken and seller offered, for additional compensation, to supply a technician for the event, which buyer declined. The court decided that the racetrack use was a particular use, but did not significantly discuss whether it was unreasonable for buyer to rely on seller's expertise when buyer had declined seller's offer of a skilled technician. Instead, it suggested that seller must disclaim expertise to assure that buyer does not rely. *Inflatable arches*, CH Trial 20021105.

A product might be suitable for ordinary use, or for an extraordinary use, but not in the place where buyer intends to use it. *Floating center*, CH Trial 19950426, raised but did not need to answer this question. A saltwater pool was to be installed by seller in a second floor room with a parquet floor that was designated by buyer. The court suggested that this might be inappropriate placement without further adjustment to prevent and reduce damage from leakage, but ventured no opinion on whether the goods were nonconforming because buyer had not provided timely notice of nonconformity.

In short, I believe that goods must always be suitable for ordinary use and, in addition, where a particular non-ordinary use is known to seller, the goods must also be suitable for that use.

§6.15 Quality Conformity Where Buyer Should Have Known of Defect; Model or Sample

CISG specifies three circumstances in which seller is not liable for art. 35(2) nonconformity because buyer should have known of the nonconformity. One is where it is unreasonable for buyer to rely on seller's skill. Usually, this requires that buyer had the opportunity to inspect the goods and had sufficient expertise to detect the nonconformity. Art. 35(2)(b).

A second, closely related situation is where buyer knew or should have known of the nonconformity at the time of contracting. Art. 35(3). The sticking point is always whether buyer should have known of the nonconformity. An Australian buyer of trucks who inspected the trucks that lacked medallions allowing their import into Australia and who knew of the requirement from previous imports could not hold the New Zealand seller liable. *Trucks*, NZ App 20100730. The court notes that similar medallions were posted in the trucks in the place usually occupied by the needed medallions, but makes nothing of that fact, which surely deceived buyers. In dicta in the purchase of a used bulldozer, the court stated that having inspected the bulldozer, buyer should have known of the defects complained of, without setting forth what the defects were or buyer's qualification to appreciate them, as it refers to buyer as a "businessperson," rather than a mechanic. *Bulldozer*, CH Trial 19971028.

The third situation is where seller provides buyer with a model or sample of the goods, and the goods conform to the model or sample even though they do not satisfy normal conformity. Art. 35(2)(c). Whether the sample should override art. 35 is discussed at §6.17.

These three exemptions from seller's nonconformity under art. 35(2) should not allow seller to escape nonconformity with the specific requirements of the contract, art. 35(1) nonconformity. Art. 35(1) conformity is like an insurance policy. For that reason, in both the cases of unusual use and samples, buyer may try to assert seller's liability by demonstrating that, considering all the evidence and especially seller's knowledge of the use, the description of the goods included the requisite requirements, so buyer can rely on specific rather than implied requirements. Whether that argument will succeed will depend on the particular facts and the disposition of the court to interpret the contract.

§6.16 Quality Conformity Due to Packaging

Goods must be packaged in a way that is adequate to protect and preserve them. Art. 35(2)(d). Packaging for bottles to be filled with wine that did not protect them from being broken or contaminated on a truck trip from Italy to Germany was nonconforming. *Wine bottles*, D App 20061214. The importance of this provision is that the bottles were in perfect condition when risk of loss passed to buyer, but the packaging was not adequate at that time. Thus buyer was able to recover even though the actual damage to the goods occurred after the risk of loss had passed.

Inadequate packaging may or may not result in damage. It did in the above case, but where the packaging was inadequate but no damage occurred, buyer derives no additional rights from the fact that the packaging was nonconforming. Where packaging is significant in marketing the product, failure to provide the agreed-upon packaging would result in damage even though the goods arrived unscathed.

§6.17 Cumulative Use of Criteria

The goods must satisfy both the ordinary use requirement and the packaging requirement in order to be conforming. Likewise, the goods must satisfy the ordinary use requirement, the packing requirement, and the conformity to the contract requirement in order to be conforming. *Ajax Tool*, US Trial.

It might, however, be argued that if an adequate sample or model is delivered, conformity to the sample or model displaces both the requirement that the goods conform to the specific requirements of the contract and that they be fit for ordinary use. The reason for this is that the sample allows buyer to determine whether the goods fit buyer's needs, and the sample is a more concrete illustration of the words of the contract.

For example, suppose buyer rejects a shipment of women's shoes because the straps result in the shoes becoming unsightly and wearing out more quickly than would ordinarily be the case. Ordinarily that would be a nonconformity. But suppose that the sample shoe sent by the manufacturer contained the same defect. Buyer should be expected to use his judgment to determine if the shoes met his requirements.

A certain amount of caution about this is advisable, which was not exercised in the leading case. There, seller provided buyer with a 10cm x 10cm sample (slightly less than 4" x 4") of the fabric from which buyer was going to make skirts. Normally, skirt fabric is delivered in a size large enough to cut both front and back in one operation, but the bolts delivered were too small to do that. In addition, when buyer washed the fabric, it billowed in a way that was unacceptable for a skirt. The court held for seller because the fabric delivered conformed to the sample, without considering that the size of the sample was too small to permit buyer to determine whether front and back of the skirt could be simultaneously cut from the material. There would have been no reason to wash the sample to discover whether it billowed, and the sample might have been too small to billow if it had been washed. *Textile sample*, D Trial 19980924.

In another case, the court recognized that the sample must be large enough to demonstrate the quality complained about. *Tulip doors*, B Trial 20060419.

A more appropriate case involved decorative rotating globes. Seller delivered a sample to buyer to use for a short time. The court held that buyer's complaint about the noise made by the finished product was precluded because the sample made the same noise. However, it found that the parties' clear intent was for the globes to operate continuously for at least three years. The cheap motors seller used made the globes nonconforming because they would fail within a year of normal use. Buyer was not obliged to do a technical inspection of the sample, which was provided primarily to confirm the suitability of the design. Because buyer could not have detected the motor deficiency in the short time the sample was used without an expert technical inspection, the sample did not oust seller's other responsibilities to deliver conforming goods. *Rotating globes*, D Trial 20020227.

Where buyer received samples of three of five juices or oils that were to be provided with Bio-Suisse certificates, the court held that the samples were delivered for taste and appearance purposes, and not intended to eliminate the certificate requirements. *Fruit juice*, CH Trial 20120614. The rule seems to be that generally conformity to a previously delivered sample will not make the goods conforming unless the parties so intended or the sample was sufficient to show a reasonable buyer that the nonconformity existed.

In *Delchi Carrier*, US App, plaintiff covered both bases. The Italian company proved that the compressors designed for room air conditioners did not conform to the sample and that they were inadequate for their ordinary use because they cooled too little and used too much electricity.

Where buyer subjected seller's crown corks to months of testing and refused seller's offer to assist with tests, the crown corks delivered were conforming even though they could not be used for buyer's particular purpose, capping wines containing sulfite, which accelerated corrosion. *Crown corks*, D App 20150813.

Also, not all buyers will be sophisticated enough to notice the defects. If the point is to transfer the risk of misappreciation at the appropriate point, each case must be decided on its own facts.

§6.18 Disclaimer of Conformity Requirements

CISG contains no detail on how conformity requirements are disclaimed, but makes it clear that they can be disclaimed. They can be disclaimed by stating the quality of the goods as "used" or "as is." Art. 35(1). Art. 35(2) begins "[e]xcept where the parties have agreed otherwise," which certainly authorizes the use of those terms to negate the conformity provisions of that article. This is a situation with which CISG specifically deals. It was argued, however, that these disclaimer clauses are a matter of validity under the laws of many countries, so should be dealt with under the appropriate domestic law. In *Norfolk Southern*, US Trial, the court did not need to make a choice of law analysis because it found that the result would not have differed, whether it used Pennsylvania or Alberta law. This is an area where domestic law is so technical, in UCC §2-316 requiring the mention of the magic word "merchantability," that it should yield to the specific language of CISG and its general principle of abolishing formalities.

§6.19 Time of Quality Conformity

The time at which the goods must conform is the time of delivery. For obvious defects, the time of most likely discovery will be when the goods arrive at their destination. For hidden defects, discovery time is likely to be somewhat later, depending on when a reasonable buyer in the position of this buyer would likely have detected the defect. The question remains whether the defect existed at delivery time. In *BP Oil*, US App, the court reversed a grant of summary judgment because, though the contract called for minimal gum content of gasoline that was confirmed on loading, the gas had significantly more gum content on arrival. It ordered a trial to determine whether the gas conformed when delivered, or whether there was a hidden defect. It did not consider whether a provision for testing the gum content on loading changed the normal rule for conformity to conformity with the test results on loading.

§6.20. Place of Quality Conformity

Usually, the place where the goods need to satisfy the requirements of art. 35 is not relevant because a tool that works in seller's country usually also works in buyer's country. However, the question becomes important because different countries have different climates, different electrical systems, and different legal rules. Since the risk of loss passes at delivery, you might think that the goods need to be usable for ordinary purposes at the time and place of delivery. You would be correct about the time. Alternatively, since these are international sales, you might think that the goods would need to be usable for ordinary purposes at buyer's place of business, or at the place to which the goods are to be delivered. One hoped that a trial court in a case where healthy plants suitable for use in seller's country, but difficult to grow in the climate of buyer's country, would tell us whether the plants were conforming. However, the expert determined that most of the plants were suitable for growth in buyer's country and, with respect to the one plant that was not, the court found this to be a special use with respect to which buyer had just as much expertise as seller, so the desired decision was not forthcoming. *Plants*, D Trial 20061212.

The leading case concerns legal regulation, though the facts do not justify it. A Swiss seller delivered to a German buyer an order of mussels containing a high level of cadmium. The mussels were not barred from human consumption, but an obscure regulation of pork with that much cadmium would have put the pork in an official category of "not harmless," though it could be sold. In a very careful opinion, the court held that the mussels were not nonconforming. It stated that seller is not obligated to comply with obscure legal rules in buyer's country. It specifically stated that it was not deciding whether seller needed to comply with legal rules in buyer's country if they were the same as in seller's country, or if buyer had informed seller of the rules, or if seller's economic penetration of buyer's country were sufficiently great that seller should have known of the rules, such as by having an office there, or repeated sales into that country. *NZ mussels*, D Sup. Ct. 19950308.

Commentators and courts immediately stated that what the German court in fact refused to decide were really exceptions to the general rule. *Medical Marketing*, US Trial.

More properly, the general rule should cover the largest number of cases, and the exceptions the smaller number. The rule should more properly be stated that seller is responsible for complying with legal regulations in buyer's country except when the rules are difficult to ascertain and seller has no good commercial reason to discover them. One might be more specific and exempt seller only where seller has not previously sold that product in the country and has no plans to do so in the future. This comports with the underlying reasoning that risks should be placed on the party who can bear them with the least cost. For most rules, that least cost bearer will be seller doing business in buyer's country, but for exceptionally obscure rules, it will be buyer.

A decision by the German Supreme Court is sometimes read more broadly. A Belgian seller delivered frozen pork to a German buyer that was shipped to Bosnia-Herzegovina at a time when the shipment was legal in all three countries. Soon thereafter, rules were in force in all three countries that Belgian pork was unfit for human consumption because of dioxin contamination if slaughtered within the period of this shipment. The court held the goods nonconforming. Closer reading of the decision reveals that the nonconformity did not result from the legal rules, but from the dioxin contamination. The court reasoned that a major shipment is intended for resale, so the question was whether the goods were merchantable, and food contaminated with dioxin, or even suspected of being contaminated with dioxin, is not merchantable. *Frozen pork*, D Sup. Ct. 20050302.

In *Wheat flour*, NL Trial 20050119, seller added a bread improver containing potassium bromide, which was prohibited in buyer's country, seller's country, and by international standards, but whose importation to Mozambique, the destination country, was tolerated. Without discussing the *NZ mussel* case, the court held the flour nonconforming.

The *Medical Marketing* case is more complicated. That case was a request to enforce an arbitrator's decision. An arbitrator's decision can be overturned in only limited circumstances, in this case if the arbitrator's decision was in "manifest disregard of the law." In addition, the sales in question were part of an agreement whereby Medical Marketing was to be seller's exclusive sales agent for mammogram imaging machines in the United States. The opinion enforcing the arbitrator's decision does not reveal whether seller had ever sold this machine, or any other product, in the U.S. Under those circumstances, one wonders whether a court, looking at the legal question de novo, would have held seller responsible for compliance with U.S. legal rules.

An entirely different route to nonconformity was found by a French buyer of Italian grated parmesan cheese. Buyer proved that seller knew of his particular purpose of selling the cheese in France. It followed that the cheese needed to be packaged in the manner usual for cheese to be sold in France, which included the French legal rule that it display a label on the sachets indicating the contents and expiration date. *Parmesan cheese*, F App 19950913.

§6.21 Inspection and Notice of Nonconformity

Buyer is obligated to examine the goods as soon as practical and to give specific notice to seller of nonconformity within a reasonable time. There is no sanction for failure to examine in a timely fashion. Buyers who do not give specific and timely notice may not assert nonconformity, unless excused. Arts. 38–40, 44. It is difficult to give timely notice of a nonconformity if buyer does not timely examine the goods.

§6.22 Reasons for Prompt and Specific Notice

CISG gives no reasons for requiring prompt notice, but they are easy to imagine.

One is to give seller the opportunity to cure. CISG seems to be designed to try to keep the contract in place as much as possible. It gives seller the right to cure with some limits. Arts. 37, 48. Notice that is prompt and specific enough for seller to plan repair would provide the best opportunity to quickly bring the goods into compliance and minimize damages. As one court put it, "the notice must [be] given in time, and in sufficient detail, to allow seller to cure the defect in a manner allowing the buyer the benefit of his bargain." *Siskyou Evergreen*, US bankruptcy.

A second is evidentiary. The time at which conformity is measured is the date of delivery. The more time that has passed since delivery, the more likely it is that the nonconformity might have occurred after the risk of loss shifted to buyer.

A third combines the first two reasons. In eventual litigation between the parties, buyer is limited to asserting the reasons set forth in the notice. This assures that the debate is about the real reasons buyer asserted nonconformity, not the reasons his lawyer invented for purposes of successful litigation.

C. Notice of Nonconformity

§6.31 Timely Notice

Unlike some domestic law systems, there is no fixed period within which notice must be given. "As soon as practical" requires a consideration of all the circumstances. One court specified notice within a week of when the defect should have been discovered without explaining why. *Waterworks cooler*, A Sup. Ct. 20020114.

When the defect should be discovered thus becomes important. An obvious defect should be discovered sooner than a hidden defect. Where the goods are perishable, inspection should take place immediately upon receipt. *Crabs & cockles*, E App 20071219; *Fish*, NL Trial 19970305. This is especially true where the defect is easy to detect by a layperson's sight or smell, *Chicago Prime Packers*, US Trial, or where buyer is to further process the goods, thereby altering them and making it difficult to determine whether they conformed at the right time. *Fish*, NL Trial 19970305.

Less satisfactorily, a French court's alternate holding was that a buyer of lift cables was obligated to inspect the goods when he repackaged them on different spools for his sub-buyer. It could not wait two months for his sub-buyer to report the defective cables. The court was not clear about how difficult it would have been to discover the defect in rewinding the cable on different spools, or what damage seller suffered from the delay. *Lift cables*, F App 20011106.

To the contrary, a U.S. court held that where the goods are to be trans-shipped and seller knows this, inspection can be delayed until receipt by the ultimate recipient. Art. 38(2); *Chicago Prime Packers*, US Trial. What constitutes reasonable knowledge by seller is in some dispute. Where a Ugandan buyer ordered shoes shipped from Germany to Mombasa, Kenya, one court held that seller was not on notice that the shoes would be trans-shipped to Kampala from the fact that Uganda has no ocean port and the normal way of getting goods to Uganda is by rail from Mombasa. *Used shoes*, D Trial 20050411.

The examination called for is a reasonable examination. Where buyer-middleman is passing nonperishable goods to ultimate customers, buyer must perform a cursory exam on receipt of the goods, but a more thorough inspection can await the goods' arrival at the ultimate customer. *Print boards*, NL App 20051011. Some courts have not adopted this view. For one, notice given 24 days after receipt and one day after notification of nonconformity from its buyer was not timely. *Adhesive foil*, D App 19970625.

Little time is provided where finding the defect would be easy, as in a situation where improper packaging would be obvious to a layperson. There a court thought that six weeks was too long. *NZ mussels*, D Sup. Ct. 19950308. Where leaks in the tank should have been obvious to anyone in the room, seven weeks was not within a reasonable time. *Floating center*, CH Trial 19950426.

Where the goods are technical and require in-depth examination requiring 75 to 150 hours for 50 models, notification within three weeks was held to be timely. *Model locomotives*, CH Trial 20040127. Notice of defects in a machine sent 12 days after a preliminary inspection at seller's plant, and notice sent five days after delivery to buyer, were held to be timely. *Grinding machines*, F App

19980129. One case involving a latent defect allowed one week after the defect was discovered, two weeks for expert examination, plus a month after receipt of the expert's report. The court does not explain why a month between discovering the cause of the defect and giving the notice is timely. *Paper grinder*, D Sup. Ct. 19991103; *Laundry machine*, CH Sup. Ct. 20031103 Where the goods are seasonal, a period of two weeks was presumed in one case, *Trekking shoes*, A Sup. Ct. 19990827, while for non-seasonal goods, eight days was normal in another. *Polypropylene granulate*, D App 19950208. The cases are inconsistent, as a shorter time is reasonable with seasonal goods than with non-seasonal because buyer is more likely to lose resale opportunities with seasonal goods.

The fact that the time allowed is not always short is demonstrated by the fact that a maximum of two years after handing over the goods is set for giving notice. Art. 39(2). This absolute limit seems to apply even to hidden defects that would not normally be discovered within two years. Nor does the obligation to give notice apply to defects seller should have known about and failed to disclose to buyer.

Contrary to the absolute language of CISG, inspection that would be unreasonable is not required. Where quantitative chemical analysis of PVC granules would have been necessary to establish whether they contained the required percentage of titanium dioxide, buyer was not required to do that analysis. *PVC granules*, D Trial 19960625. The degree of inspection required is a reasonable one, so the purchaser of a large quantity of shoes would be expected to have a shoe expert randomly examine them. *Trekking shoes*, A Sup. Ct. 19990827. On the other hand, where goods are to be processed, a full inspection of the entire shipment is required. *Fish*, NL Trial 19970305. A reasonable inspection will depend on the ultimate use of the goods and the prevalence of particular defects. Where apple juice cannot be sold as apple juice if it contains glucose syrup and mixture of glucose and apple juice concentrate was not unusual in apple juice concentrate sold at the time and place, buyer must test the apple juice concentrate for sugar content. *Apple juice concentrate*, D App 20010312.

Timeliness may also depend on the identity of buyer. A buyer who is involved in the trade seems to have an obligation to inspect on arrival. Where buyer is not involved in the trade, "as soon as practicable" asks when a reasonable buyer of the same type would inspect. A company buying a framed Warhol print that was not in the business of dealing in art was not obligated to inspect for defects hidden by the framing until it either re-framed or sold the work. The court stated in dicta that had buyer been a professional art gallery, it would have been obligated to unframe the print on arrival to inspect it for defects. *Warhol print*, A App 20151216. A buyer who has no expertise with the goods and relies on seller's engineers to use the equipment justifies a longer reasonable time to inspect. *Shuttle Packaging*, US Trial. On the other hand, where a dredging amphibious shovel with a hidden defect was sold through a jobber to a company that did major construction, there was no suggestion that either the jobber or its ultimate customer was obligated to promptly inspect to find the defect, and notice was given within the maximally allowed two-year period. *Amphibious shovel*, F App 20130421.

What is troubling about these decisions is that none of them relate to the reasons for requiring prompt notice in determining how soon "prompt" might be. The fact that the time is short for perishable goods goes to the evidentiary question of establishing whether the goods conformed when risk of loss passed. The fact that time is short for seasonable goods goes to the ability of seller to repair defects and minimize damages. In other cases, it is unclear that timely notice is anything more than a box to check, and the consequences of not giving timely notice are disastrous.

Parties have argued that responding to a notice of nonconformity after the expiration of time is a waiver of that requirement, but courts have not so decided. *Wood*, A Sup. Ct. 20000321. Responding is an action of good faith trying to keep the contract alive, which is not inconsistent with eventually invoking the time limit. For the same reason, it should not be regarded as amending the contract.

The parties can fix the notice requirement in their contract. In *MCC-Marble Ceramic*, US App, the written contract required notice of defect within 10 days of delivery by certified letter. It can also be fixed by an applicable trade custom or usage between the parties. In *Wood*, A Sup. Ct. 20000321, the court held that both applied to fix the timing at 14 days, and both were also applicable in *Fish*, NL Trial 19970305.

§6.32 Specificity of Notice

Simply stating that the goods do not conform is not specific enough. *Shoes*, D Trial, 199331201. The notice must be unambiguous. In the sale of a printer system including printer, computer, and software, notice of printer documentation missing could mean documentation for the printer (which was supplied in response to the notice) or documentation for the entire system, buyer's actual complaint. *Computerized printer*, D Sup. Ct. 19961204. The notice must be sufficiently specific that seller can plan to bring the goods into conformity.

With machinery, this requires relating the symptoms, but does not require buyer to divine the ultimate cause. Stating that steel splinters appeared on paper processed is sufficient. *Paper grinder*, D Sup. Ct. 19991103. Where the complaint is about packaging, buyer need not specify the underlying cause of the inadequate packaging; stating that the packaging was insufficient to prevent breakage and contamination of wine bottles on a truck journey from Italy to Switzerland was enough. *Wine bottles*, D App 20061214. Where the contract called for blankets of different designs, failure to specify which designs were short made the notice insufficiently specific. *Acrylic blankets*, D App 19970131. Another court stated, "[I]n this day and age of electronic communication the seller can be expected to ask questions in any case if he desires more precise instructions. . . ." *Laundry machine*, CH Sup. Ct. 20031113.

In a case involving a claim that a car sold was stolen, notification to seller two months after police seized the car was not timely. It also did not serve as notification of the claim of the true owner received later because it did not indicate who the claiming owner was, which would have allowed seller to attempt to remove the claim. *Stolen car*, D Sup. Ct. 20060111. But in a similar stolen car case where the auto was seized by police, three months after the seizure was held to be a reasonable time in which to secure all the relevant information necessary. *VW Golf*, D Trial 20020822.

In short, given the difficulty of being certain whether a court might hold any delay to be unreasonable, notice should be given as quickly and as specifically as possible.

§6.33 Form of Notice

No form of notice is specified in CISG.

One court allowed notice by e-mail, rejecting the argument that notice meant filing a suit. The court cautions that the parties consistently used e-mail to communicate, but it is not clear why. The implication is that consistent use is consent to continued use, but that hardly seems necessary. *Amphibious shovel*, F App 20130421. The parties could have provided a particular form for notice, thereby derogating from the lack of form required by either art. 27 or 39, but they did not do so. Communication by e-mail, telex, letter, phone, or carrier pigeon should suffice. This is especially true since a general principle of CISG is doing away with formal requirements. However, proving both the date and the content of the communication will be easier if it is dated and done in writing.

§6.34 Notice of Inadequate Repair

While arts. 38 and 39 seem to be designed for the initial delivery of goods, the wording would also apply to nonconformity resulting from repairs, and one court has so held. *Bakery freezers*, B App 20081114.

§6.35 Relief from Notice Requirement for Nonconformity

The consequence of failure to give timely and specific notice is draconian—buyer is deprived of all relief for nonconformity. It is not surprising that CISG provides relief from every part of the notice requirement (including the two year limit) in two ways.

Buyer need not give timely or specific notice of art. 35 nonconformity if seller could not have been unaware of the defect and did not inform buyer of it. Art. 40. In some cases, there is evidence from test results showing that seller was aware of the defect. *Kaolinite*, D Sup. Ct. 20120926. One seller bought trees of lower grade to fulfill his order. *Siskyou Evergreen*, US bankruptcy. In many cases, the deviation from conformity will be so great that seller could not have been unaware of it. That should have been the case where seller shipped shoes to his Ugandan buyer that were in such bad condition that they had to be destroyed, but it does not appear that buyer argued this provision. *Used shoes*, D Trial 20050411. Tribunals have gone much further, in one case holding that a seller could not have been unaware of the risk (unquantified) that buyer would improperly install a part. *Rail press*, S Arb 19980605. If that case is not an outlier, buyer should have been able to avoid the notice requirement in each of the cases discussed above.

In one case, seller invoiced a quantity in excess of the amount ordered. Buyer argued that she was excused from the notice requirement because seller should have known of the discrepancy, but the court held that buyer had been notified by the documents, so art. 40's exemption did not apply. *Shrimp*, D App Rostock 20020925. Such a strict reading would eliminate art. 40 from CISG except in cases of seller deceit.

The second exception provides only partial relief. If buyer can show reasonable excuse for failure to give timely and specific notice, buyer retains the remedies of price reduction and damages (but not for lost profits). Reliance on a reputable international inspection company's report has been held to be reasonable excuse. *Coke*, ICC Arb 9187/1999. Again, the question of what is reasonable seems to depend on many factors. "Relevant factors include the severity of the infringement, the type of goods, the type of deficiency and some lack of experience.... Art. 44 CISG is especially applicable for buyers who are retail sellers, craftsmen, farmers or those who practice a liberal profession. Larger companies like the [Buyer], whose business must be prepared for swift and punctual settlement of transactions, will generally not be excused...." *Polypropylene granulate*, D App 19950208. This is interesting guidance, but the court's rejection of buyer's reasonable excuse would have been more persuasive had the court revealed what the excuse was.

It is not entirely clear that either of these cases should have been decided under art. 44 because the court's discussion in each case make it seem like a situation where the notice was given within a reasonable time, so buyer should have been protected by art. 39.

D. Title and Intellectual Property Claims

§6.41 Non-IP Right or Claim of Third Party

Seller must deliver the goods free from any unexcepted right or claim of a third party. While one normally thinks in terms of an ownership claim, it would also require seller to clear up any liens encumbering the goods, or any restrictions on their use. Where seller's seller prohibited export of the goods to Belgium, the goods were not free from a right. *Propane*, A Sup. Ct. 19960206.

What is troublesome under this provision is that a mere unsupported (and possibly frivolous) claim is enough to permit buyer to exercise remedies for breach of the contract. Presumably, a court would not permit this where buyer induces a third party to make the claim.

§6.42 IP Right or Claim of Third Party

Seller must also deliver goods free from any unexpected right or claim based on intellectual property such as copyright, trademark, patent, or know-how in buyer's state, or a state where the parties contemplated that the goods would be resold or used, but only if seller knew or could not have been unaware of the right or claim by the time the contract was concluded. Buyer's success does not depend on the claim being justified; it is seller's responsibility to remove the claim. *Blank CDs*, A Sup. Ct. 20060912.

Seller is relieved of this responsibility if buyer should have been aware of the right, or if the claim results from seller's compliance with buyer's instructions. Where Spanish seller produced shoes violating a French trademark pursuant to directions from a French buyer, the court said first that seller should have been aware of the claim, bringing it within art. 42, and then held that the claim resulted from buyer's fault, so there was no breach of art. 42. *Shoes Fouille*, F App 20000217. Another court held that buyer, being a professional and the proprietor of six retail clothing stores, should have been aware that a third party had "commercial rights" (though not a registered trademark) to the fabric with which the blouses were made. *Blouses*, F App 20021113. The court does not say why buyer should have been aware other than the fact that he was a "professional"; that would include many buyers under CISG, and render most sellers not liable.

The geographic and knowledge requirements above may relieve seller of liability. If this is seller's first sale to buyer's country or to the country where the goods are to be delivered, seller will argue that he had no reason to know that the goods transgressed the intellectual property law of that country, and may cite *NZ mussels*, D Sup. Ct. 19950308, for that proposition. There seems to be a clear theoretical conflict between that case, where seller is not responsible for complying with the law of the destination state, and art. 42, where seller is.

§6.43 Excuse from Notice Requirement

The same excuses for failure to give timely notice that apply to art. 35 nonconformity also apply to right or claim nonconformities, with one exception. For art. 35 nonconformities, buyer is excused from giving notice if seller actually knew or could not have been unaware of the nonconformity. For right or claim nonconformities, buyer is only excused if seller actually knew. This change is probably necessary because repeating "could not have been unaware" with intellectual property nonconformities would be congruent with seller's liability and thereby remove all notice requirements.

A second difference is that with nonconformities, notice must be given within two years of delivery of the goods. No such limitation applies to property or intellectual property defects; the only limit is the applicable statute of limitations on bringing suit, four years from delivery in countries that have ratified the *UN Limitations Convention* or the domestic forum rule for other nations.

E. Partial Breach

§6.51 Partial Breach

If seller delivers only part of the quantity of goods promised, a breach exists with respect to the undelivered goods. If all the goods are delivered, but some of them are nonconforming, a breach occurs for the nonconforming goods, but not for the conforming goods delivered. However, if the delivery shortfall or the nonconformity of some of the goods amounts to a fundamental breach of the entire contract, buyer may declare the contract avoided. Art. 51. Where buyer ordered 11 computer parts and only five of them were delivered, buyer could not avoid the contract. Buyer gave seller a reasonable additional period to deliver the missing parts, which seller failed to do. There was no fundamental breach of the contract because buyer was able to buy and did buy substitutes for the six missing parts on the open market at a higher price in order to fulfill buyer's obligation to his sub-buyer. *Computer parts*, D Trial 19920703.

But another case drew a different line, distinguishing between an order for a number of products, and an order for a single product. In that case, the sale was of a spinning mill. Some parts of the mill were not delivered. Without those parts, the mill would not operate, but those parts were freely available in the market. The court held that there was a fundamental breach of the entire contract because the mill would not work without the missing parts. This seems misguided. If the contract had been for any single one of the parts and it was delivered nonconforming, it would not be a fundamental breach because of the availability of substitute parts in the market. The fact that a number of parts were involved should not change that result if all the missing parts were available in the market. *Spinning mill*, CH Sup. Ct. 20120716.

CHECKPOINTS

You should have learned that:

- Seller's main obligation is to deliver physical possession and the ownership of the goods or documents agreed upon free from known intellectual property claims.

- The time and place of delivery are crucial to many aspects of seller's performance. They determine where and when the goods or documents must conform, where and when seller must fulfill other obligations, and where and when buyer must pay.

- Seller must deliver the goods or documents where and when the contract provides. Usually, parties will provide the place of delivery and passage of risk of loss by using a recognized trade term.

- When the contract does not provide and if carriage of goods is involved, seller delivers by handing the goods to the first carrier. The first carrier is someone other than seller or buyer.

- Passage of risk of loss from seller to buyer generally occurs on delivery.

- Delivery is often made by delivering documents conferring the right to eventual possession of goods.

- Trade terms usually do not include a time for delivery. CISG provides that delivery must be within a reasonable time unless the parties have otherwise provided.

- Where trade terms are used that can be derived from more than one source, it is important to specify the source.

- Students should know the different responsibilities that go with trade terms fob, cif, and the d terms.

- In the European Union, there is generally adjudicatory jurisdiction at the place of performance of a sales contract.

- Goods must normally conform to the contract. This means that they must comply with the quantity and quality called for by the contract, and be accompanied by any required documents.

- Goods must be fit for the purposes for which such goods are ordinarily used.

- In the absence of other specifications, the goods must be marketable.

- Seller is liable for failure of the goods to be fit for any unusual purpose known to seller before conclusion of the contract, except where it was unreasonable for buyer to rely on seller's skill.

- Where seller provides buyer with a model or sample of the goods sufficient to discover any nonconformity, seller is not liable for failure of the goods to conform in ways that should have been discovered from the model or sample.

- Seller is not liable for nonconformity of which buyer was aware when the contract was concluded.

- Seller is not liable for nonconformity where it was unreasonable for buyer to rely on seller's skill.

- Seller is liable for failure to package the goods adequately for their anticipated transport.

- Conformity requirements can be disclaimed by mutual agreement.

- Goods must conform at the time and place where risk of loss passes.

- Seller is responsible for complying with legal regulations in buyer's country except when the rules are difficult to ascertain and seller has no good commercial reasons for discovering them.

- Buyer is obligated to examine the goods in a reasonable manner as soon as practicable and to give specific notice to seller of nonconformity within a reasonable time.

- Prompt and specific notice is required in order to give seller opportunity to cure, to provide reliable evidence of the nonconformity and when it occurred, and to limit disputes about conformity to the nonconformities listed in the notice.

- The timeliness of the notice depends on the nature of the goods, whether the defect is obvious or hidden, the examination required to discover it, and the status of buyer. Less time is allowed for perishable or seasonal goods. Hidden defects should be reported as soon as a reasonable buyer would have discovered them. A person who does not regularly deal in the goods concerned has longer to report nonconformities than a person in the business.

- The notice of nonconformity must relate the symptoms, but does not require buyer to divine the ultimate cause.

- Buyer who does not give timely and specific notice of nonconformity cannot rely on any remedies provided for nonconformity unless excused. Buyer is excused if seller could not have been unaware of the defect and did not inform buyer of it. If buyer can show reasonable excuse for failure to give timely and specific notice, buyer retains the remedies of price reduction and damages (but not for lost profits), but not the remedies of specific performance or avoidance.

- Seller must deliver the goods free from any unexcepted non-IP right or claim of a third party.

- Seller must also deliver goods free from any unexpected right or claim based on intellectual property in buyer's state, or a state where the parties contemplated that the goods would be resold or used, but only if seller could not have been unaware of the right or claim, there was no reason for buyer to be aware of the claim, and the claim did not result from following buyer's instructions.

CHAPTER 7

Buyer Accepts and Pays

ROADMAP

After reading this chapter, you should understand:

- Buyer is obligated to accept conforming goods and pay for them.
- The only way for buyer to assure inspection before payment is to provide for it in the sales contract or to provide for payment at a later date.
- Payment is made in the currency specified. In the absence of specification, it is made in the currency of the place of payment.
- Buyer taking delivery of more goods than ordered is obligated to pay for the excess. Buyer can refuse the excess, but must take care to prevent the goods from being exposed to theft or damage.
- Buyer can likewise refuse to take delivery of nonconforming goods, but must take care to prevent the goods from being exposed to theft or damage.

§7.01 Buyer's Obligations

Buyer is obligated to accept conforming goods and pay for them. The time and place for buyer's acceptance and payment are usually specified by contract because the parties either specify the time and place of delivery or select a trade term that states a place. In the absence of other specification, the time and place for payment is the time and place for delivery. In the case of a credit sale, unless otherwise stated, payment is to be at seller's place of business. Arts. 57–59; *Urea*, CH Trial 19971203; *Carpets*, D App 20031210.

While in theory payment must be in cash unless other arrangements are made, a buyer is unlikely to show up with a sack of coins, or even a stack of bills, at the place of delivery to pay for an international sale. Since in most cases delivery will be by handing the goods to the first carrier or putting them aboard a ship, this would involve either a trip by buyer to seller's country, or the employ of an agent there. In the real world, payment is likely to be either by letter of credit, by wire transfer, or by the agreed extension of credit. If payment is to be by letter of credit, wire transfer, or on credit, the details should be provided in the contract. If buyer asserts the right to pay by wire transfer, buyer should be prepared to prove a contract provision or that there is a custom of the parties or in that international trade of payment by wire transfer to satisfy art. 9.

Buyer must take steps necessary to effect the payment called for in the contract and absorb any costs necessary to do so. This may involve securing foreign exchange in countries where it is limited, currency conversion charges, and transfer fees. Where the contract calls for issuing a letter of credit, failure to do so by the time specified is a breach. *Scrap steel*, AUS Sup. Ct. 20001117.

CISG fixes the place of payment for goods as the place agreed to by the parties; in default of an agreement, where transfer of goods or documents and payment are simultaneous, the place of delivery; or seller's place of business. Art. 57; *Carpets*, D App 20031210. Much litigation has ensued over this question, but not because of payment in the wrong place. The litigation derives from the Brussels regulation discussed above, which authorizes judicial jurisdiction at the place of performance. Regulation 1215/2012, art. 7(1). The place of performance under CISG has been deemed to be buyer's place of business where buyer was seeking refund of an overpayment, *Industrial equipment*, F App 19961023, but another court thought CISG irrelevant in determining jurisdiction if the Brussels reg or domestic law applied because it has its own determination, and held that there was no jurisdiction over buyer in seller's country. *Violins*, A Sup. Ct. 20080403. In deciding whether to use a trade term and which trade term to use, parties should consider that they may be subjecting themselves to suit at the place of performance.

Seller must bear any additional expense of payment caused by a change in seller's place of business after conclusion of the contract. Art. 57(2). The implication is that if payment must be made at seller's place of business, it is at the new place of business (presumably only after seller has notified buyer of the place change). Where seller has removed from one country to another, it does not seem appropriate for that move to destroy jurisdiction if it was determined by seller's place of business because a general principle of CISG seems to be that, barring amendment, all aspects of the contract are determined on the conclusion of the contract. Even less is jurisdiction to be changed because seller has assigned his claim to a third party located in a different state, as one court has held. *Orange juice*, D App 19981111.

Buyer needs to pay at the right time and place. Buyer also needs to pay the right person. In a contract with a standhostess representing seller at a trade fair, the standhostess later delivered the goods to buyer at buyer's place of business and was paid by buyer. The time and place of payment were correct. But the standhostess did not transfer the payment to seller. The court held buyer liable for the purchase price because buyer did not pay the correct person, seller. It held on the basis of German law that the standhostess was authorized to conclude the contract, but not to amend it or to accept payment, and CISG requires that buyer pay seller. *Tiles*, D Trial 19950512.

Buyer may agree to obligations other than payment and taking delivery, and often does. It is common for a manufacturer to restrict the geographic area of a buyer's resales because seller already has exclusive distributorships in other areas, as occurred in *Jeans*, F App 19950222.

In the case where the goods are damaged, destroyed or stolen, CISG obligates buyer to pay the purchase price only when that damage occurs after the passage of the risk of loss, and then only if the damage is not caused by seller. Art. 66. The exact operation of this provision is difficult to understand, especially when combined with art. 70, which preserves all of buyer's remedies in the event of a fundamental breach by seller. My best guess is that if the damages occur before the risk of loss passes from seller, art. 66 is unnecessary because seller has breached the contract and buyer has adequate remedies for that breach. The situation where damage occurs after the risk of loss passes due to an act or omission of seller is likely to be where the goods are delivered, buyer notifies seller of nonconformity, seller attempts to cure, and damages or destroys the goods. If the goods are destroyed, buyer need not pay the purchase price, but if they are only damaged, one would think that the normal remedies for nonconformity should suffice.

§7.02 Buyer's Right to Inspect

Art. 58(3) says buyer need not pay until he has been able to inspect the goods. This provision is meaningless, as the clause adds "unless the procedures for delivery or payment agreed upon by the parties are inconsistent with his having such an opportunity." The procedures are usually inconsistent with inspection before payment unless it is a sale on credit because seller may, and usually does, make payment a condition for handing over the goods or documents. Art. 58(1) & (2). The only way for buyer to assure inspection before payment is to provide for it in the sales contract, or to provide for payment at a later date.

While some commentators have suggested that provisions calling for simultaneous performance, such as art. 58(2), provide additional justification for buyer's right to inspect before paying, such a right would be unusual absent a specific contract provision.

Because most delivery occurs when seller delivers the goods to the first carrier or the ship in seller's country, buyer is usually not physically present to inspect. A typical contract provision would provide for inspection and certification by a trusted third party.

§7.03 Currency of Paying Contract Price

In most cases, the currency of payment will be specified in the contract because the contract specifies the price to be paid in a currency. This will not be the case where the specification is ambiguous. Such a situation might occur in a contract between U.S. and Canadian firms. Both countries' currencies are the dollar, and they use the same dollar sign ($). A contract that did not specify whether the dollars to be paid were Canadian or U.S. would be ambiguous. A second ambiguous situation is where the contract is formed by an exchange in which each party designates the price in its own currency. A third situation is where the contract sets no price, with the price to be set either by a formula that does not indicate the currency to be used, or a price set by Art. 55.

The problem is likely to occur most severely when the relative values of the currencies change between the signing of the contract and the date of payment. Absent a change in relative values, there is still a problem because no one converts currencies without imposing a charge. That charge will either increase buyer's cost of the goods or reduce seller's profits on them.

Absent indication of the parties' intent, CISG has no specific rule for fixing the currency, but the question is certainly one that CISG should govern. Art. 7(2) calls for application of the general principles of CISG, but it is difficult to imagine any general principle that would apply to this situation other than one that specifies the place of delivery as the place of payment. If that is not an adequate general principle, one should then do a choice of law analysis and apply the law of the country selected. In fact, the cases have settled on the currency of the country where payment is to be made, without satisfactorily explaining whether it was using general principles of CISG or domestic law chosen by choice of law rules. *Wire rod*, CH Trial 20140917; *Wine*, D App 19940124; *Computer chip*, D App 19930917. One reason might be that the only currency that is legal tender for payment in many countries is the currency of that country. Once the time and place of payment are settled, it is presumed that payment would be made in a currency that is legal for discharging debts at that time and place. However, one court held that the currency is determined by the appropriate choice of law rule, which indicated the currency of seller, in a case where seller delivered the goods to buyer so concurrent payment using the place of payment would have called for buyer's currency. *Hotel oven*, CH Trial 20070427. However, payment was not made simultaneously, so payment would necessarily be made at seller's place of business.

§7.04 Taking Delivery

Buyer must take delivery of the goods as prescribed by the contract. Art. 60(b). In most cases, the point is prescribed by the contract because the parties have used a delivery term, and the CISG provision is simply a back-up. Where buyer's wrongful refusal to take delivery of iron ore sent CFR resulted in demurrage charges, buyer was responsible for those charges. *Iron ore*, ICC Arb 13492/2006, 200607. The court finds liability based on both Incoterms and CISG, but the Incoterm liability would have been sufficient.

Buyer must take delivery of the goods within the time specified in the contract or within a reasonable time under the circumstances. Failure to take delivery within the prescribed period constitutes a breach of contract. This is especially true where the goods are perishable. In a situation where buyer could not take possession because buyer had not caused the required letter of credit to be issued, buyer was in breach for failure to take possession because payment was buyer's risk. *Grape must*, E Trial 20030607. In other words, failure to procure the letter of credit was a breach of contract by buyer.

It has been argued that taking delivery includes ordering the amount of goods set forth in the contract, but a court confined taking delivery to a situation where seller puts the goods at the disposition of buyer at the place of delivery. *Beer*, D App 20081118.

Seller's overperformance is not usually a problem, but it might be. Buyer is not obligated to take delivery when the delivery is made before the date fixed in the contract. Art. 52(1). Buyer might not have adequate storage space to accommodate the early delivery. Where there is a fixed date, that is the date upon which seller must deliver. Where there is no fixed date, seller can deliver at any reasonable date, and buyer must accept delivery.

Another overperformance is the delivery of a greater quantity of goods than had been ordered. If that occurs, the buyer has a choice: she can either accept or reject the overage. If she accepts the overage, she must pay for it at the same rate called for in the contract. Art. 52(2).

The buyer who wishes to refuse the overage must do something to so indicate. Buyer must physically take in the goods; otherwise buyer is violating her art. 86 obligation to preserve. That looks to the onlooker as though buyer is accepting the goods. So buyer must notify seller within a reasonable time that buyer is rejecting the overage and holding that part of the goods for seller. Otherwise, a court is likely to find that the overage was accepted and the contract was so modified, as it did in *Artframe mouldings*, CDN Trial 19990831. In theory, no significance should be attached to buyer's physical taking of the goods because buyer is obligated to do that, and should not be barred from rejecting the excess goods because of it. But the wise buyer will quickly notify the seller that he is not accepting the excess goods.

The same advice is appropriate when buyer is refusing to take delivery because the goods are nonconforming. Buyer should physically receive the goods and notify seller that buyer is rejecting delivery and holding the goods at seller's instruction.

CHECKPOINTS

You should have learned that:

- Buyer is obligated to accept conforming goods and pay for them.
- The only way for buyer to assure inspection before payment is to provide for it in the sales contract or to provide for payment at a later date.
- Payment is made in the currency specified. In the absence of specification, it is made in the currency of the place of payment.

- Buyer taking delivery of more goods than ordered is obligated to pay for the excess. Buyer can refuse the excess, but must take care to prevent the goods from being exposed to theft or damage.

- Buyer can likewise refuse to take delivery of nonconforming goods, but must take care to prevent the goods from being exposed to theft or damage.

CHAPTER 8

Breach

ROADMAP

After reading this chapter, you should understand:

- CISG distinguishes between breaches and fundamental breaches.

- A fundamental breach entitles the aggrieved party to avoid the contract. With other breaches, the aggrieved party must perform as best he can, and his remedies include damages, price reduction, and specific performance, but not avoidance.

- Any failure to adhere to the contract is a breach.

- A fundamental breach occurs when the other party is substantially deprived of what he is entitled to expect under the contract, provided this is foreseeable.

- The parties can specify in their contract breaches that will constitute a fundamental breach.

- Some courts define substantial deprivation as a percentage of completion, but there is no agreement about the percentage needed.

- Other courts define substantial deprivation as a situation where the aggrieved party has no reasonable use for what has been promised.

- Goods that can be easily and inexpensively repaired are not a fundamental breach.

- Goods that can be easily resold are not a fundamental breach if seller regularly does business in such goods.

- Failure to deliver seasonal goods by a date early enough for the seasonal market is a fundamental breach.

- A defect in documents that would prevent their transfer is likely to be a fundamental breach.
- Failure of buyer to pay anything is a fundamental breach.
- Buyer may commit a fundamental breach by reselling the goods in a prohibited territory.
- The party committing the breach must be able to foresee that it will be fundamental.

§8.01 Breaches and Fundamental Breaches

The thrust of CISG is to keep contracts in force if possible. This contradicts the instinct and desire of most businesspeople when they realize that they cannot resolve their differences. They want out of the relationship as quickly as possible so that they can get on with their business, and the lawyers will sort out who owes whom what. Before the parties reach what one might call the point of no return in the relationship, CISG wants them to try to resolve their dispute so that the contract can be effectuated as much as possible. To do this, CISG distinguishes between breaches and fundamental breaches. If the contract is breached, the parties move ahead with the contract and sort things out later; only if there is a fundamental breach can one of the parties call the contract off, not perform, and get damages. The party who is the victim of a fundamental breach must follow a prescribed pattern correctly. For this reason, the difference between a breach and a fundamental breach is, well, fundamental.

This reflects a policy choice. Some domestic systems provide that any non-conformity entitles buyer to refuse the goods and rescind the contract. This places the risk on seller in a domestic situation where seller will not likely incur huge costs in retaking the goods, and will probably have in place a marketing system that can dispose of them. With international sales, neither may be the case. Significant and unrecoverable costs may have been expended in transporting the goods or paying customs duties and clearance charges, and seller is less likely to have a marketing network in buyer's country. For this reason, CISG permits avoidance only in extreme cases.

In case of doubt, a breach will not be fundamental. *Egyptian cotton*, CH Sup. Ct. 20000915.

Some legal systems draw a distinction between nondelivery and the delivery of nonconforming goods. CISG also draws that distinction, but not as part of deciding whether there has been a fundamental breach. *Military shoe leather*, PL Sup. Ct. 20070511.

§8.02 Breach

Any failure to adhere to the contract is a breach. That is true whether it is failure to adhere to the express words of the contract, failure to follow a trade usage or a custom between the parties that is applicable to the contract, or failure to comply with a CISG requirement such as delivering property that works for its ordinary usage or property that is not subject to a hostile claim of title.

§8.03 Fundamental Breach

A *fundamental breach* is a breach that "results in such detriment to the other party as substantially to deprive him of what he is entitled to expect" unless a reasonable person in the position of the breacher would not have foreseen such detriment. Art. 25. The parties can specify in their contract what constitutes a fundamental breach. It is less certain that the parties can, by specifying the intended ultimate use of the goods, or several possible uses, reduce the scope of arguments about whether a breach is fundamental. To find a fundamental breach, the elements are substantial detriment and foreseeability. Courts repeat that they should assume that a breach is not fundamental because avoidance is an exceptional remedy. Damages or price reduction are preferred. E.g., *Packaging plant*, CH Sup. Ct. 20090518.

However, it should be clear that nonperformance, coupled with a declaration to never perform, is a fundamental breach because the aggrieved party will receive no part of what was bargained for.

§8.04 Substantial Detriment

Substantial detriment is defined by some courts as only relating to the degree to which the product delivered falls short of the contract's demands. Other courts require that buyer have no reasonable use for the product before finding substantial detriment. The argument that a fundamental breach exists where it is not possible for seller to make the goods conforming has been rejected as too strict. *Cobalt sulfate*, D Sup. Ct. 19960403. If that were the case, even a trivial breach would make the breach fundamental if it could not be corrected.

The courts that believe the goods must be useless to buyer often define substantial detriment by what it is not.

A safety defect in an industrial furnace that could be easily corrected by installing metal sheeting at little expense was not a substantial detriment. *Industrial furnace*, CH App 20070726. The same is true of a leaking salt water isolation tank. *Floating center*, CH Trial 19950426. Neither court revealed the number of hours an easy correction would require, nor whether the little expense was in absolute terms or in comparison to the purchase price. The general rule these courts apply is that there is no substantial detriment when the defect can be easily or inexpensively repaired. It is unclear whether the repair needs to completely eliminate the nonconformity, or simply needs to make the goods usable or salable, but the latter is preferable. It is clear that it does not matter whether the repair is done by buyer, seller, or a third party. *Injection-moulding tools*, D Sup. Ct. 20140924; *Cobalt sulfate*, D Sup. Ct. 19960403. But there are also cases holding that there is a fundamental breach despite the fact that substitutes for the defective parts are readily available on the market. *Spinning mill*, CH Sup. Ct. 20120716.

There is some suggestion that no breach is fundamental if seller makes a credible offer to cure it. *Designer clothes*, D App 20021014. While the court's statement is broad, it refused to credit seller's promise of cure because seller said it would "try to" cure, and did not provide a delivery date to buyer for high-fashion clothes where time was of the essence.

A breach is not fundamental if buyer could put the goods to another use. *Cobalt sulfate*, D Sup. Ct. 19960403; *Designer clothes*, D App 20021014. It is likewise not fundamental if buyer offers to accept the goods at a reduced price. *Meat*, CH Sup. Ct. 19981028.

Where the goods can be resold by someone who sells goods of that type, it is not a substantial detriment, *Apple juice concentrate*, D App 20010312, *Petroleum coke*, CHN Sup. Ct. 20150707, as long as the resale does not entail unreasonable expense. *Designer clothes*, D App 20021014. However, a person who does not normally sell goods of that type is not obligated to go into that business. *Packaging plant*, CH Sup. Ct. 20090518, *Warhol print*, A Sup. Ct. 20151216; *CISG-AC 5*. Goods that are custom-made for buyer may have only a limited market. *Packaging plant*, CH Sup. Ct. 20090518.

Where seller had added a prohibited substance, potassium bromide, to wheat that could not be separated from the wheat economically and that made the wheat dangerous for human consumption and unsalable in many countries, it was a fundamental breach. *Wheat flour*, NL Trial 20050119.

Evidence that seller, a professional art dealer, later tried to sell the print for eight months without generating any interest, and that it was entered in an auction but received no bids, was sufficient to prove that the goods could not be resold. *Warhol print*, A Sup. Ct. 20151216. For that reason, the breach was fundamental.

Sometimes failure to deliver by the date specified in the contract is a fundamental breach. Where the date was December 3 and buyer had told seller that the goods were needed for the Christmas season, non-delivery by December 3 was a fundamental breach. *Knitted goods*, I App 19980320. Where buyer has a re-sale contract to supply the goods to a sub-buyer by a certain date, failure to deliver in time to fulfill that contract would be substantial detriment. *Iron molybdenum*, D App 19970228.

In *Delchi Carrier*, US App, air conditioning compressors defective both in cooling power and in energy use were a fundamental breach because of the importance of those criteria, but the court did not ask whether an easy or inexpensive fix was available (though it recites that there were several unsuccessful attempts to fix the compressors), or whether they could be resold on the open market.

Some courts have suggested that the test is whether the breach impairs the other party's expectations so much that its interest in performance ceases to exist. *Injection-moulding tools*, D Sup. Ct. 20140924.

Courts that have looked solely at the degree of nonconformity have not set any fixed percentage. An assembly and packaging plant consisting of 10 devices that performed at 40% to 71% less than the contract specified was a substantial detriment. *Packaging plant*, CH Sup. Ct. 20090518. Where buyer resold about half the boots, and received complaints about cracked leather, loose seams and soles, and dissolved glue after minimal wear from 22% of the sales, the court said that this was a substantial detriment for the entire order because of buyer's reasonable fear that a like percentage of the boots remaining unsold would have similar defects. It also suggested that this might not be a fundamental breach for a large discount store where shoddy merchandise is to be expected, but was a fundamental breach for a small retailer because being known for quality is a larger part of buyer's professional reputation. *Boots*, D App 20071121. A 35% devaluation of a screenprint was a substantial detriment. *Warhol print*, A Sup. Ct. 20151216. On the other hand, where the contract called for the purchase of 400,000 hectoliters of beer a year for three years and buyer only ordered 90,000 hectoliters in the first year, the court found that a shortage of 7% in the entire contract was not enough to be a substantial detriment to seller, even though it was 21% of the order contracted for in that year, proving that there is more than one way to do math. *Beer*, D App 20081118.

An interesting discussion of fundamental breach took place in *Valero Marketing*, US trial. The question was whether delivery of naphtha to be made into 87 RFG two days late was a fundamental breach. The court speculated that had the two-day delay pushed the sale of 87 RFG into a much lower October market, it would have been a fundamental breach. Since the two-day delay did not prevent seller from putting its 87 RFG on the market in September, the delay was held not to be a fundamental breach. The court did not discuss other potential uses (including resale) of the naphtha. If the court is suggesting that the price at the time the naphtha was delivered was so low that no reasonable manufacturer would have made 87 RFG from it and there was no other use of it, including resale, I agree that it is a fundamental breach.

Documentary sales of commodities pose special problems because it is to be expected that the goods will be resold in transit by transfer of the documents, and because the commodities market is volatile. Any defect in the documents that impedes resale will be a fundamental breach, *CISG-AC 5*, subject to the possibility that the documents can be corrected before potential sales are lost.

Cases of buyer's breach tend to be simpler. Failure to pay anything toward the purchase price is a fundamental breach. This follows from a case where buyer failed to pay "large sums due," though it is not possible to determine from the opinion how the sums due compared with the amount already paid, and why the shortfall is a fundamental breach. *Shuttle Packaging*, US Trial. There are no cases on whether refusing delivery after paying the purchase price in full is a fundamental breach.

Reselling the goods in a place other than the one promised was a fundamental breach where seller had already licensed another exclusive dealer in that country. *Jeans*, F App 19950222.

There are other breaches by buyer that may not be fundamental. Attempting to pay in the wrong place or paying in a currency not called for by the contract would be breaches. Those breaches would probably not be fundamental unless seller could not retrieve or exchange a significant part of the payment.

§8.05 Foreseeability

Foreseeability is a requirement for remedies in two distinct cases. First, to be liable for damages, art. 74 specifically provides that the damages must be foreseeable by the conclusion of the contract. In general, sellers tend to be held to take the risk of most things that might interfere with obtaining or delivering the goods they have promised. That foreseeability will be discussed more fully with damages.

Second, the foreseeability here is that the breach would be a fundamental breach. For instance, it is foreseeable that the late delivery of a perishable and seasonal item, like Christmas trees ordered for October but delivered in January, would be useless to buyer and a fundamental breach.

CISG does not specify the time at which the breacher needs to be able to foresee that the breach will be fundamental. It is strange that there is no case law on this question. Many times set by CISG are the time of the conclusion of the contract, and most commentators think this is the appropriate time because that is the time at which the breacher has priced his risk. I believe that the better rule is that the consequences of the breach must be foreseeable at the moment the breach occurs, because that is the time when the party decides whether to breach or not to breach. It should also be the time when the party calculates the consequences of the breach.

§8.06 Fundamental Breach and Party Autonomy

It has been stated that the parties can by agreement declare what breach of the contract is to be considered a fundamental breach. *Injection-moulding tools*, D Sup. Ct. 20140924; *Cobalt sulfate*, D Sup. Ct. 19960403, *CISG-AC 5*. That is certainly true when the parties stipulate that failure to deliver the goods on time is a fundamental breach. *Clothing*, ICC Arb 8786/1997. It is probably true within reason, and very useful where a decision about whether substantial detriment or foreseeability exists depends on all the facts and circumstances. Whether it would be true of an extreme contract providing that any breach by seller is fundamental and no breach by buyer is, one might doubt.

CHECKPOINTS

You should have learned that:

- CISG distinguishes between breaches and fundamental breaches.
- A fundamental breach entitles the aggrieved party to avoid the contract. With other breaches, the aggrieved party must perform as best he can, and his remedies include damages, price reduction, and specific performance, but not avoidance.

- Any failure to adhere to the contract is a breach.
- A fundamental breach occurs when the other party is substantially deprived of what he is entitled to expect under the contract, provided this is foreseeable.
- The parties can specify in their contract breaches that will constitute a fundamental breach.
- Some courts define substantial deprivation as a percentage of completion, but there is no agreement about the percentage needed.
- Other courts define substantial deprivation as a situation where the aggrieved party has no reasonable use for what has been promised.
- Goods that can be easily and inexpensively repaired are not a fundamental breach.
- Goods that can be easily resold are not a fundamental breach if seller regularly does business in such goods.
- Failure to deliver seasonal goods by a date early enough for the seasonal market is a fundamental breach.
- A defect in documents that would prevent their transfer is likely to be a fundamental breach.
- Failure of buyer to pay anything is a fundamental breach.
- Buyer may commit a fundamental breach by reselling the goods in a prohibited territory.
- The party committing the breach must be able to foresee that it will be fundamental.

CHAPTER 9

Excused Performance

ROADMAP

After reading this chapter, you should understand:

- CISG generally requires parties to perform their contractual obligations.

- Performance is excused if a party rightfully avoids the contract.

- A party may suspend performance temporarily if it becomes apparent that the other party will not perform a substantial part of his obligations as a result of: (a) a serious deficiency in his ability to perform or in his creditworthiness; or (b) his conduct in preparing to perform or in performing the contract. The suspender must immediately give notice of the suspension. If the other party provides reasonable assurance of performance, the suspender must perform.

- A party may avoid the contract if it is clear that the other party will commit a fundamental breach (anticipatory fundamental breach). Requirements for this are substantively the same as for suspension, and the result is more to the party's liking.

- A fundamental breach of one installment of an installment contract permits the aggrieved party to avoid the contract for that installment.

- A fundamental breach of one installment may, under appropriate facts, constitute a fundamental breach of the entire contract.

- Liability for damages is temporarily excused if: (1) the failure is due to (2) an impediment that is (3) beyond his control and (4) he could not reasonably have been expected to have taken into account and (5) whose consequences for the contract he could not have avoided or overcome. The party must give prompt notice to avoid damages. All these terms should be interpreted in the context of what is commercially reasonable.

- An impediment is not unforeseeable if it is within the party's normal sphere of operation.

- The exemption from liability for damages disappears with respect to actions after the impediment is removed or it could be overcome.

- Other remedies such as price reduction or avoidance are available to the aggrieved party.

- There is no doctrine of excuse for hardship in CISG.

- It is unclear what adequate assurance might be. Performing the contract is adequate assurance where the complaint is failure to perform, but a party cannot demand more than the contract requires as adequate assurance. It appears that adequate assurance may be an oral or written statement that the party will perform the contract.

- A party is excused from performing if prevented from doing so by the other party.

§9.01 Introduction

In many domestic legal systems, rules like the "perfect tender" rule provide that even the slightest deviation from contractual requirements on the part of one party will release the other party from the contractual obligations. CISG does not follow that rule. Under CISG, a party must perform its contractual obligations unless it is entitled to avoid the contract, usually because the other party has committed a fundamental breach. That strict rule is relaxed in only a few situations detailed in this chapter.

Several different provisions of CISG excuse partially or entirely, temporarily or permanently, one of the parties from performing his obligations under a sales contract. Each carries special obligations, which means that they are perilous to invoke. Failure to meet all of the obligations for excuse likely means that the party seeking to be excused has himself breached the contract.

The reasons for excusing performance are several. Suspension and anticipatory breach require that the parties keep in touch when performance is in doubt. This should lead to more contract completion than if the parties took unilateral action because they will be acting on the basis of fact rather than rumor. In a situation where performance is not going to occur, it is economically efficient for the other party to mitigate at the earliest possible time as the cost of doing so is likely to be less.

§9.02 Suspending Performance

A party may suspend performance temporarily if it becomes apparent that the other party will not perform a substantial part of his obligations as a result of: (a) a serious deficiency in his ability to perform or in his creditworthiness; or (b) his conduct in preparing to perform or in performing the contract. The suspender must immediately give notice of the suspension (and presumably the reasons for it) and must continue performance if the other party provides adequate assurance of performance. A seller who has already dispatched the goods may prevent the delivery to buyer (if he can). Art. 71.

This provision is a demonstration of CISG's preference for keeping the contract in existence if at all possible.

A brief read of the requirements shows the difficulty of suspending performance. First, it must become apparent that the other party will not perform. The evidence of this must not have been available before the contract was signed; it must result from the other party's ability, conduct, or creditworthiness; and notice must be given. This only temporarily suspends the performance obligation, pending the other party's presentation of adequate assurances.

The courts have applied these requirements very strictly. After years of smooth operation, a seller of umbrellas was not paid by buyer for eight months. Because of that, seller was unable to pay his suppliers. The court reports that buyer had suffered deteriorated financial conditions, but did not reveal what seller knew of that other than failure of payment. Buyer told seller that buyer had ordered a bank payment, so seller resumed deliveries. Buyer stopped the payment, and seller stopped the deliveries. In holding seller's suspension of delivery unjustified, the court set up a strict standard: delayed or sluggish payments, or even the revocation of a payment order, are insufficient to show lack of creditworthiness. Insolvency proceedings for buyer would have been sufficient. The court also suggests that ceasing to make payment would be sufficient, but how is seller to know if payments are stopped or only sluggish if delayed for eight months? *Umbrellas*, A Sup. Ct. 19980212. In *Doolim Corp.*

v. R. Doll, US Trial, the court held that being in arrears of payment for three months was enough to show lack of creditworthiness, but the authority of that case is weakened because it was a default judgment. In another case, the court never decided whether a disputed debt of buyer to seller of US$7 million was enough to show that buyer lacked creditworthiness, because the trial court found that seller did not adequately prove that the debt was owing, and failed to prove that buyer's financial position was worse at the time seller suspended delivery than it had been when the contract was concluded. *Scooters*, CH Sup. Ct. 20070717. In neither case did the court consider whether seller was justified by buyer's conduct of not paying.

On the other hand, a court stated that a seller who was promised a letter of credit could suspend delivery until he received the letter of credit or a substitute payment. However, the ability to suspend delivery for the two weeks seemed to make no difference in the final result because seller suspended delivery for longer than permitted. *Styrofoam machines*, Canada B.C. Sup. Ct. 20030821.

One difference between the two cases is that the failure in *Styrofoam* was with a requirement of the contract at issue, whereas the alleged failure in *Scooters* was with a previous contract. Nowhere is that distinction mentioned in CISG.

Notice is a vital element of suspension. Failure to give notice invalidates the suspension, and means that the party who suspends performance has breached the contract. *Rijn blend*, NL Arb 2319, 20021015; *Italian shoes*, D Trial 19910131.

If a suspending seller has already sent the goods, seller may prevent their delivery if he can. As a practical matter, seller will be able to prevent delivery only in one of two ways. If seller still has the shipment documents, seller can refuse to deliver them to buyer (or the bank). If seller has already delivered the shipping documents, the carrier is unlikely to refuse to deliver the goods to the person presenting the documents unless a court orders the carrier to refuse delivery. Obtaining a court judgment takes time and increases seller's cost of stopping delivery, but may be worthwhile. To be effective, that court judgment needs to be issued (and perhaps widely publicized) before buyer transfers the documents to a holder in due course or an inventory financer, as the right to recall delivery only applies between buyer and seller.

It is not clear why anyone would invoke art 71's suspension when the exact same proof is required to invoke art. 72's anticipatory breach provision, and the result does not leave the suspender in suspense, but permits him to avoid the contract.

§9.03 Anticipatory Breach

A party may avoid the contract if it is clear that the other party will commit a fundamental breach. Art. 72.

Under art. 71, a party may act if "it becomes apparent that the other party will not perform...." Under art. 72, a party may act if "it is clear that one of the parties will commit...." That is a different wording, but the same standard of proof will be required to establish "it becomes apparent" as "it is clear."

In both cases, the person who invokes the excuse must prove that the other party "will" commit the breach.

Art. 71 requires that the other party "will not perform a substantial part of his obligations," whereas art. 72 requires that the other party "will commit a fundamental breach." There may be a slight difference there, as art. 71 looks to the substantiality of the obligations of the breacher, while the requirement of art. 72 looks to fundamental breach, which is when the victim is substantially and foreseeably deprived of what he is entitled to expect under the contract. So one looks to how substantial the shortfall will be in the obligation of the breacher, while the other looks to how substantial the detriment is to the victim. In practice, the proof required will likely be the same, regardless of theoretical differences.

The consequences are quite different. A party who suspends must immediately give notice; a party who invokes anticipatory breach must give notice "if time allows." In both cases, the excuse can no longer be relied upon if the other party provides "adequate assurances." Under both provisions, the party invoking it must be prepared to resume performance if the other party provides adequate assurance of performance within a reasonable time, or within the time set in the invoker's notice so long as that is a reasonable time. For anticipatory breach, the remedy is avoidance if adequate assurances are not forthcoming. It is unclear what the remedy is for suspension of performance. Presumably, nonliability for failure to perform.

Courts confuse the two situations. *Military shoe leather*, PL Sup. Ct. 20070511, talks about anticipatory breach, which is art. 72, repeatedly citing art. 71.

The clearest situation for anticipatory breach is where the other party notifies you that he will not perform. That notification can be express or implied, but one should be careful about implying too much. For instance, a communication from seller that he will have difficulty performing without an increase in the price may be interpreted as a statement that he will not perform, or it may be simply an invitation to negotiate. In the latter case, you will not be able to prove that he will not perform. *Jute*, E Sup. Ct. 20000128. On the other hand, the statement that seller will sell the goods to others unless buyer agrees to do things not required by the contract was held to be notification that seller would not perform. *Magellan Int'l*, US Trial.

One case is instructive of facts meeting the requirements for anticipatory breach without a declaration of refusal to perform. A Swedish seller promised a medicine packaging machine to a Chinese buyer. The parties agreed that seller would develop a difficult-to-imitate medicine container. Buyer was to provide package samples, but did not provide satisfactory samples. Seller did not deliver the machine at the date specified, pointing out that buyer had purchased two filling machines from seller's competitor without notifying seller. Buyer gave seller notice of a time to perform. Seller did not deliver. Buyer avoided the contract and asked for return of its deposit. The arbitral tribunal held that buyer could not avoid the contract. Seller was justified in failing to deliver the machine because buyer did not present proper samples and because of the risk of patent infringement by buyer or buyer's other supplier of machines. While the tribunal did not discuss anticipatory breach, one might well think that buyer's secretive purchase of substitute machines from a competitor might make it clear that buyer would commit a fundamental breach by not accepting delivery. *Medicine packaging machine*, CHN Arb 20021227.

§9.04 Installment Contracts

Excuse from installment contracts may be treated by individual install-ments, or as a whole. A fundamental breach for one installment triggers the remedies for fundamental breach for that installment. Performance that amounts to fundamental breach on one installment may give the other party "good grounds" to declare an anticipatory breach for subsequent installments. The breach on one installment may be such a substantial detriment to the other party that he is substantially deprived of the purpose of the entire contract so as to constitute a fundamental breach of the entire contract. Art. 73. Like other avoidance, avoidance of installment contracts requires notice within a reason-able time. A reasonable time to give notice of avoidance for a single installment may be shorter than a reasonable time to give notice for the entire contract because it may not initially be apparent to a reasonable person in the position of the aggrieved party that the breach of the installment provides grounds for anticipatory breach or constitutes a fundamental breach of the entire contract.

An installment contract is a contract providing for either delivery of goods or payment at different times. Two contracts executed the same day between the same parties providing for different delivery dates and different payments may be regarded as an installment contract. *Malting barley*, A Arb 19971210.

Breaches on one part of the contract may be considered in deciding whether the entire contract has been fundamentally breached. So may the likely reputational effects of the quantity of defective merchandise. *Boots*, D App 20071121.

It has been suggested that the use of different terms for the certainty required in arts. 71–73 indicates that the drafters intended a different level of likelihood of a future fundamental breach, and I agree in theory. In the real world, I doubt that it will make any difference. A delivery of two defective installments of malting barley was said to provide good grounds to believe that future installments will be similarly defective in the absence of some assurance from seller, even though the court said that the burden of proof is on buyer. *Malting barley*, A Arb 19971210.

§9.05 Unforeseeable Impediment

The drafters took a novel approach to the problem of the unforeseen circumstance that hinders performance of the contract. Domestic laws contain concepts such as *force majeure*, impossibility of performance, frustration, impracticability, or hardship. CISG avoids all those terms for fear that the use of any of them would make autonomous interpretation less likely, and courts would interpret the term in accord with domestic law. Instead, the drafters set up five conditions that would excuse a party from damages for defective performance while those conditions lasted. Performance is temporarily excused if: (1) the failure is due to (2) an impediment that is (3) beyond his control and (4) he could not reasonably have been expected to have taken into account and (5) whose consequences for the contract he could not have avoided or overcome. Unlike many similar domestic law doctrines, the party is not relieved of the obligation to perform. His obligation to perform is intact; only his liability for damages is obliterated until the impediment is removed or its consequences for the contract overcome. Art. 79.

The principal U.S. interpretation of art. 79, *Raw Materials*, US Trial, is a disaster for which the parties bear responsibility. Seller promised to deliver used Russian railroad rail from the port of St Petersburg by June 30, which was then postponed by mutual agreement to a time that the parties dispute, around

December 31. What is undisputed is that the port of St. Petersburg froze, preventing the departure of ships sometime in December. The annual freeze does not normally close that port because it uses icebreakers, but icebreakers were useless that year due to extreme weather. The parties, represented by large multinational law firms, both argued that since no U.S. court had interpreted art. 79, it should be interpreted on analogy to the comparable provision of the UCC. The court obliged.

This is wrong under art. 7! Uniformity of interpretation internationally is to be sought. There were many decisions from other countries available, and no one was prevented from grammatical interpretation of the plain words of art. 79.

It was especially wrong in this case! The problem with this approach is that UCC §2-615 is worded very differently, has only three requirements instead of five, and permanently discharges the party from performance. The UCC requires that a contingency occur that makes performance impractical and that was unforeseen. The court refused to grant summary judgment on grounds that there was a conflict in the evidence on whether the freezing of the port made performance impractical. That decision was proper; the court's alignment of CISG and the UCC was not.

The court never discusses whether seller could have overcome this impediment by sending the rail by a different route, such as by railroad, or by shipping it from a different port that was not frozen, or by buying scrap rail from a different supplier that could be sent from a non-frozen port.

Also, the court does not discuss the fact that the port is only closed temporarily. Eventually, "spring is coming and the ice will break" and under CISG seller will be obligated to pay damages if it does not perform at that time.

It should be noted that U.S. courts are not alone in interpreting CISG as identical to domestic law when it is not. A German court equates art. 79 with *force majeure*, though with more justification. *Iron molybdenum*, D App 19970228.

In an art. 79 case, the first decision to make is whether an impediment has occurred. There are many things that can cause an impediment, such as strikes, unavailability of raw materials, or transport difficulties. It is usually not difficult to find an impediment.

The impediment must have caused the failure to perform. Where seller failed to deliver dried sweet potatoes claiming that it was because of government-imposed export restrictions or crop failure, this requirement failed. The export restrictions were not imposed until after the date for delivery, and the crop failure occurred before the contract was signed, so could not have been unforeseen. *Sweet potatoes*, CHN Arb 19960314.

More difficult is to find that the impediment is beyond the party's control. Where the car sold had been stolen and was confiscated from buyer's buyer, the court held that seller should have been aware from the facts surrounding his agent's purchase that it was possible that the car was stolen, such as the price, the frequent theft of that model, and the vague identification of the person with whom the agent was dealing. This, plus seller's successful efforts to verify title through two police checks, seem to indicate that seller foresaw the risk that the car had been stolen, and assumed them. *Stolen car*, D App 20080305. Where seller ordered the manufacture of black vine wax that did not adequately protect vines but did not test it before selling it, the court held that the impediment of faulty design could have been overcome by a prudent testing program that was within seller's control. *Vine wax*, D Sup. Ct. 19990324.

Some cases have faltered because the impediment is one that seller is expected to have considered when the contract was concluded. For instance, the fact that seller or his supplier may be in financial difficulty may be neither beyond the party's control, nor something that seller had no reason to take into account. *Chinese goods*, D Arb 19960321. Failure of seller's supplier to deliver is normally seller's responsibility. *Fertilizer*, ICC Arb 8128/1995. If strikes are not unusual in seller's area, the possibility of a strike is something seller should anticipate.

Since seller is usually responsible for making or procuring conforming goods, it will be difficult for seller to establish that delivering non-conforming goods was the result of an impediment that he had no reason to take into account.

However, it would be pushing matters too far (though in literal conformity with the words) to require an impediment that is not humanly foreseeable or its results avoidable. The provision is designed for commercial contracts, and should be interpreted to mean reasonably foreseeable or avoidable within the context of the contract. There are few things that are not avoidable if one can use unlimited resources to avoid them. Rather, the question should be whether the impediment was reasonably foreseeable or avoidable within the commercial context in which the contract was designed to operate.

It is unclear whether things like market fluctuations or increased costs do not qualify because they are not impediments, or because they are part of the normal risks a seller must consider in setting his price, but it is clear that they will not exempt seller from damages. While CISG Advisory Council suggests that there might be a case for extreme hardship as an exemption, it could cite no case where that argument had succeeded. *CISG-AC 7, 20.* The only apparently successful invocation of hardship was with a 70% rise in the price of steel, and that was under French domestic law. *Steel pipes*, B Sup. Ct. 20090619. The decision was much criticized both for using domestic law and for finding an impediment where the price only rose by 70%. In other cases, a 300% difference in price was insufficient to constitute an impediment where industry prices had been speculative. *Iron molybdenum*, D App 19970228. In short, there is a theory that extreme hardship might be an impediment, but the case has yet to occur, and the consequence is simply that failure of performance does not result in liability for damages until the hardship ceases to be extreme. The parties are under no obligation to renegotiate the contract, nor can a court or arbitrator force a new contract on them or terminate the existing contract. *CISG-AC 20*. The aggrieved party could avoid the contract if the failure to deliver were a fundamental breach, and likely would.

If all of that can be overcome, one must satisfy the requirement that the party must have been unable to avoid the consequences of the impediment. Even if adverse weather conditions reduced the harvest and there were export restrictions as a result, nothing in the contract prevented seller from acquiring the goods from an area where the weather was fine and there were no export restrictions. *Sweet potatoes*, CHN Arb 19960314. Such a result would not be available if the contract specified the area or supplier from whom the goods were to be supplied and buyer refused to waive that provision. Where chicken was contracted to be delivered to Romania but Romania closed its borders to foreign chicken due to bird flu, seller could have delivered the chicken to buyer at a nearby port as buyer had requested. *Macromex SRL v. Globex*, US Trial.

CISG recognizes that often a party, usually seller, cannot perform because of the failure of some other independent supplier, usually an independent contractor, that seller has hired to supply the goods for which seller is obligated directly to buyer. In that case, both the supplier and seller must meet all the requirements of art. 79. In *Vine wax*, D Sup. Ct. 19990324, seller commissioned a third party to produce a black vine wax to protect vines from disease after pruning. The wax produced turned out not to be protective. The court held that neither seller nor his supplier met the requirements of art. 79. This double burden will not apply if the contract specifies the person who must perform because an alternate supplier is not possible under the contract.

If a party wants *force majeure*, impossibility of performance, frustration, impracticability, or hardship to apply to the contract, it needs to be specified in the contract, as it was in *Iron molybdenum*, D App 19970228 or *Sweet potatoes*, CHN Arb 19960314. Given the vagueness of these standards, the contract might want to be a bit more specific about what satisfies the standard, and whether the consequences are release from the obligation, or only its suspension. But a word of caution is appropriate. Specifying the standards means that the party must comply with them. In *Sweet potatoes*, CHN Arb 19960314, the *force majeure* clause required that the party provide a certificate from the government, which seller failed to do.

§9.06 Notice Requirement

The notice requirements differ for these sections, though in each case the person invoking the benefit is expected to give notice. For suspension, notice must be given "immediately" or the suspension is invalid because the notice calls on the other party to provide adequate assurance of performance. If adequate assurance is provided and the other requirements are met, the suspension is valid but is terminated on the receipt of adequate assurance. For anticipatory breach, "reasonable" notice must be given "if time allows" in order to permit the other party to provide reasonable assurance, but notice need not be provided if the other party has declared that (s)he will not perform. There is no need to perform a senseless notice when the other party has declared. For installment contracts, no notice is specifically provided, but if the offended party wishes to exercise the most desired remedy, avoidance, that carries a requirement of declaration of avoidance within a reasonable time after learning the facts. Art. 49(1), 64(1). No provision states to whom that declaration must be made, but it is more logical to make it to the other party rather than, like Hamlet, deliver it as a soliloquy from the ramparts of his castle. For an impediment, notice must be given of the impediment and its impact on performance, but if the other party does not receive notice within a reasonable time, the suspension is still valid. The un-notified party's remedy is damages for the delay. Art. 79 still excuses the person who is impeded from paying damages.

§9.07 Remedies Available

If someone succeeds in being excused under art. 79, the only result is exemption from the remedy of damages. Presumably, that excuse from damages is only for the period during which the impediment persists. Other remedies are available. Art. 79(5). What might they be?

Surely not specific performance. Arts. 46, 62. If an impediment prevents performance, it will also prevent specific performance. Price reduction is a potential remedy, but how would that operate if the other party is going to perform after the impediment is removed? The only remedy that seems practical is avoidance, and that is the remedy the injured party is likely to prefer.

§9.08 Adequate Assurances

I have found no case satisfactorily defining what adequate assurances might be. One arbitral tribunal found that adequate assurances included statements by the other party, combined with partial performance. In *Lanthanide Metal*, CHN Arb 19960918, buyer was obligated to have a letter of credit issued by 15 March, and subsequent letters of credit every 30 days before five later specified delivery dates. Buyer promised a letter of credit on 17 April, which seller rejected and declared avoidance. Buyer's bank produced the letter of credit that day. The tribunal is not clear whether buyer's statement is adequate assurance, which it should not be, or whether the tribunal is deciding that there has been no anticipatory breach of the later installments because seller said nothing about them.

If it is seller who is seeking assurance, presumably payment in full or a payment guarantee would be an adequate assurance. That raises the problem that the contract does not require buyer to pay that soon or to provide the guarantee. If seller can receive early payment or a guarantee for which he was unable to bargain in the initial contract, he has been able to unilaterally amend the contract to his advantage simply by raising doubts.

If it is buyer seeking assurance, that assurance will need to vary with the reasons advanced by buyer for believing that seller will not perform. If the reason relates to seller's solvency, it is unclear what adequate assurance might be other than permitting buyer to examine seller's books and assets, something seller is unlikely to authorize and that buyer has no right to under the contract.

§9.09 Other Party's Act or Omission

A party is excused from performing if prevented from doing so by the other party. Art. 80. A contract for propane specified that buyer would procure a letter of credit and seller would specify the port of loading. Buyer could not secure a letter of credit because seller never specified a port of loading, which was necessary for the letter of credit to issue. As a result, seller could not rely on buyer's failure to open the letter of credit to escape liability. *Propane*, A Sup. Ct. 19960206.

The other party's omission should be something that the other party is obligated to do. In a case where seller delivers nonconforming goods, seller may lack the money to procure substitute conforming goods, and may allege that his failure to perform was the result of buyer not paying him. If buyer is not obligated to pay yet, seller will not prevail. *Military shoe leather*, PL Sup. Ct. 20070511. If the contract requires buyer to make an advanced deposit, failure to do so may excuse seller's performance.

This provision can be analogized to the fact that CISG limits damages to those caused by the breach. It may be true that the breach caused the loss, but CISG regards the injured party's action as the cause of the breach and therefore the cause of the loss.

A case where both parties breached their obligation and the damage complained of would not have occurred if either had acted as it was obligated to act is not properly decided under this rubric unless the breach by one party caused the breach by the other. A sale of kaolinite was made to prepare a bath to separate starch-rich potatoes to be used for human food from starch-poor potatoes to be used for animal feed. The kaolinite had too high a concentration of dioxin, which was seller's fault, but buyer did not inspect the kaolinite as required by art. 38 and agricultural regulations. Had buyer known of the dioxin contamination, an easy remedy of rinsing the kaolinite was available. The court ended up reducing but not eliminating damages due to buyer based on general principles of CISG derived from arts. 77 and 80. *Kaolinite*, D Sup. Ct. 20120926. This case seems questionable. The remedy for buyer failing to inspect and give notice of nonconformity is that buyer cannot use any remedy for nonconformity. Art. 39. However, the court found that buyer gave proper notice within a reasonable time, which varied from one to four months. It also found that buyer failed to inspect its outgoing product for impurities as required by law. There is no warrant to invoke general principles of CISG, as arts. 74 and 77 specifically cover damages and mitigation. Justification for the decision should be the aggrieved party's obligation to mitigate. Mitigation is required only when the aggrieved party knows of the breach, or should have known of it. If buyer had tested the first batch for impurities, buyer would have discovered the breach when it sent out the product derived from the earlier deliveries, so it is difficult to see why buyer's notification about the early deliveries was timely. The best explanation for the case is practical. The court thought both parties were at fault, so gave reduced damages.

CHECKPOINTS

You should have learned that:

- CISG generally requires parties to perform their contractual obligations.

- Performance is excused if a party rightfully avoids the contract.

- A party may suspend performance temporarily if it becomes apparent that the other party will not perform a substantial part of his obligations as a result of: (a) a serious deficiency in his ability to perform or in his creditworthiness; or (b) his conduct in preparing to perform or in performing the contract. The suspender must immediately give notice of the suspension. If the other party provides reasonable assurance of performance, the suspender must perform.

- A party may avoid the contract if it is clear that the other party will commit a fundamental breach (anticipatory fundamental breach). Requirements for this are substantively the same as for suspension, and the result is more to the party's liking.

- A fundamental breach of one installment of an installment contract permits the aggrieved party to avoid the contract for that installment.

- A fundamental breach of one installment may, under appropriate facts, constitute a fundamental breach of the entire contract.

- Liability for damages is temporarily excused if: (1) the failure is due to (2) an impediment that is (3) beyond his control and (4) he could not reasonably have been expected to have taken into account and (5) whose consequences for the contract he could not have avoided or overcome. The party must give prompt notice to avoid damages. All these terms should be interpreted in the context of what is commercially reasonable.

- An impediment is not unforeseeable if it is within the party's normal sphere of operation.

- The exemption from liability for damages disappears with respect to actions after the impediment is removed or it could be overcome.

- Other remedies such as price reduction or avoidance are available to the aggrieved party.

- There is no doctrine of excuse for hardship in CISG.

- It is unclear what adequate assurance might be. Performing the contract is adequate assurance where the complaint is failure to perform, but a party cannot demand more than the contract requires as adequate assurance. It appears that adequate assurance may be an oral or written statement that the party will perform the contract.

- A party is excused from performing if prevented from doing so by the other party.

CHAPTER 10

Non-Judicial Remedies

ROADMAP

After reading this chapter, you should understand:

- If seller performs early and buyer notifies seller that the goods or documents are non-conforming, seller may cure the nonconformity up to the time of performance if the cure does not cause buyer unreasonable inconvenience or unreasonable expense.

- After the time set for performance, seller may still cure subject to the above and also on condition that buyer has not avoided the contract and that buyer is certain of reimbursement for cure expenses that buyer advances.

- A credible offer to cure makes a fundamental breach non-fundamental.

- Buyer loses the remedy of price reduction if buyer refuses a cure.

- Where seller offers to cure, if buyer fails to respond within a reasonable time, seller may perform within the time he has specified.

- Buyers can call on sellers to repair the goods to make them conform, as long as this is not unreasonable.

- Repair would be unreasonable if it were more costly than replacement.

- Buyer can only demand replacement goods if the breach is fundamental.

- A U.S. court is unlikely to order repair or replacement because it is a form of specific performance.

- CISG has no provision giving buyer the right to cure defective performance, but one might be implied because most remedies accorded to either buyer or seller are reciprocal.

- Either party may fix a reasonable additional period for the other party to perform their contractual obligations. This is called *nach-frist*. Granting additional time is strongly advised as a practical matter because it demonstrates reasonableness.

- Setting a date for performance to which the other party does not timely object raises a presumption that the period is reasonable.

- It is unclear whether a reasonable time is computed from what is reasonable for buyer, what is reasonable for seller, or what is reasonable for both.

- In determining whether the time given was reasonable, courts have included the time after the expiration of the time stated but before the contract is declared avoided in determining whether the time was reasonable.

- Where seller breaches, buyer may reduce the price to an amount that bears the same proportion to the contract price as the value of the goods delivered bears to the value that conforming goods would have had.

- Price reduction is a substitute for damages suffered when the value of goods delivered (or not delivered) is less than the value of the goods ordered. Damages may not be collected for that loss, but price reduction can be combined with damages for other losses.

- Price reduction may be hard to use in cases where it is difficult to value the goods. A cover transaction is likely to be more persuasive than opinion evidence of value.

- Where the contract gives buyer the right to make choices about the goods but buyer refuses to choose, seller may make the choice subject to buyer's objection.

- A party can avoid the contract if the other party commits a fundamental breach, or if the other party does not deliver, the injured party grants additional time (*nachfrist*), and the other party does not deliver within the reasonable additional time.

- To avoid the contract, one party must send timely notice of avoidance to the other. Courts have construed notices liberally to find that they are notices of avoidance.

- When a contract is avoided, buyer returns the goods, seller returns the purchase price, and neither price reduction nor specific performance is a permissible remedy.

- Delivering nothing is non-delivery. Delivering the wrong quantity of the goods ordered, or delivering the right quantity of nonconforming goods, or paying only part of the purchase price, is not non-delivery. Whether delivery of entirely different goods than those ordered is non-delivery remains to be seen.

- With an installment contract, whether there has been delivery is determined installment by installment.

- Buyer may not avoid the contract if buyer cannot return the delivered goods to seller in substantially the same condition in which buyer received them. However, buyer can still avoid the contract if part of the goods have deteriorated as a result of the required examination on arrival; if they have been sold, processed, or transformed in the ordinary course of buyer's business before buyer ought to have discovered the lack of conformity; or if the inability to restore goods to seller is not due to buyer's act or omission.

- Seller's return of the purchase price must be accompanied by interest. Courts have used a number of different measures to determine the rate of interest and whether it is simple or compound.

- Buyer must account to seller for any value received as a result of having possession of the goods.

- Buyer in possession of the goods must preserve them and arrange to convey them to seller. The cost of doing so is likely to be part of the damages suffered.

- Goods may be sold if they are likely to spoil before the other party can obtain and dispose of them. All goods may be sold if the other party does not take possession within a reasonable time.

- A party who properly elects avoidance after a breach may also collect damages suffered.

§ 10.01 Introduction to Non-Judicial Remedies

CISG contains a number of opportunities for the parties to settle any disagreements they may have without resort to litigation or arbitration. The point is to encourage performance of the contract as nearly as possible, and to avoid reliance on the expense and delay of court or arbitral decisionmaking. While this is a laudable goal, the parties still retain the right to litigate about whether the particular non-judicial remedy could be pursued, or was properly pursued. They do litigate. No statistics are available that would indicate whether the existence of these non-judicial remedies has reduced litigation.

One may categorize the remedies as repair, replacement, granting time, price reduction, and avoidance. These remedies are contrasted with, and may be intermediate steps on the way to, the judicial remedies of specific enforcement or damages.

A. Cure

§ 10.02 Cure Before Performance Time

Seller is not obligated to perform before the date when performance is due. Sometimes seller does perform early. If he performs early and buyer notifies seller that the goods or documents are non-conforming, CISG gives seller the right to cure the nonconformity up to the time of performance if the cure does not cause buyer unreasonable inconvenience or unreasonable expense. Arts. 37, 34. Note that since the goods are in buyer's possession, as a practical matter the parties need to communicate about a cure. Buyer retains the right to claim damages. The nonconformity can be small or fundamental, and it is not clear whether seller's right to cure or buyer's right to avoid in the case of a fundamental breach would take precedence. I think seller's right to cure would prevail because there is no reference in art. 37 to the right to avoid, and because CISG tries to keep contracts alive if at all possible. There is also the doctrine noted above that a credible promise by seller to cure will prevent a breach from being fundamental. *Designer clothes*, D App 20021014.

Usually, buyer will not suffer unreasonable inconvenience or expense as a result of a cure that occurs before the time for performance because buyer would have been without the goods at that time. Buyer might suffer damages from a cure, such as the expense of processing replacement goods through customs. Greater damages might have occurred if the goods are one machine in a production line. It might be necessary to shut down the entire production line to repair or replace the defective machine, which might entail significant loss to buyer. Or buyer may have used the goods in her production line before discovering the nonconformity.

This provision is not much used, perhaps because of its time constraints. The number of deliveries before the delivery deadline is probably small. Of those cases, the number of nonconforming deliveries is even smaller. Only some of those will be notified by buyer quickly enough to permit seller to cure before the contract's delivery date.

§10.03 Cure After Performance Time

More likely to occur is the situation where seller delivers nonconforming goods on time, late, or not at all.

In this case, seller still has the right to cure, but is subject to two additional contingencies.

Buyer cannot be placed in a position of uncertainty of reimbursement for expenses he advances. Art. 48. This seems to contemplate cure by buyer or seller or both to be financed eventually by seller. It would not be unusual for buyer to participate in a cure, even though that is seller's responsibility.

The second condition is more serious. Art. 48 begins "subject to article 49," which is the section authorizing avoidance in the case of a fundamental breach or non-delivery within additional fixed time. This seems to cut off seller's right to cure if the breach has been fundamental and buyer avoids. However, a credible offer to cure prevents a breach from being fundamental. *Designer clothes*, D App 20021014; *Acrylic blankets*, D App 19970131; *Inflatable arches*, CH Trial 20021105.

§10.04 Credible Offer to Cure

A cure may involve either repair or replacement. Art. 37. It is unclear whether seller's offer to cure must include a specific date for effectuating the cure, but that should certainly be a requirement when the goods are seasonal. *Designer clothes*, D App 20021014. If the cure is replacement, buyer must return the goods originally delivered in substantially the same condition in which they were received. Arts. 82, 84. See the discussion below for a fuller account and exceptions.

§10.05 Unreasonable Expense or Unreasonable Delay

One court has opined in dicta that unreasonable inconvenience can be that buyer is faced with damage claims from customers, or that seller seems to lack the ability to successfully make repairs by past unsuccessful repair attempts. *Injection-moulding tools*, D Sup. Ct. 20140924. As to damage claims, once buyer knows of the defect, no additional damage claims will accrue if buyer ceases to use the goods until the defect is corrected. Unsuccessful repair attempts may or may not indicate that seller is incompetent to fix the defect. Typically, when there is a defect, one dresses a list of possible fixes and proceeds based on a balance between the cost of the fix and the likelihood of its success. Failure to succeed may simply mean that the least expensive fixes did not work. Besides, the ability of seller is not one of the criteria on the basis of which buyer can refuse to permit seller to cure.

But granting the right to cure freezes buyer's options. Buyer may suffer unreasonable expense if buyer has re-sale commitments and buyer's buyer must shut down a production line for lack of the goods. *Tetracycline HCL*, D Trial 19950623. One might argue that this is reparable by damages, but obtaining damages in the U.S. requires the expenditure of legal fees that will not be reimbursed absent a specific clause in the contract, may take years, and may be quite limited with an insolvent seller.

Buyer should not refuse a cure lightly. No matter how justified the refusal, buyer loses the remedy of price reduction if buyer refuses a cure. Art. 50.

§10.06 Buyer's Silence as Acquiescence

The exchange of communication that is implicit before the performance date is explicit afterward. It appears that seller must request permission to cure, and buyer can refuse on any of the grounds set forth above. Art. 48(2) & (3). Buyer's failure to respond to seller's proposal of cure is acceptance, but seller's notice is not effective until actually received, contrary to art. 27's statement that notices are effective when sent. Art. 48(4).

Where seller offers to cure, if buyer fails to respond within a reasonable time, seller may perform within the time he has specified. Art. 48(2). Where the contract called for delivery by August 14 and seller's letter promising to deliver by September 10 arrived before then but was not answered, the court found that the September delivery was within the permitted cure period. *Italian shoes*, D Trial 19940614.

§10.07 Buyer's Right to Have Seller
Cure—Repair or Replacement

All the above assume that seller wishes to cure, and talks about seller's rights against a presumably unwilling buyer. Buyers also have rights. Buyers can call on sellers to repair the goods to make them conform, as long as this is not unreasonable. Art. 46(3).

Unreasonable as compared to what? If the cost of repair exceeds the cost of replacement, it is unreasonable to demand repair unless the time required for replacement would be significantly longer than repair and would significantly disadvantage buyer.

Buyer should usually prefer replacement over repair because with replacement, buyer receives new goods. The value of new goods is always more than the value of repaired goods, even if their function is identical. Buyer can only demand replacement goods if the breach is fundamental. Art. 46(2). The reason for the limit on demanding replacement is that usually replacement will be more costly than repair. Replacement not only incurs the cost of substitute goods, it also requires the return of the nonconforming goods originally provided. That return may incur additional transport, insurance, and customs costs. CISG tries to reduce the total costs of contracting by limiting buyer's replacement right to fundamental breaches.

Buyer may demand replacement or repair, but in the U.S. there are few situations where a court will force an unwilling seller to do either. That is because repairing or replacing is a form of specific performance, which CISG generally authorizes, but which a court is not obligated to order unless it would do so in a comparable case not involving CISG. As detailed below, specific performance is rarely ordered by U.S. courts.

Buyer's right to repair or replacement depends on buyer's making a demand for it either with the notice of nonconformity, or within a reasonable time thereafter. If the first repair is unsuccessful, buyer should give a new notice and request for repair. *Grinding machines*, F App 19980129.

Buyer's right to replacement goods is further qualified by the obligation to return the nonconforming goods originally provided, with the same exceptions set forth in the discussion below of returning goods on avoidance.

§ 10.08 Buyer's Right to Cure

There is none. No provision gives buyer a right to cure. Presumably, if buyer makes an incorrect payment in advance, buyer will have the right to cure as the time set for performance has yet to arrive. CISG is silent on the question. Presumably, buyer only has a right to cure after the date fixed for performance if seller grants it, as set forth in the following section. In a system that tries to treat buyer and seller in parallel, this is a major departure.

B. Granting Additional Time

§ 10.11 Granting Time (*Nachfrist*)

None of the previous remedies should be endorsed by buyer without the formal grant of time. Art. 47(1) says "buyer may fix an additional period of time of reasonable length for performance by the seller of his obligations." (Art. 63 is comparable for seller.) This clause is thought by some commentators to apply only to non-delivery, but both by its wording and judicial decisions, it applies to all performance defects, such as failure of a delivered gluing press to operate properly. *Gluing press*, A App 20121122.

The practical reason for buyer to grant extra time is that failure of seller to deliver the goods within the period permits buyer to avoid the contract without needing to prove that the breach is fundamental. Art. 49(2). A good example of this occurred in *Laser cutter*, D App 20160215. Seller tried to avoid the contract, but the court found that buyer's failure to pay on time was not a fundamental breach where buyer asked for payment instructions. Not having granted reasonable additional time, seller could not rely on the other grounds for avoiding the contract—failure to comply within reasonable time granted—so seller's failure to deliver was a fundamental breach.

It is not so clear that failure by seller to correct nonconformities in some of the delivered goods permits buyer to avoid the contract without proving a fundamental breach. In *Computer parts*, D Trial 19920703, seller delivered five of eleven parts. Buyer gave seller a reasonable time to deliver the other six, which seller did not do. Buyer bought the other six elsewhere at a higher price. The court held that buyer could not avoid the contract because there was no fundamental breach of the entire contract.

The setting of a date for performance provides at least a presumption, if seller does not object, that the date is within a reasonable time. It also provides an opportunity to put in writing the fact that by setting an additional time for performance, buyer is not amending the original contract, as occurred in *Valero Marketing*, US App. Another advantage is that if the contract ever comes to litigation, it makes your client look like a reasonable person who is trying to keep the contract alive as long as possible.

Tribunals have been liberal in finding the grant of additional time. A Russian buyer complained that the goods delivered were short in quantity and the goods were unusable. Buyer suggested that seller either refund buyer's prepayment or that seller deliver conforming goods that correspond to the value of buyer' prepayment within a time fixed by buyer. The tribunal held this to be the grant of additional time even though phrased as an alternative. *Egyptian goods*, R Arb 20040528.

A wise party granting extra time will be as precise as possible about what needs to be done and when it must be done. A Sup. Ct. 20190705.

While cases state that buyer cannot declare the contract avoided without first giving seller extra time to perform, *Autumn textiles*, D Trial 19900424, *Shoes*, D App 20020701, that is correct if the nonconformity has not been a fundamental breach, but incorrect as a broad statement that buyer must always give seller extra time to perform. The provision says "buyer may," which is definitely permissive. *Gluing press*, A App 20121122.

That leaves the question of how a reasonable time is to be calculated. In *Printing presses*, D App 19950524, the court speculated that 11 days might be too short a time to find a ship from Germany to Egypt because of the necessity of locating a ship leaving within that time that had available space. A French case suggested that a reasonable time might depend "on the complexity of the problems encountered and the stakes." *Grinding machines*, F App 19980129. However, in that case, seller could not complain that the time was unreasonable because it was too long, especially as seller had requested the time. It also appeared that buyer and seller were both hoping to work out a fix. In neither case did it appear that buyer had any time constraints. *Apple juice concentrate*, D App 20010312, states in dictum that 28 days is a reasonable time, but does not explain why. An Italian seller only granted 15 days to perform, but the grant came 73 days after the date set for buyer's payment, and was repeated, so the court counted the reasonable time from the date set in the contract for performance to the date seller declared the contract avoided. *Printing press*, I App 19981211.

Imagine a case where buyer has ordered goods that are unlikely to sell outside the Christmas season that, given the delay in delivery that has already occurred, seller would have difficulty delivering by the Christmas season. Only a short time would be reasonable for buyer, but any time that would be reasonable for buyer would be unreasonable for seller.

In *Printing presses*, the court did not find the shortness of the period prohibitive because buyer did not in fact take action to avoid the contract until seven weeks had passed. Similarly, buyer of a car provided a delay of only eight days to deliver from Germany to Denmark and the court did not decide whether that was a reasonable period because buyer waited 25 days before avoiding the contract. *Automobile*, D App 19990427. The court in both cases must have thought that the failure to grant a reasonable time was cured by the fact that avoidance was not declared until a reasonable time from the original default had expired.

While they did not express this, they must have looked to the purpose, to provide a reasonable time for performance before the contract was avoided.

C. Price Reduction

§10.21 Price Reduction

One remedy buyer may elect is price reduction, a remedy unknown at common law. Price reduction is a remedy applied by buyer on a formulaic basis. Buyer may reduce the price to an amount that bears the same proportion to the contract price as the value of the goods delivered bears to the value that conforming goods would have had. Art. 50. (Note that the English version has this backward, but the French and Spanish versions state it correctly.) The result of that formula may be more, less, or the same as the actual damages buyer has suffered, depending largely on the two values. Damages should produce more in a rising market. In a falling market, price reduction advantages buyer.

There is no way other than the above formula to compute the price reduction. Where nonconforming art books were delivered, buyer could not use the cost of repair or an estimate of the value of the goods actually delivered by itself. *Art books*, CH Trial 19990210.

This remedy has the advantage that buyer need not mitigate damages. Price reduction may be available where avoidance is not, either because a timely notice of avoidance was not given, or because the breach was not fundamental. *Coffee makers*, A Sup. Ct. 20050523.

If buyer has not paid the purchase price, buyer can simply reduce his payment, placing the burden on seller to sue him. If buyer has paid, buyer will likely need to sue to recoup the price.

It might be argued that buyer can have both price reduction and damages based on art. 45(2), which says that buyer is not deprived of damages if buyer pursues other remedies. It is better to regard that statement as confirming the many other places stating that buyer reserves the right to damages if he avoids the contract, seeks specific performance, or offers any cure discussed in this chapter. Arts. 37, 47(2), 48(1), 81(1), or 83. There is no such statement attached to price reduction reserving the right to damages in addition. Price reduction seems to be a substitute for damages, even though it may produce different results.

However, it appears to be a substitute for only one kind of damages—damages suffered by buyer due to the value difference between what was ordered and what was delivered.

There are several other situations where price reduction and damages are compatible.

Where nonconforming goods are delivered late, it seems appropriate to permit price reduction for the nonconformity while also allowing damages for the loss incurred as a result of the tardy delivery.

Where buyer suffers consequential damages from the nonconformity, such as where buyer's or a sub-buyer's production line must be shut down because of the nonconformity, or where people are injured due to buyer's incorporation of the nonconforming goods into a defective product, buyer should be able to reduce the price and collect the consequential damages.

The assumption of price reduction is that something has been delivered. However, the value of that something might be nonexistent. While it is often difficult to believe that something has no value, even as scrap, it was held that the coffee makers had no value, so the price could be reduced to zero. *Coffee makers*, A Sup. Ct. 20050523. It is questionable whether broken or contaminated wine bottles had no value, even as recyclable scrap, but a court so held. *Wine bottles*, D App 20061214. The implication of these cases is that the remedy of price reduction to zero is also available if seller fails to deliver anything.

The difficulty with price reduction is determining the values. The value of conforming goods on the date (and presumably at the place) of delivery will be easy for fungible commodities, but may be more difficult for other goods that are less frequently sold. This information may be in the hands of seller, who may have sold identical goods at the same time. Even more difficult is determining the value of the nonconforming goods that were delivered. If buyer has re-sold the goods, information about the re-sale will be in the hands of buyer. In order to decide whether a price reduction was in the appropriate amount, both buyer and seller may be required to disclose details about other transactions under U.S. discovery law. *Interag*, US Trial.

The starting place for the value of conforming goods is likely to be the contract price. The party suggesting that the value of conforming goods at the time of delivery is something other than the contract price probably bears the burden of proof. For fungible, frequently traded goods, proving a change in price may be easy. For all other cases, and perhaps even for fungible, frequently traded goods, the wise buyer will hire an expert at the time of the breach to opine in writing both on the value of conforming goods and on the value of the goods actually delivered.

Price reduction has an advantage over some other remedies because it lacks a requirement of notice except in one situation. If buyer fails to give prompt and precise notice of defects, all remedies are barred, including price reduction, unless notice is dispensed with. Arts. 39, 40, 44. Some remedies require other preconditions. Avoidance requires that a declaration of avoidance be made within a reasonable time. Art. 49(2). It also requires that buyer be able to restore the goods to seller, with certain exceptions. Art. 82. A buyer who cannot avoid the contract for either of those reasons may still reduce the price. *Wine bottles*, D App 20061214. Sometimes a buyer who can avoid the contract may prefer to reduce the price because she can keep the goods or because there is no mitigation requirement.

Price reduction also has an advantage over damages. If a seller is excused from paying damages because of an impediment under art. 79, buyer can still reduce the price because art. 79 only excuses from damages (and presumably specific performance).

Buyer cannot reduce the price if seller corrects the nonconformity, or if buyer refuses seller's request to cure the nonconformity. Art. 50.

D. Seller's Option if Buyer Does Not Choose

§ 10.31 Buyer's Option Clause

Art. 65 presents what appears to be a strange possibility. It is a situation where buyer has an option "to specify the form, measurement or other features of the goods." This is strange because one's first reaction is that if the form, measurement, or other features of the goods are not fixed in the contract, there may not be a contract because of the lack of definiteness. However, the assumption is that a contract exists because the options available to buyer are limited, or because giving buyer certain options is a way of making the goods definite. The drafters might have been thinking about something like whether the door of a refrigerator opens from left to right or from right to left.

Assuming a valid contract, the question dealt with by this provision is where buyer does not make a choice. The drafters thought that this should not result in there being no contract. The provision goes on to permit seller to ask buyer to specify. If buyer does not specify within a reasonable time, seller may specify according to the needs of buyer known to seller. Seller must then notify buyer of seller's choice, which will be binding if buyer fails to contradict that specification within a reasonable time of receiving it. (Note that this adopts a different rule than art. 27, where communications are effective on dispatch; here the communication is only effective on receipt.)

One court applied this provision somewhat more broadly than its express language. The contract provided that buyer would have warehouse space at seller's factory, into which seller would deposit goods. Buyer would notify seller when taking goods from the warehouse and have the option to either pay for them or replace them at a later time. Buyer took significant amounts of goods and did not tell seller. Seller invoiced the goods taken, and gave buyer a reasonable time to notify seller whether buyer would elect to pay or replace the remaining goods. Seller indicated that if buyer made no election, seller would elect to sell the goods to buyer. Buyer made no election, so seller elected that buyer should keep the items and pay, justifying this by art. 65. The court barely invokes art. 65, but bases its decision for seller on an interpretation of the intent of the parties under arts. 8 and 18, and says that silence can be an act that can constitute consent under the circumstances of this case. *Aerosol can production line*, CH Trial 20130408.

E. Avoidance

§10.41 Avoidance: General

CISG spends more time and more sections on avoidance than on any other remedy. That is because CISG views avoidance as the remedy of last resort, preferring damages, specific performance, or price reduction because these keep the contract in effect. On the contrary, most breach victims who get to litigation want to get out of the relationship by avoidance and to secure damages for past breach. For that reason, avoidance has been surrounded by significant rules and restrictions, and many contract parties who have tried to avoid the contract have instead found themselves in breach.

§10.42 Avoidance Prerequisites

A party can avoid the contract when either of two things occurs. One is that the other party commits a fundamental breach. We have already seen how difficult it is to draw the line between a breach and a fundamental breach. That route is perilous. The more cautious route is to give the breacher a reasonable period to perform. If the breacher does not perform within that time, the victim can declare the contract avoided if there is non-delivery. Art. 49. In *Wire rod*, CH Sup. Ct. 2015, buyer could not avoid because seller had not committed a fundamental breach and, though seller was late in delivering documents, buyer had not granted seller the required extra reasonable time to perform. The granting of additional time is likely to be seen by a court that might later decide the case as reasonable behavior negating any suggestion that the party is being opportunistic. A good example of this is *Egyptian goods*, R Arb 20040528, where seller delivered goods that were both short on quantity and unusable, did not correct the nonconformities within the extra time granted, and the tribunal held the avoidance valid without discussing whether the breach was fundamental.

If the breach is fundamental, the fact that risk of loss has already passed to buyer is irrelevant. Buyer still has the right to avoid the contract. Art. 70. When buyer avoids the contract, the risk of further price changes for the goods reverts to seller, as buyer is entitled to return of her purchase price and damages.

The party injured by either a fundamental breach or by a failure to deliver within extra time granted may declare the contract avoided. When that occurs, the goods should be returned to seller and the purchase price to buyer. There are detailed provisions on effectuating that. For most purposes, the contract ends, subject to the right to seek damages, for which there are special rules.

§ 10.43 Qualification for Avoidance—Fundamental Breach

If there has been delivery, avoidance still requires a fundamental breach. While the criteria for fundamental breach have not changed, the circumstances may have changed. What was not a fundamental breach might, with the passage of time, have become a fundamental breach.

§ 10.44 Qualification for Avoidance—Delivery

One might ask what delivery actually is. If seller delivers nothing or buyer pays nothing, there is clearly no delivery. If seller delivers the correct goods in the wrong amount or correct documents that are defective, or buyer pays the wrong amount, there is likewise delivery, though a shortage on either side may or may not be a fundamental breach. *Cobalt sulfate*, D Sup. Ct. 19960403. If the delivery is a very small portion of what is due, a court might hold that there has been no delivery, or that the nominal delivery is a fundamental breach. If buyer orders 100 computers and seller delivers 100 printers to a wholesaler of computers and printers, one might argue that there has been no delivery of the goods ordered and, if seller does not rectify the misdelivery within a reasonable time, there is still no delivery, even though there has been no fundamental breach because buyer is in the business of selling what seller has delivered and there is a market into which buyer can sell the printers. Courts have stated that delivery of anything is not non-delivery, *Apple juice concentrate*, D App 20010312, but in the context of delivery of apple juice concentrate with added sugar when the contract called for it without added sugar. Whether the courts would adhere to that opinion if the delivery were a very different product, or a token amount, remains to be seen.

However, where an installment contract is involved, whether anything has been delivered is considered separately for each installment. A perfect delivery for the first installment does not prevent non-delivery on the second installment. *Printing presses*, D App 19950524.

§ 10.45 Qualification for Avoidance—Declaration

Arts. 49 and 64 simply state the conditions on which buyer or seller may declare the contract avoided. The declaration is to be made to the other contracting party. Art. 26. There is no specification of how that declaration is to be made. Since CISG generally does away with many of the contract formalities of national law, the declaration can be made in any fashion, but must be definitive. It is effective when dispatched. Art. 27. Likewise, the declaration need not mention avoidance. A buyer who says that he will refuse delivery and wants his money back has declared avoidance. *Printing presses*, D App 19950524. A seller who gives extra time for performance but warns that failure to perform is one possible consequence, then makes a statement of claim that includes the consequence of avoidance, has made a proper declaration of avoidance, *Jewelry*, A Sup. Ct. 20000428. Simply stating that avoidance is an option if the other party fails to perform should not be a notice of avoidance. *Coke*, D App 19940302. Courts have also dispensed with notification when the other party has declared that he will not perform on grounds that this would be a mere formality. *Furniture leather*, D App 20040915. But it is not a mere formality. It is an election of remedies between avoidance, specific performance, damages, and in the case of a defaulting seller, price reduction. Knowing which remedy the aggrieved party is pursuing is important to the breacher.

Once again, for purposes of proving the date, the content, and the fact that it was done, written communication is preferable.

The declaration must be timely or the victim loses the right to avoid. While the breacher was at fault, CISG does not wish to give either party the ability to speculate on changes in the market at the expense of the other. A breaching seller is most likely to be able to minimize damages from retaking the property if it is done as close to the sale as possible.

For seller's breach, CISG envisions two situations, completely neglecting the third.

First is where there is delivery and a fundamental breach. Notice must be given within a reasonable time after the party ought to have known of the breach, or after the expiration of additional time given or promised, or after declaration by the other party that he will not perform. It is unclear whether it is the first or the last of these alternatives to occur. *Floating center*, CH Trial 19950426, says that a reasonable time begins at the time of delivery, but that will seldom be true, and probably should not have been in that case. The fact that the center was leaking and might cause damage to the structure does not tell buyer that it cannot be easily repaired. The party must have a reasonable time after the party ought to have known that the breach was fundamental, because it may take some time to appreciate the true consequences of the breach. *Packaging plant*, CH Sup. Ct. 20090518. In *Boots*, D App 20071121, buyer of defective boots received the first complaint from retail customers in July. More complaints were received in September and October, so by the end of October, complaints had been received about 15% of the boots sold. The declaration of avoidance sent six weeks later was held timely.

Second, where there is late delivery, within a reasonable time of becoming aware that delivery has been made.

CISG provides no time for notice of avoidance if the reason for the avoidance is non-delivery. Nonetheless, the party wishing to avoid should give the other party notice soon after the extra time for performance has expired because giving notice within a reasonable time may be a general principle of CISG.

One court said that as a general rule, a period of one to two months would be reasonable absent special circumstances. *Packaging plant*, CH Sup. Ct. 20090518. Another said that two and a half months was too long in the case of a car where the defect was noticed immediately. *Repainted car*, D App 20080331. It thought that a reasonable time depended on all the circumstances, such as whether the defect was easy to evaluate, whether the parties were engaged in settlement negotiations that might lead to resolution, or whether the decision-makers were away at the time the defect was discovered. Another court added that when there were ongoing attempts that might reasonably rectify the nonconformities, the time for a declaration of avoidance does not begin to run until it is obvious that those attempts will not succeed. *Orica Australia*, US Trial. One court allowed three and one-half months without discussion, saying only that seller could not be expected to decide "during the last remaining days of the year." *Venison*, D App 19991028.

If it is buyer who is in breach and buyer has paid some of the purchase price and the defect is late performance, seller can only avoid the contract if seller declares avoidance before learning that buyer has performed. For other buyer breaches, seller loses the right to avoid the contract unless he declares avoidance within a reasonable time after seller should know of the breach, the expiration of the extra granted time, or buyer's declaration that he will not perform. Art. 64(2).

In situations where buyer has not paid the purchase price or seller has not delivered, CISG imposes no specific requirement that notice of avoidance be timely. Whether a court would impose one as a general principle of CISG is unknown, but it should. This defuses the case that occasionally occurs where one party believes that the other party is in default, while that other party thinks he has performed. Seller sends the goods, but they are delivered to the wrong place, as happened in *ECEM European Chemical*, US Trial. Or buyer pays electronically but it is credited to the wrong account. The requirement of notice will permit clearing up the facts and keep the contract in effect.

§10.46 Disqualification for Avoidance

Buyer may not avoid the contract if buyer cannot return the delivered goods to seller in substantially the same condition in which buyer received them. However, buyer can still avoid the contract if part of the goods have deteriorated as a result of the required examination on arrival; if they have been sold, processed, or transformed in the ordinary course of buyer's business before buyer ought to have discovered the lack of conformity; or if the inability to restore goods to seller is not due to buyer's act or omission. Art. 82.

The last condition is ripe for dispute if the goods have deteriorated. Buyer will argue that the goods deteriorated because of their nonconformity or because of the passage of time; seller will argue that buyer's improper maintenance resulted in the deterioration. *Orica Australia*, US Trial.

Exceptions to the obligation to return may result in unusual cases. Buyer and seller agreed that buyer could not determine conformity of the goods without processing them as buyer would normally have done. Early processing revealed nonconformity of some of the goods. Buyer avoided with respect to the nonconforming goods. None of the goods could be returned in substantially the same condition in which they were received, but the court held that buyer could avoid because art. 38 obligated buyer to discover which part of the goods were nonconforming. *Stainless wire*, D Sup. Ct. 19970625. The processing of the goods increased their value, even though the goods were nonconforming. In avoiding the contract, buyer must restore the goods to seller in their current condition, and can claim credit for the increased value if buyer can prove the increase. Buyer can also claim as damages the reasonable processing cost, given the circumstances.

§ 10.47 Avoidance Consequences

The result of successful avoidance is that buyer returns the goods and accounts for any benefits received, seller simultaneously returns the purchase price with interest, and the person who breached will be liable in damages. Arts. 81, 84. Neither specific performance nor price reduction are available remedies once avoidance has been elected, as either would be inconsistent with the contract's avoidance. When neither side has performed, it is easy to return to the position of the parties before the contract was breached. It is not so easy once the contract has been partially performed by seller because the goods are with buyer. When buyer has partially performed, restoration of the purchase price may not be as simple as it seems.

While the return of the goods and the purchase price should be simultaneous, CISG says nothing about where this is to occur. The place of return involves costs, such as packaging, freight, insurance, customs duties, and currency conversion charges. Controversy has developed as to whether CISG articles on passage of risk of loss and delivery establish general principles of CISG to be applied here. If that is the case, buyer's return of the goods depends on whether carriage is involved. If so, return is accomplished by buyer's delivery to the first carrier. If carriage is not involved, buyer returns by making the goods available to seller.

If the parties have used a trade term for the initial shipment of the goods, the same trade term might be applied to their return.

If there is no general principle of CISG applicable, one turns to the domestic law of the country indicated by the forum's choice of law rules. But since litigation has not been initiated, there is no forum, so one hopes that the choice of law rules of the two countries involved both point to the same country's law.

Even then there may be problems because the obligation to return is so specific to CISG that the country involved may have no rules on the question.

Several provisions further detail the obligations of both parties.

§10.48 Seller Returns Amount Buyer Paid with Interest

Seller must repay the amount buyer paid with interest from the date of receipt. Art. 84. It is clear that CISG does not set an interest amount. What is not clear is how that amount should be set. Art. 7(2) says to look to general principles of CISG, and some have suggested that a general principle of CISG regarding avoidance is that no one should profit from the transaction. This is derived from the fact that buyer gives back the goods and seller returns money received. In that view, the interest rate might be computed on the basis of what seller in fact earned on the money received. But it is likely to be impossible to trace the investment, if any, made by seller of the money received. The best approximation would be the return that someone in seller's position would have earned at seller's place of business. *Sunflower oil*, CH Trial 19970205.

Another tribunal, without any discussion, found no general principle of CISG applicable, so used the conflicts law of the forum (Russia) to determine that interest should be measured by the law of seller's principal place of business, which was Egypt. It applied the official Egyptian rate, which was 5%, instead of the 14% that buyer claimed it paid to borrow in Russia. *Egyptian goods*, R Arb 175/2003, 20040528.

A minority of courts have used the interest rate of buyer's place of business on grounds that it is a better measure of the damage buyer suffers from not having had the money. This mistakes the purpose of avoidance, which is restitutionary. For that reason, the rate of interest should be the rate at the payor's place. *CISG-AC 9*.

It should be clear that this is a notional interest. No attempt will be made to trace the income that seller actually derived from having buyer's money for this period of time. Seller is not relieved of the obligation to pay even if seller proves that he earned nothing that can be specifically tied to buyer's money.

§10.49 Buyer Accounts for Actual Benefits

If buyer has received any benefits from having the goods, buyer must transfer the benefits to seller. This would be the case if buyer could use some of the goods in manufacturing products. Those benefits should be a portion of buyer's net profits after expenses. However, the amount derived by buyer from selling the goods delivered to a third party do not count as benefits if buyer is obligated to refund the third party's purchase price. *CISG-AC 9.*

The most likely situation where buyer derives net benefits is where buyer is the breaching party because of nonpayment of part of the purchase price and has resold the goods received before discovering the breach.

In a somewhat analogous case where seller thought buyer would refuse the goods sold on a cif contract so did not ship them, the portion of the sales price that would have gone for insurance and freight was not recoverable on grounds that this was seller's benefit. *Pakistani goods*, R Arb 340/1999, 20000210. This result is difficult to sustain because seller is retaining the cost of freight and insurance that he has neither earned nor expended.

§ 10.50 Buyer Returns the Goods/ Seller Retains the Goods

CISG is concerned that the value of the goods be maintained to the extent possible in order to preserve the value of the contract and to reduce the damages from breach. Depending on the circumstances, this may impose obligations on buyer, seller, or both.

Transfer of goods may invoke a delicate minuet designed to assure that the value of the goods will be preserved. On avoidance, the parties should concurrently restore what they must, but that frequently does not occur because one party or the other is unwilling to restore when the other party wants to restore, or is unwilling to restore at all.

The party in possession of the goods must take reasonable steps to preserve them. Suppose goods have been delivered to buyer. Buyer's employees examine the goods on the loading dock and determine that they are nonconforming and a fundamental breach. Buyer cannot simply leave the goods on the loading dock or outdoors in an unfenced area unless the goods are both impervious to weather and impossible to steal. It would be reasonable under the circumstances to bring the goods into buyer's premises. But that would use buyer's resources for an unpredictable period. Buyer could place the goods in storage and add the reasonable cost of transporting them to storage and the reasonable storage charges to seller's bill. Art. 87.

This provision confronts buyer with a dilemma. Keeping the goods herself imposes costs on buyer, but those costs are not easily measured. What is the fair rental value of buyer's space, security, and climate control that those goods are occupying? This is probably not easy to compute. Placing the goods in storage with an unrelated third party provides an easily ascertainable figure. It also increases buyer's risk, in case seller's financial position is so precarious that he cannot pay any damages that might be due, leaving buyer as a practical matter with an even greater loss.

The same rule applies if seller is in possession of the goods. Assume that the goods are sold Ex-works, meaning buyer will pick them up at seller's plant. Buyer determines at the plant that the goods are nonconforming and a fundamental breach. Seller believes that the breach is trivial, not fundamental. Buyer leaves without the goods. Seller must store them himself or put them in commercial storage.

The possessor, either buyer or seller, with a preservation obligation must sell goods subject to rapid deterioration. Meat is clearly subject to rapid deterioration if left at room temperature, but a court held that freezing would prevent deterioration, so a seller who froze the meat was not obligated to make a quick sale. *Venison*, D App 19991028.

Perhaps the strangest situation involved the sale of a CNC production plant that was inoperable because it had rusted. The court endorsed buyer's avoidance, but refused buyer permission to destroy it and required buyer to return the plant and seller to accept it. There are no figures indicating that the value of the plant exceeded the cost of returning it, nor did seller appear to request return. *CNC production plant*, CH App 20050221.

§10.51 Possessor Sells the Goods

A party in possession of goods destined for the other contracting party is not a permanent custodian. The party holding the goods may do so until the other party takes possession or pays the price or the cost of preservation, as the case may be. If the appropriate action by the other party is not forthcoming within a reasonable time, the party preserving the goods may sell them in a reasonable manner "provided that reasonable notice of the intention to sell has been given to the other party." Art. 88(1). The hitch here is that there are two reasonable times to consider: the reasonable time after which the possessor may sell the goods, and the reasonable time before sale that the possessor must give notice. The prudent possessor will give actual notice to the other party of the time after which she intends to sell the goods. Failure to object that the time is not reasonable is likely to be persuasive in a later dispute. It would then be wise to allow additional time to transpire after the expiration set in the notice, but not so much as to be construed as a waiver. While not a CISG case, the arbitrators cite the CISG provisions as "recognized international law of commercial contracts" in *Watkins-Johnson*, Iran/US Claims Tribunal 19890728. In *Garments*, A App 20020916, seller notified buyer by fax and phone to take delivery within 14 days, which buyer did not. The court held that seller's re-sale of the goods was appropriate.

The possessor must immediately sell the goods if they are perishable or if their preservation involves unreasonable expense. Where a significant portion of the goods spoiled in seller's warehouse, seller violated this obligation and could not collect the sale price for them. *Pakistani goods*, R Arb 340/1999, 20000210. The preserver must give notice to the other party of his intent to sell "to the extent possible." Art. 88(2).

If a sale occurs, the possessor may retain from the sale proceeds an amount equal to the reasonable expense of preserving and selling the goods. Art. 88(3). Anything in excess of those reasonable expenses must be returned to the other party. Think of this as a kind of security interest, but a limited one. The possessor has security for his preservation and sales expenses, but cannot keep the excess funds received as security for any damages that might be awarded in the future. As a practical matter, however, the aggrieved party who sells the goods will be suing for damages or return of the purchase price, an amount likely to be greater than the amount retained. This will all be netted out at the end of the litigation unless superseded by the applicable insolvency law.

CHECKPOINTS

You should have learned that:

- If seller performs early and buyer notifies seller that the goods or documents are non-conforming, seller may cure the nonconformity up to the time of performance if the cure does not cause buyer unreasonable inconvenience or unreasonable expense.

- After the time set for performance, seller may still cure subject to the above and also on condition that buyer has not avoided the contract and that buyer is certain of reimbursement for cure expenses that buyer advances.

- A credible offer to cure makes a fundamental breach non-fundamental.
- Buyer loses the remedy of price reduction if buyer refuses a cure.
- Where seller offers to cure, if buyer fails to respond within a reasonable time, seller may perform within the time he has specified.
- Buyers can call on sellers to repair the goods to make them conform, as long as this is not unreasonable.
- Repair would be unreasonable if it were more costly than replacement.
- Buyer can only demand replacement goods if the breach is fundamental.
- A U.S. court is unlikely to order repair or replacement because it is a form of specific performance.
- CISG has no provision giving buyer the right to cure defective performance, but one might be implied because most remedies accorded to either buyer or seller are reciprocal.
- Either party may fix a reasonable additional period for the other party to perform their contractual obligations. This is called *nachfrist*. Granting additional time is strongly advised as a practical matter because it demonstrates reasonableness.
- Setting a date for performance to which the other party does not timely object raises a presumption that the period is reasonable.
- It is unclear whether a reasonable time is computed from what is reasonable for buyer, what is reasonable for seller, or what is reasonable for both.
- In determining whether the time given was reasonable, courts have included the time after the expiration of the time stated but before the contract is declared avoided in determining whether the time was reasonable.
- Where seller breaches, buyer may reduce the price to an amount that bears the same proportion to the contract price as the value of the goods delivered bears to the value that conforming goods would have had.
- Price reduction is a substitute for damages suffered when the value of goods delivered (or not delivered) is less than the value of the goods ordered. Damages may not be collected for that loss, but price reduction can be combined with damages for other losses.

- Price reduction may be hard to use in cases where it is difficult to value the goods. A cover transaction is likely to be more persuasive than opinion evidence of value.

- Where the contract gives buyer the right to make choices about the goods but buyer refuses to choose, seller may make the choice subject to buyer's objection.

- A party can avoid the contract if the other party commits a fundamental breach, or if the other party does not deliver, the injured party grants additional time (*nachfrist*), and the other party does not deliver within the reasonable additional time.

- To avoid the contract, one party must send timely notice of avoidance to the other. Courts have construed notices liberally to find that they are notices of avoidance.

- When a contract is avoided, buyer returns the goods, seller returns the purchase price, and neither price reduction nor specific performance is a permissible remedy.

- Delivering nothing is non-delivery. Delivering the wrong quantity of the goods ordered, or delivering the right quantity of nonconforming goods, or paying only part of the purchase price, is not non-delivery. Whether delivery of entirely different goods than those ordered is non-delivery remains to be seen.

- With an installment contract, whether there has been delivery is determined installment by installment.

- Buyer may not avoid the contract if buyer cannot return the delivered goods to seller in substantially the same condition in which buyer received them. However, buyer can still avoid the contract if part of the goods have deteriorated as a result of the required examination on arrival; if they have been sold, processed, or transformed in the ordinary course of buyer's business before buyer ought to have discovered the lack of conformity; or if the inability to restore goods to seller is not due to buyer's act or omission.

- Seller's return of the purchase price must be accompanied by interest. Courts have used a number of different measures to determine the rate of interest and whether it is simple or compound.

- Buyer must account to seller for any value received as a result of having possession of the goods.

- Buyer in possession of the goods must preserve them and arrange to convey them to seller. The cost of doing so is likely to be part of the damages suffered.

- Goods may be sold if they are likely to spoil before the other party can obtain and dispose of them. All goods may be sold if the other party does not take possession within a reasonable time.

- A party who properly elects avoidance after a breach may also collect damages suffered.

CHAPTER 11

Judicial Remedies

ROADMAP

After reading this chapter, you should understand:

- No tribunal may grant either buyer or seller extra time to perform the contract. The parties may agree to extra time, and are encouraged to use the *nachfrist* procedure.

- Specific performance of the contract is an available remedy. There are few decided cases about it, as aggrieved parties usually prefer avoidance and damages.

- Both avoidance and price reduction are inconsistent with specific performance, so an aggrieved party who elects either remedy may not seek specific performance.

- Requesting a cure and granting extra time are both consistent with specific performance.

- A court need not order specific performance where it would not order it in a similar case under domestic law.

- Under U.S. law, specific performance is usually available only when the remedy at law is inadequate, usually because the goods are unique or it would be difficult for the aggrieved person to secure a substitute transaction.

- However, a U.S. court is likely to enforce an arbitral decision calling for specific performance.

- Damages may be awarded for all losses suffered as a result of contract breach, including lost profits.

- Damages are limited to those that the breacher ought to have foreseen as possible when making the contract. They do not include damages that the victim could have avoided by mitigation. Damages only include losses that are reasonably certain.

- Damages are intended to put the parties in the economic position they would have occupied had the contract been performed. In easy cases, that might only be the cost to repair the goods to be equal to what was promised, or the difference in value between what was promised and what was delivered.

- Damages may include seller's cost of reselling goods buyer has refused; buyer's liability to sub-buyers for malfunction of goods buyer has resold; or loss of buyer's resale profits.

- There are two special provisions for damages when the contract is avoided. When the aggrieved party reasonably covers, the aggrieved party may claim damages as the difference between the contract price and the cover price. When there is no cover, it is the difference between the contract price and the fair market value. The aggrieved party is not limited to these measures of damages.

- Even where there is no avoidance, parties have successfully used those damages measures.

- To be liable for damages, the breaching party must have been able to foresee the type of damages that would result from the breach by the time the contract was concluded. It is less clear that he must foresee the amount of those damages.

- Some cases have questioned whether resale of the goods by buyer is foreseeable.

- The aggrieved party is charged with mitigation, reducing the amount of damage caused by the breach as much as is commercially reasonable. In a declining market, an aggrieved buyer is charged as though he had found substitute goods within a reasonable time at the then-prevailing market price.

- The aggrieved party must even be willing to mitigate with the breacher, or with the aggrieved party's competitor.

- Damages for buyer's breach should be paid in the currency called for in the contract. Damages for seller's breach should normally be paid in buyer's currency. Some courts order damages paid in the currency of the court.

- Damages include general dispute resolution costs. They do not include attorney's fees. Whether attorney's fees of the prevailing party in the breach of contract action can be recovered depends on the domestic law of the forum. Attorney's fees incurred to defend suits resulting from the breach are included in damages.

- Damages include compensation for lost volume of sales.

- The parties may limit or modify their liability for damages, or provide for liquidated damages, to the extent that such a provision would be valid under domestic law.

- Interest is due on any sum in arrears. Alternatively, interest can be recovered as damages when it can be proven.

- Most courts hold that interest on damages begins to accrue at the time of breach, even though the amount of the liability is unknown at the time.

- Courts are in disagreement about whether interest is simple or compound and the rate of interest.

- Interest is paid in the currency in which the sum on which interest is calculated is paid.

A. No Extra Time

§11.01 No Court-Ordered Extra Time

CISG specifically prohibits tribunals from granting either buyer or seller extra time to perform the contract, arts. 45(3), 61(3), so the granting of extra time is not a judicial remedy that either can seek as a matter of right in the absence of an amendment to the contract. In some countries, mandatory domestic law requires that courts grant extra time. In the U.S., a bankruptcy filing automatically stays all action under contracts. 11 U.S.C. §362. Under CISG, either party may accord the other party extra time under arts. 47(1) and 63(1), but no court can order it. In *Helen Kaminsky*, US Trial, it appeared that the bankruptcy stay and the prohibition on a tribunal granting extra time came into conflict, but the judge avoided that conflict by holding that the sale involved was under a distributorship agreement to which CISG does not apply. As an interpretive matter, that is clearly wrong, because there was a purchase of a specific quantity of particular goods, so CISG should apply. On the substantive question, there does not appear to be a conflict with the bankruptcy stay. It is a stay preventing further legal action. It does not affect the rights of the parties except that it forces them into the bankruptcy proceeding and limits the timing of remedies. The breach for late payment is not transformed into a nonbreach, so the automatic bankruptcy stay is not the granting of extra time to perform.

B. Specific Performance

§11.11 Specific Performance in General

CISG lists specific performance as a remedy for both buyer and seller, unless the party has already elected a remedy that is inconsistent with specific performance. Arts. 46(1), 62. However, a court is not bound to order specific performance if it would not do so in a comparable domestic case.

It is doubtful that specific performance is a universal remedy for buyers. Buyer's request for substitute goods is limited to fundamental breaches. Art. 46(2). For anything less than a fundamental breach, buyer is limited to repair, and repaired goods are not considered as valuable as new goods.

While the words specific performance may be the same, the mechanics of the remedy may differ significantly from country to country. For instance, a U.S. court order of specific performance is enforced by the court's contempt power. A person ordered to specifically perform who refuses may find himself the guest of the U.S. or a state government in one of its carceral facilities until he performs. That is not the case in France, where the courts lack similar contempt powers. What assures specific performance in France is the institution of *astreint*. The judge can order a payment by a person for every day that the specific performance order is not complied with. These payments usually amount to considerably more than damages would be if specific performance does not occur within a reasonable time.

One great advantage of specific performance over damages is that specific performance imposes no obligation on the injured party to mitigate his loss, as he must do with damages. A second advantage is that while damages are limited by foreseeability, causation, and certainty, specific performance is not. With specific performance, the promisee receives what she is promised.

In the real world, there are few cases where the injured party requests specific performance. Except where buyer cannot secure the goods elsewhere, by the time the case gets to litigation, the aggrieved party usually wants nothing further to do with the breacher except to avoid obligations under the contract and to collect any damages owed.

§11.12 Remedies Inconsistent with Specific Performance

Timing is important here. If the injured party has already resorted to an inconsistent remedy at the time he files suit, he may not have specific performance. The same is probably true if he institutes a competing remedy before the trial concludes and specific performance is granted.

It appears that many other remedies are inconsistent with specific performance. Avoidance is inconsistent. Its basic premise is that the contractual obligations mostly no longer exist; they are replaced by damages. Specific performance assumes the contract's continuance. Price reduction assumes that the contract has been performed, though in a nonconforming way, and the price reduction is buyer's remedy for the breach. The same is true of damages if some damages are claimed before the suit for specific performance is filed. However, a party should be able to claim specific performance, with an alternative claim for damages if specific performance is not granted. It is not inconsistent to claim both specific performance to receive the goods ordered, and damages to compensate for losses resulting from the fact that the performance was late.

Some remedies are consistent with specific performance. Requesting a cure, either by way of repair or replacement goods, is consistent. So is granting extra time, as long as that grant does not indicate that failure to perform within the time granted will result in an inconsistent remedy. Suspending performance or an anticipatory breach would not be inconsistent as long as it has not led to a declaration of avoidance. Excuse from performance because of an impediment is not inconsistent because the assumption is that when the impediment is removed, the contract will be performed, and because excuse from performance is not something that the other party has elected.

One might ask whether installment contracts present special problems of inconsistency. Breach of contract for one installment gives remedies for that breach, but a fundamental breach on one installment may (or may not) be a fundamental breach of the entire contract. Whether an inconsistent remedy has been elected for a breach of an early installment that bars specific performance on a later installment probably depends on whether the victim of the breach has decided to treat the earlier breach as a breach of an installment or a fundamental breach of the entire contract. In the latter case, even if the court holds that it is not a fundamental breach of the whole contract, an inconsistent remedy has been elected and the injured party is barred from specific enforcement. If the party has sought damages or avoidance or reduced the price only for the early breached installment, seeking specific performance for breach of a later installment would not seem inconsistent.

§11.13 Specific Performance in U.S. Courts

Art. 28 provides that a court need not order specific performance where it would not order it in a similar case under domestic law. This provision as written leaves the decision to the court's appreciation. The court may grant specific performance if it would not order specific performance in a similar case, but it need not, and probably will not.

In the U.S., a prerequisite for specific performance by seller is a finding that the remedy at law (damages) is inadequate. That is usually the case where the goods are unique, or where it is difficult to find substitute goods. UCC §§2-709 and 2-716 generally conform to these principles. Seller may recover the purchase price if buyer accepts the goods or the goods are lost when at buyer's risk, or when seller is unable to resell goods identified to the contract, though that is usually thought of as a damages remedy rather than specific performance. Buyer may have specific performance if the goods are unique "or in other proper circumstances." Unique goods include artwork, antiques, some wines, and some jewelry. Other proper circumstances include supply or requirements contracts, as well as situations where cover is difficult.

It is entirely possible that cover will be more difficult in international contracts for seller than in domestic contracts. The goods are in buyer's country where seller may have no marketing ability. If the costs of exporting the goods to a place where seller can market them are prohibitive, this may be a place for specific performance even though there would be no such order in a domestic case. United States courts retain discretion to either order it or not. In *Magellan Int'l*, US Trial, the court kept its option to order specific performance when plaintiff alleged that cover was difficult.

A similar case might be the sale of the same goods between two domestic parties, or it might be an international sale where one of the parties is located in a state that has not ratified CISG.

This provision might motivate a claimant who wants specific performance against a U.S. firm to obtain it by suing in a foreign state (if there is jurisdiction over defendant there) that routinely grants it. To make it truly effective, plaintiff would then need to have the judgment recognized and enforced in the U.S. That route might not work, as enforcing a specific performance judgment might be seen as the equivalent of entering the judgment, which a U.S. court is not obligated to do.

§ 11.14 Specific Performance in Arbitration

Art. 28 applies only to courts specifically. Arbitral tribunals are not courts. They are creatures of the contract. The remedies available in arbitration depend on the contract. The contract usually incorporates rules of an arbitral tribunal. It may also set forth special rules agreed to by the parties. In the absence of a prohibition, an arbitral tribunal is likely to believe that it can order any appropriate remedy. Even if there is a choice of U.S. law, an arbitral tribunal is probably bound to order specific performance in most fundamental breach cases because art. 28 only releases courts from that obligation.

Whether a U.S. court will enforce such an arbitral order is another question. While it can be argued that a U.S. court should not enforce an arbitral order in a case where it would not grant specific performance, the better rule would ask what art. 28 asks: would the court enforce an arbitration award of specific performance in a domestic sales case, or in an international sales case not governed by CISG? It is difficult to see a court's justification for refusing to do so, as the grounds for refusing to enforce an arbitration award are quite limited, mostly to corruption or other misconduct by the arbitrators. *Federal Arbitration Act*, 68 P.L. 401, 43 Stat. 883, §§ 10–11.

C. Damages

§ 11.21 Damages in General

The general principle is that damages may be awarded for all losses suffered as a result of contract breach, including lost profits. These are expectancy damages designed to put the victim of a contract breach in the position she would have occupied had the contract been performed. This is referred to as "full compensation."

It thereby excludes punitive damages, since that would be more than full compensation. However, one court was willing to cumulate damages for breach of contract under CISG with damages for the tort of abuse of process arising from the same facts plus the litigation about them. One might view this as a species of punitive damages, though it is more accurately characterized as compensatory contract damages for breach of contract plus tort damages for abusive litigation. *Jeans*, F App 19950222. As we will see, one is seldom compensated for all losses resulting from a breach, but CISG tries to come close.

Since these are damages "for breach of contract" without requiring fault on the part of the breacher, it is intended to provide for damages regardless of whether the breach occurred through some fault of the breacher or otherwise. Some countries require fault for contract damages; CISG does not. Art. 74.

There are three exceptions to full compensation: foreseeability, avoidability, and certainty. Damages are limited to those that the breacher ought to have foreseen as possible when making the contract. They do not include damages that the victim could have avoided by mitigation. Damages only include losses that are reasonably certain.

There are some special rules for computing damages when one party avoids the contract.

The general rule is that the parties can modify CISG at will. Parties frequently specify remedies for breach, sometimes limiting remedies, sometimes imposing special conditions or time limits on them. It is not clear how far the parties' ability to write their own rules reaches before the matter becomes a question of the validity of the provision, subject to domestic law.

One way to think about damages is to divide them into three categories: incidental costs, consequential damages, and lost profits.

Another conceptual framework is to think of restitutionary damages, reliance damages, and expectancy damages.

A third conceptual framework would divide damages between spending wasted because of the breach, additional spending caused by the breach such as cover, damage for ancillary breaches such as confidentiality, territorial limits, human rights or environmental requirements, change in currency valuation, reputation damage, loss of profit, loss of opportunity, or future loss.

CISG uses no framework. Damages are damages are damages. Classification matters not. The questions instead are: was there a loss? Was it caused by the breach? Was the loss foreseeable? Does the loss meet the certainty test? Was the loss avoidable? Is the claimed loss duplicative of another loss for which the innocent party is to be compensated?

§ 11.22 Damages: Benefit of the Bargain

Damages include lost profits. Art. 74. That means that damages are intended to put the parties in the economic position they would have occupied had the contract been performed.

How this should be done forms the basis of numerous litigated cases.

Take a case where the contract calls for an easily valued product and seller delivers another easily valued product instead. Seller is to deliver a $50,000

Mercedes and actually delivers a $30,000 Volkswagen. The measure of damages is the difference between the value of what should have been delivered and what was actually delivered, or $20,000 in this case. That measure of damages is valid even if the contract price was only $30,000. Buyer is entitled to the benefit of her bargain, which would have yielded a $20,000 profit.

In another case, seller delivers machinery that, because of inadequate packaging, suffers damage in transit. In one day, buyer fixes the defect in the machinery caused by the poor packaging for $5,000 in parts and labor, and the value of the repaired machine is equal to the value of the machine if it were new. Assuming that buyer suffered no damages by the day's delay in use, buyer's damages are $5,000. *Waterworks cooler*, A Sup. Ct. 20020114.

If buyer pays the purchase price late, seller's damages probably equal the cost of funds for the intervening period.

Not all cases are as easily resolved. In the first case, the product delivered, or the product specified in the contract, or both, may not be easily valued. In a fourth case, nothing may be delivered. In the repair case, it may not be possible to bring the damaged machinery up to the value of a new machine. More legal tools are needed, especially when it comes to computing lost profits. One court took seller's average profit margin of 10% and applied it to the contract price to determine seller's lost profit. *Venison*, D App 19991028.

§11.23 Incidental and Consequential Damages

Incidental loss and consequential damages are both recoverable because CISG does not single out either for exclusion.

Incidental losses are costs that would not have been incurred but for the breach, such as the additional costs of reselling the goods, *Venison*, D App 19991028, seller's storage charges if buyer refuses to accept the goods, or buyer's duplicate customs charges if seller's initial nonconforming order is followed by a second shipment from a different seller to provide the goods required and mitigate damages. *Delchi Carrier*, US App. Incidental losses do not necessarily represent cash out of pocket. Where a seller of venison would normally pay a commission to an independent broker who arranged the resale after buyer's breach, seller who handled the resale himself was entitled to claim the commission even though never actually paid. *Venison*, D App 19991028,

Consequential damages include downstream losses imposed on buyer. For instance, if a defective air conditioner that was installed in buyer's automobile exploded, killing the driver and buyer was held liable for the lost life, that would be consequential damages.

The timing of the damages is not dispositive. Where seller breached a contract to sell a printing press, buyer had purchased a supplemental press shortly before the breach occurred. After the breach, buyer used the supplemental press to reduce the damages it would have otherwise suffered as a result of seller's failure to deliver, and sold after acquiring another. The court allowed the cost of buying the press less the receipt from selling it as damages. *Printing press*, E App 20050926.

§11.24 Damages—A Real and Illustrative Case

Rotorex (U.S.) promised to sell 10,800 compressors to Delchi (Italy) to be placed in air conditioners. Ninety-three percent of the first shipment was rejected for insufficient cooling capacity and excess energy use. Several attempts to fix the problems were unsuccessful. Delchi asked for replacement compressors, which were not provided; then Delchi avoided the contract. Delchi had already ordered additional compressors from Sanyo, the delivery of which it was able to expedite. It was unable to purchase other replacement compressors for delivery for that air conditioning season, which ended August 1. Delchi claimed as damages:

1. Shipping, customs, storage, and incidental costs for the rejected compressors, and obsolete insulation, wiring, and tools bought specifically for use with the Rotorex compressors. The trial court held that these expenses were not recoverable because they were duplicative—they were recovered as lost profits. The appeals court disagreed. It thought that those costs would not have been included in calculating profits that Delchi would have made had the compressors been conforming. That is clearly true of the costs connected to storing and returning the nonconforming compressors. The shipping to Delchi's plant for inspection, cost of inspection, tools, wiring, and insulation were costs that would have been incurred had the compressors conformed and been used. Whether replaced by similar costs of acquiring the Sanyo compressors or not, they are incidental costs. If similar costs were incurred for the Sanyos, they are duplicative; if not, they are a dead weight loss. It is unclear why Dechi was claiming them as lost profits. Similarly, in *Sweet potatoes*, CHN Arb 19960314, the tribunal refused to award buyer the cost of arranging for a letter of credit because that cost was already included in figuring buyer's lost profits, and would have been incurred had the contract been performed.

2. Cost of modifying electrical panels to use with the Sanyo compressors. The District Court held that Delchi did not prove that this was not a normal

cost of using Sanyo compressors, which it would have incurred regardless of the Rotorex breach. This was upheld.

3. Lost profits, calculated by subtracting variable costs from lost sales. Lost sales were calculated on the basis of unfilled orders. While there was testimony from agents that they would have ordered more units had they been available, the trial court found this testimony too indefinite. The unfilled orders were sufficiently definite because they represented orders actually placed for which the buyers were willing to pay. Whether the court would have accepted the testimony of the agents as sufficiently definite if backed up by surveys or actual results from previous or following years is unknown, because that evidence was not offered.

There is general agreement that one subtracts variable costs, but not fixed costs, from the lost sales. One subtracts variable costs because they are an expense that would have been incurred in earning the profit, so would have reduced the lost profits. One does not subtract fixed costs because there would have been no change in those costs had the contract been fulfilled and the extra products sold. Examples of fixed costs are depreciation, executive and legal salaries, and property and business licensing taxes to the extent that they do not depend on turnover. Normally, hourly labor costs of production line workers are variable costs, but if the employer is required to pay them regardless of whether there is work for them to do, they may become fixed costs. *Delchi Carrier*, US App.

However, if fixed costs can be assigned to the breached contract, they may qualify as damages because they are an expenditure that is wasted if the contract is breached. Factory construction is normally a fixed cost, but a factory built to fulfill this contract that is decommissioned when buyer breaches will be part of the damages. Or if the breach is serious enough, a substantial amount of administrative time and talent must be devoted to its repair and that should be compensated because that is attention that is diverted from other projects because of the breach. *Computer graphic cards*, CDN Trial.

In short, determining lost profits is a fact-intensive process that tries to assess the true loss without giving double compensation.

Costs of repair may also be disputed. Where a small percent of seller's computer graphic cards installed in buyer's computers malfunctioned and buyer recalled and replaced all the graphic cards, the court held the full cost to be recoverable because it was impossible to predict which graphic cards would go bad in the future. *Computer graphic cards*, CDN Trial.

§11.25 Damages on Avoidance

CISG provides two special provisions for damages when the contract has been avoided.

Where the injured party reasonably covers, damages include the difference between the contract price and the cover price. Art. 75. Where seller states that he will not deliver the goods and buyer properly avoids the contract, buyer can purchase the same goods in the market within a reasonable time for a reasonable price and collect the difference in damages from seller. Likewise, where buyer refuses to pay the contract price and seller properly avoids the contract and resells the goods within a reasonable time at a reasonable price, the difference between the contract price and the cover price makes up part of seller's damages.

The second damage provision is where there is no cover, but there is a current price for the contracted goods at the time and place of required delivery. The injured party may measure damages by the difference between the contract price and the current price at that time and place. Art. 76. If the injured party takes over the goods, the contract price is measured against the current price at the time and place where the goods are taken over.

The current price method usually works well for the aggrieved seller and for the aggrieved buyer when there has been no delivery. When there has been a delivery, but the defect is not discovered immediately, it seems inappropriate to date the current price before buyer has had the opportunity to discover that the goods are so badly out of conformity as to constitute a fundamental breach.

The difference between the substitute transaction method and the current price method is clear. In one, there is an actual transaction to measure the damages; in the other, the figures are based on the existence of a market. The current price computation is attractive because the victim of the breach need do nothing, nor need it incur sales or purchasing expenses that may or may not be compensated in damages (depending on the breacher's solvency). The risk is that the aggrieved party may be unable to prove the current price. This should not be a problem where commodities are regularly traded on an exchange, with sales prices published daily, so long as freight from the place of delivery to the place used on the exchange can be calculated.

There is not a current price for all goods, or even for all commodities. In *Coal*, ICC Arb 8740/1996, the contract called for coal of at least 32% volatile matter. Seller delivered coal with 20.4%. Buyer was unable to prove a current price for either the coal ordered or the coal delivered. Coal can have different heating and other properties. There is no commodity trading in coal. There are transactions in coal of various sorts, but buyer could not cite comparable transactions, probably because traders do not often publicize their prices. It is difficult to believe that no current price could be figured out for that particular type of coal. Granted that different coals have different heating properties, one might have been able to derive a price for that type of coal from the prices of other types. Or perhaps there were not sufficient transactions in coal at the appropriate time to adjust to a current price for that coal at that time. CISG seems to anticipate that current price can be derived by adjustment, as it specifies that if there is no current price at the proper place, it can be derived from the price at another reasonable place with adjustment for the cost of transport. Art. 76(2). This might properly be extended to a situation where the goods are not identical.

A more liberal court found a current price, even though the expert could not identify Pony or Madras leather, but opined that the price of furniture leather increased about 30% from the contract signing to seller's repudiation. *Furniture leather*, D App 20040915.

The current price method does not seem to contemplate its use in documentary transfers, as it refers only to goods. It is common, especially with commodities, for the ownership of goods to be transferred by means of documents during their shipment. In that case, the appropriate time and place should be the time and place of the documentary transfer.

Failure to establish a current price does not doom the party as a matter of theory, as CISG specifically says that damages can be secured in addition to the measures of arts. 75 and 76. In practice, failure of evidence for either section will usually mean insufficient proof of general damages.

An illustration of such supplementary damages might occur where seller delivers nonconforming goods to buyer late, and buyer avoids the contract, then buys conforming goods at the market price. The difference between the contract price and the price paid for conforming goods establishes damages for the nonconformity, but buyer may also be entitled to damages resulting from the lack of conforming goods between the delivery date and the date when buyer secured the replacement goods.

The damages provided by arts. 75 or 76 will usually compensate seller for loss, including loss of profit. They are unlikely to do so for a buyer who is a reseller. Damages for an advantageous purchase are covered, but computing damages for loss of the subsequent resale requires recourse to art. 74.

The injured party need not prove foreseeability of damages because the calculation of a loss by a substitute transaction or reference to the market is always foreseeable.

Determining a reasonable time will vary with the goods, the situation of the injured party, and the market. One court held that a delay of two weeks between seller's refusal to deliver and buyer's cover was justified for orientation and solicitation of bids. *Iron molybdenum*, D App 19970228. In *Scrap Metal*, AUS Sup. Ct. 20001117, two months was considered reasonable where seller immediately began looking for buyers. On the other hand, one does not want the injured party to be able to speculate at the expense of the breacher.

A reasonable price is determined by what a party in the position of the injured party could obtain in the market at the time.

If there is a cover transaction, it may be that an injured party pressed for time will not be able to obtain the very best price in the market. The pressure of time limits one's negotiating options. The price received should be considered a reasonable transaction even though in hindsight it might not have been the best possible price. *Fertilizer*, ICC Arb 8128/1995. Some slack should be allowed to the aggrieved party who needs to act quickly.

If the injured party has made a cover transaction, but the transaction is not reasonable, the injured party cannot rely on art. 75; the specific language of art. 76 seems to prevent its use; and the injured party would be remitted to damages under art. 74. Unanimous opinion, however, is that art. 76 can be used.

Likewise, art. 76 should be used when the injured party is a repeat dealer in the goods involved, so that it is impossible to pinpoint which of its many transactions in those goods is the cover transaction. This appeared to be the situation in the somewhat confused *Furniture leather*, D App 20040915. An aggrieved party who deals repeatedly in the goods should specify which transaction is the cover, preferably the first one after learning of the breach.

If goods purchased before the breach in fact replace the goods subject to the breach, that is not a qualifying substitute transaction because the substitute must occur after the breach. The aggrieved party can use the current price, but that may not provide the same result as using the cost of the goods actually used as replacements.

The substitute transaction need not be exactly the same as the original contract as long as the difference in value can be easily calculated. For instance, a cif purchase replacing an fob buy can easily be equated by backing out the cost of freight and insurance.

When these measures of damages are used, there is no specific requirement for mitigation. Mitigation is supplied by the requirement that the resale be in a reasonable manner and within a reasonable time. The same is true when the current price method is used. One court and the CISG Advisory Council, however, did not recognize this difference, and discussed whether the substitute transaction for the sale of shoes was done in a reasonable manner in the context of mitigation. *Shoes*, D App 19940114; *CISG-AC 8*.

§11.26 Certainty and Causation

Damages are only awarded if they are certain, and if they result from the breach. It is the "loss suffered by the other party as a consequence of the breach." Art. 74. How direct the causation must be, and how certain, is a matter of some dispute. The better rule is that they cannot be speculative, *Orica Australia*, US Trial; they must be reasonably certain to occur and to be the responsibility of the injured party. *Norfolk Southern*, US Trial. They need not have already been paid. *Propane*, A Sup. Ct. 19960206. In *Sweet potatoes*, CHN Arb 19960314, buyer's liability to his sub-buyer for failure to deliver the potatoes promised by seller had been determined by an arbitral tribunal, but had yet to be paid. The tribunal held that buyer could recover those damages from seller. The amount need not be proven with precision, as often damages will occur after the trial has been concluded. A reasonable prediction is enough. In other words, certainty means reasonable certainty, not absolute certainty.

Damage to professional reputation or goodwill is compensable, *Powerturf carpets*, SF App 20001016, but only if reasonably certain. In *Cardin shoes*, F App 19991021, seller's failure to deliver caused buyer to cancel contracts with its retailers. Experts estimated that buyer would lose some retailers and would need to provide deeper discounts to retain others, but the court denied the damages in the absence of proof of actual pecuniary loss.

What needs to be proven with reasonable certainty is both the fact of the loss and its amount. Often, the proof of one will also be the proof of the other, but not always. Proof of the amount of lost profits often involves a bit of speculation about the future based on the past because, as a result of the breach (or perhaps other facts), the profits did not occur. Proof of lost profits by written or oral testimony showing the cancellation of customer orders tends to be more persuasive than salespeople's speculation about orders they could have secured had they possessed sufficient inventory. *Delchi Carrier*, US App.

§11.27 Foreseeability

Damages are only due if the damages were foreseeable by the breaching party as possible at the time of contracting.

It can be argued that the time of foreseeability should be the time of the breach, rather than the time of contracting, because at that point the potential breacher will know more and will be able to make a better assessment of the economics of breaching. Such an interpretation is precluded by CISG's language, but the time of contracting should mean the time of any modification of the contract, as well as its initial conclusion, if the modification is relevant to the consequences of the breach.

This formulation differs from the Anglo-American rule that damages must be foreseeable by both parties as probable. Whether the wording difference between probable and possible or the change from foreseeable by both parties to foreseeable by the breacher results in difference in any individual case is debatable.

Formulating the test as to whether the type of damage is possible is not helpful. That the damage occurred proves that it was possible. The real question is whether the possibility of the damage was so reasonably foreseeable that the breacher should have taken it into account in pricing the contract. As an empirical matter, it is doubtful that most sellers, when entering into a contract, price it on the basis of the kind of damages they will need to pay if they breach. That is economic theory, not reality. It is much more likely that sellers price the contract based on their anticipated costs of performing the contract, their anticipated profit, what they expect their competitors might charge, and what would be required to finalize the contract.

Most of the cases have involved breaching sellers.

Some courts have suggested that both the type and the size of damages must be foreseeable. *Waterworks cooler*, A Sup. Ct. 20020114, *Cloth*, D App 19990131, *Russia-England*, R Arb 406/1998 20000606. In the latter case, the tribunal did not dismiss the arbitration, but reduced the profit from the 50% that buyer had arranged on its resale to the 10% it thought foreseeable. Supporting this rule, it is argued that when businesspeople calculate risks, they do so on the basis of likely amounts.

The better rule requires only that the type of damage be foreseeable. The reason for this is that many contract breaches occur because of a significant change in the price of the contracted item between the time of contracting and the time of performance. A strict interpretation of foreseeability of probable amount would not grant the innocent party damages at all, not even the smaller part of the actual damages that were foreseeable as possible, because on concluding the contract, there is less than a 50% probability that the price of the goods will move in that direction. The greatest probability is that the price will not change. If it does change, the likelihood of upward change is usually balanced by the likelihood of downward change. An interpretation of possible amount of change would allow anything.

It is to be noted that arts. 75 and 76, providing damages formulae in case of avoidance, do not impose any limits on foreseeability of amount.

Also, the drafters of CISG refused to include any provision on hardship or force majeure. Requiring consideration of the magnitude of the actual damage should not be relevant because it would sneak those considerations in the back door.

While there is no specific discussion of considering the magnitude of the damages, it is clear that the court in *Delchi Carrier*, US App is only considering the foreseeability of the type of damages.

Foreseeability should be viewed from two angles. The text says "damages which the party in breach foresaw or ought to have foreseen." This corresponds to the two interpretations of intent, subjective by the person speaking in art. 8(1), and objective "according to the understanding that a reasonable person ... would have had in the same circumstances." in art. 8(2). In the real world, foreseeability is more likely to be viewed objectively than subjectively because it is easier to prove what the person should have known than what the person actually knew.

There have been a surprising number of cases asking whether resale by buyer is a possibility that is reasonably foreseeable. Given the large number of cases of resale, it seems appropriate as a general rule to consider resale as foreseeably possible without need for any proof because buyers can only be users or resellers. Some courts have found a likelihood of resale based on the quantity of goods ordered (objective standard), *Frozen pork*, D Sup. Ct. 20050302, or based on the fact that seller knew that buyer was a trader or a wholesaler that lacked appropriate storage facilities. *Chicago Prime Packers*, US Trial. Others assume that resale is a foreseeable possibility. *Propane*, A Sup. Ct. 19960206.

Where a late delivery of cloth forced buyer to process the cloth in Germany rather than in lower-cost Turkey, the court refused to include the extra processing cost as damages because seller was not informed before the contract was concluded that this was a possible consequence of late delivery. *Cloth*, D App 19990131, It did not consider whether a seller should objectively know that a late delivery raises the possibility of changes in production to meet sales commitments. The case raises the question of the specificity with which seller should foresee damages. It would be unusual for buyer in the process of negotiating the contract to detail to seller of a raw material the specifics of buyer's production process. It should be clear to a businessperson that late delivery may occasion extra cost where buyer may have made resale arrangements. Whether those extra costs involve payments for overtime or for Sunday work, or for processing in a pricier location, should make little difference.

TeeVee Tunes, US Trial, ordered a production line to make record boxes from Schubert, who delivered a nonconforming line that could not be fixed. Among the damages claimed was the cost of relocating to a new plant. The court, using objective criteria, held that it was not foreseeable that possible damages for failure to deliver a working production line would trigger the need to move to a new plant. However, increased administrative costs and loss of profits from being unable to sell boxes were foreseeable. This followed the admission of Schubert's president that he knew that boxes were to be produced for sale in the Christmas season, giving foreseeability in that case a subjective nature.

There appears to be a split of opinion about how much foreseeability will be assumed, and how much must be proven.

Some courts seem to require exacting proof of why the damages that occurred were foreseeable. Where buyer had resold the cyclohexane at a profit and sub-buyer had done the same, buyer's suit for damages for late delivery was dismissed because buyer did not prove that seller knew that buyer was a trader, rather than an end user. *Citgo Petroleum*, US Trial. The court spent most of its opinion talking about the Texas law on foreseeability, presumably on the unstated and mistaken assumption that Texas law and CISG are identical.

Others seem to take judicial notice of what a reasonable party would have known. For instance, in *Al Hewar*, US Trial, the court held that a foreseeable result of the breach of a contract to supply a large quantity of hay was that buyer would resell the hay and might suffer the loss of a security bond posted for fulfilling that contract.

Parties to contracts should foresee common business realities, such as that November and December may produce 25%–30% of the yearly sales for toy, hobby, and game stores, and an even larger share of the annual profit, or that a shortfall of sales is likely to produce a much larger decline in profit because of fixed costs.

The moral of the story is that if the breacher will not stipulate that he should have known about the possibility of resale, use, or seasonality of the goods, claimant should be prepared to prove that a reasonable person in the business should know of these possibilities with the expert testimony of a business school professor, preferably one who teaches in the city of the breacher.

§11.28 Mitigation

The general principle of mitigation is simple: the aggrieved party must take whatever reasonable opportunity exists to reduce the loss that results from the breach. Normally, this means that if seller defaults, buyer should purchase the goods ordered at the best price she can within a reasonable time; if buyer defaults, seller should sell the goods at the best price he can within a reasonable time. If the goods are nonconforming, they might be repaired or replaced. The application of the rule sometimes leads to situations that defy normal business practices.

Where seller refused to deliver watches to buyer because seller had made buyer's competitor seller's exclusive dealer, the court said that buyer should have bought the watches from his competitor and reduced the damages to the difference between the contract price and what the competitor would have charged. This is presumably because anything in excess of what the competitor would have charged (which was probably nothing because the competitor was charging retail) would have been earned by buyer had he made the substitute purchase. *Watches*, CH Sup. Ct. 20091217. The decision is probably correct in theory, but flies in the face of common practice to ask a merchant to buy from his competitor at the price at which she must resell to her customers. It is the ultimate triumph of formalism over substance, unless there is evidence that the competitor would have sold to the aggrieved party at less than a retail price.

A Spanish court held that the injured party must mitigate with the breacher without any adjustment in terms, and this is accepted law. Buyer refused to accept the contracted jute at the contract price and proposed to pay the then-prevailing lower market price "with a view towards giving once and for all a solution to this regrettable matter." Seller would accept buyer's offer if buyer paid in advance, but buyer declined and seller covered at a lower price. The court reduced seller's damages to the difference between the contract price and buyer's reduced offer, saying that seller should have mitigated with the breaching buyer without attaching new payment conditions. *Jute*, E Sup. Ct. 20000128.

The opinion is troubling for a number of reasons.

It does not find that seller avoided the contract, yet it proceeds under art. 75, which requires avoidance. It does not talk about art. 75's reasonable time and manner test, but quotes art. 77's "reasonable in the circumstances to mitigate" test. The court says that the sale was made a few days after buyer's breach, but in fact it was three weeks.

It is also clear from the "solution" language that buyer's offer is not a cover offer, but a proposal to amend the contract that would negate seller's right to damages in the amount of the price difference.

The court, in questioning seller's demand for assurance of payment in advance, gives no weight to the fact that this buyer has just breached the contract, which should cause a reasonable seller to wonder about the chance of payment occurring if the cover is with the same party. On the other hand, the parties had dealt with each other for five years without payment problems, which might reassure seller about payment in the absence of knowledge of buyer's possible financial problems. Seller did not demand advanced payment in the cover transaction from a first-time client with whom seller covered, which seems to indicate that advanced payment is not an industry custom. But where the buyer has breached this contract, surely a reasonable seller would demand extra assurance that the breaching buyer will perform this time, like advanced payment.

Ultimately, the court may have reached the right conclusion for the wrong reason because the cover transaction was at a price considerably lower than buyer's offer. It is stipulated that buyer's offer was at the then-market price. The court might have found that seller could have sold to any number of other buyers at the market price, and should have, which would have made more sense.

In *Pharmaceutical glycerin*, A App 20170227, the court stated "[T]he seller must also accept an offer from the contract-breaking buyer to accept part of the goods at a lower price if this price is still higher than the price to be obtained from a cover sale." The court goes on to find that "[s]uch a concrete offer was never made by [buyer]." That seems to have been the situation in the *Jute* case also.

The problem is in fact very common. Frequently, when there is a disadvantageous change in price one party will ask the other to adjust the price. E.g., *Iron molybdenum*, D App 19970228. This is properly regarded as a request to amend the contract, not an offer to mitigate, because it would serve no purpose for the breacher to help the injured party mitigate without a contract modification. *Steel bars*, ICC 6281.

In the real world, if seller is to cover with buyer, he must preserve his rights with a clause in the purchase contract that the purchase does not amend the original contract and seller reserves the right to collect damages under it. Buyer will not agree to such a clause because it negates buyer's purpose in refusing the goods, obtaining them for a lower price.

Some mitigation is unusual. Seller delivered nonconforming goods that needed to be accompanied by seller's report of test results. Buyer did not timely report the test results to seller so that it could certify them. The tribunal found that buyer's failure to report reduced the price at which buyer could resell by 50%, so reduced buyer's damages by that amount. *Russia-US*, R Arb 54/1999 20000124.

Continuing to use a product after learning that it is nonconforming and causing damage is failure to mitigate. This was alleged to be the case where buyer continued to use nonconforming vine wax after realizing that it was not protecting pruned vines. *Vine wax*, D Sup. Ct. 19990324. Another way to conceive this is that the additional damage was not caused by the nonconformity, but by the aggrieved party's continuing to use the product.

Clearly, an aggrieved party is not obligated to cover by engaging in a substitute transaction. However, if cover would have been reasonable under the circumstances, the aggrieved party's damages will be reduced as if he had covered. But when is it reasonable to not cover? *Venison*, D App 19991028, says that CISG prefers to keep as much of the contract in place as possible. For that reason, it is perfectly reasonable for the aggrieved party to not cover as long as there is a chance that the contract might be fulfilled. In that case, seller need not seek a replacement buyer for the venison until buyer refused to accept it and seller had a reasonable time in which to decide whether to avoid the contract. Otherwise, if seller had a limited stock of the goods, he might find himself unable to deliver them either in the substitute sale or to the party who breached the contract. The court makes it clear that until seller elects avoidance, seller continues to have the right to demand specific performance, which would necessitate delivering the venison.

An aggrieved party is not obligated to notify the breacher before the mitigation either of its intent to mitigate or the specifics of the mitigation. *Steel bars*, ICC 6281. If, however, notification is made and the breacher does not protest, the breacher may be barred from arguing that the mitigation was unreasonable.

Factors weighed to determine whether an aggrieved buyer's actions were reasonable include the length of time between the breach and the time buyer needs to use or deliver the goods, as well as evidence of the difficulty in finding an alternate supplier. *Chinese goods*, D Arb 19960321. Buyer need not act perfectly, only reasonably. *Computer graphic cards*, CDN Trial. Buyer is not obligated to violate the law, even if that would provide a better price. *Doolim*

Corp. v. R. Doll, US Trial. A party is not obligated to take significant financial risks or to incur extraordinary expenses to mitigate, because lurking at the back of the injured party's mind is the possibility that the breacher will be unable to pay any judgment in the situation because of bankruptcy. Nor is the aggrieved party obligated to adopt a mitigation that its tests fail to show will fix the problem, or that seem to fix the nonconformity temporarily, but not permanently. *Computer graphic cards*, CDN Trial.

A peculiar problem of mitigation arises where buyer defaults on a contract to purchase goods made with buyer's intellectual property. This will most often occur where buyer's trademark is to be attached to the goods. Seller fears that selling the goods in a cover transaction will be trademark or patent or copyright infringement. One can argue that implied in the contract is a license to sell the goods ordered if buyer defaults. Uncertain of its rights, one seller awaited a favorable court decision before disposing of the clothing. *Doolim Corp. v. R. Doll*, US Trial. This caused a delay of 15 months that, in some markets, would not have been cover within a reasonable time.

The cost of mitigating damages is an additional item that must be factored into the aggrieved party's planning. If the cost of mitigation exceeds the benefits of mitigation, the action should not be taken. Where a product that should be dry is delivered wet, buyer might ask whether buyer should spend $10,000 to dry it. If drying the product would increase its value by $20,000, buyer is obligated to dry it, but not if it only increases its value by $5,000.

The cost of mitigation should be added to the aggrieved party's damages. Said another way, the breacher only gets the benefit of the net mitigation—the amount saved less the cost of saving it.

§11.29 Currency in Which Damages Are Paid

One would think that damages would be in the currency in which the purchase price was to be made because that is the closest analogy. Damages are not necessarily in the currency of payment because the purpose of damages is full compensation for loss. Where the breach is failure to pay the purchase price, damages should indeed be in the currency of the purchase price. To the extent that the aggrieved party experienced the loss in another currency, payment should be in that other currency. Damages will usually be in the currency of the person who is owed the damages because that is the place where the loss is suffered. *Wire rod*, CH Trial 20140917, *Wire rod*, CH Sup. Ct. 20150402.

Most courts, however, work in their own national currency. When that is the case and the award is to be paid in another currency, when should the conversion from the court's currency to the payment currency be made? In *Schmitz-Werke*, US App, the court found that CISG did not govern that question, either specifically or by general principles, that Maryland choice of law was appropriate and led to the application of Maryland law, but there was no Maryland law on the question. Under those circumstances, the appeals court thought it inappropriate to overrule the trial judge, who made the conversion at the rate applicable on the date of the breach, rather than the date on which the judgment was rendered.

§11.30 Dispute Resolution Costs as Damages

Parties have argued that the general principle of full compensation requires that all costs of dispute resolution be paid by the breaching party because these are incidental expenses that would not have occurred but for the breach. Others have argued, less persuasively, that these are not costs resulting from the breach, but costs resulting from a decision to litigate. One might divide those costs between attorney's fees, court costs, fees for providing notices, and internal research and personnel costs.

The greatest of these is attorney's fees. In the landmark case of *Zapata Hermanos*, US App, Judge Posner held that attorney's fees could not be recovered as damages. He doubted that Congress intended to change the general American system, where each party pays its own legal fees unless specifically provided otherwise, which CISG does not. Less persuasively, he also noted that this would set up an unfair system, because a successful plaintiff could recover legal fees, but a defendant who proved that he was not in breach would be left to pay his own legal bills. *CISG-AC 6* adopts the latter reason. In fact, in most cases where the claimant is unsuccessful in proving breach, the court holds that it is the claimant who has breached, e.g., *Scooters*, CH Sup. Ct. 20070717, or that both parties have breached. E.g., *Rijn blend*, NL Arb 2319, 20021015. In the absence of that situation, one might argue that claiming a breach where there is none is a breach of the contractual obligation to act reasonably, but that is an argument that has never been adopted (or advanced that I have found).

Posner also posited that no general principle of CISG was applicable, so the matter must be decided by domestic law. He did not consider whether full compensation for loss was a general principle of CISG, whether it should apply here, or whether it is counterbalanced by a CISG principle of equality between buyers and sellers.

The result is that attorney's fees are recoverable in countries where they are normally recoverable in litigation (most of the world), and not in those countries where they are not (the U.S.), but they are recoverable as part of the legal system, not as damages. That result is probably correct as a matter of U.S. interpretation, but it does raise the possibility of forum shopping by an informed and confident plaintiff. Fees for litigation between the parties are also recoverable if provided by contract or by the rules of the chosen tribunal. It should be noted that in some countries where legal fees are recoverable, such as Germany, a party may contract with his lawyer for whatever fee they can agree on, but the amount of reimbursement will be limited to a statutory formula that is principally based on the amount in controversy.

However, this result only applies to attorney's fees in the breach of contract action between buyer and seller. If a buyer incurs attorney's fees in an action with a sub-buyer, those reasonable fees are damages that buyer can recover. The same should be true where buyer had to litigate with the tax authorities because seller did not provide evidence of the goods' origin. *Stemcor*, US Trial, enforced attorney's fees for the litigation between buyer and the Mexican authorities for return of taxes paid, and in the arbitration because the arbitral rules left that discretion to the tribunal. There was no discussion of the attorney's fees expended to resist in court seller's attempt to nullify the arbitration award

Pre-litigation attorney's fees also seem to be deductible, *Stemcor*, US Trial, though one court questioned whether the use of an attorney in his own country to make the initial demand was a failure to mitigate when he would need a lawyer in the breacher's country to file suit. The court did not explain why this was a failure to mitigate. *Tiles*, D Trial 19950512.

Arbitration fees imposed are recoverable as damages. *Chocolate*, R Arb 200/1994 19950425.

There have been no cases challenging other litigation costs such as court costs, perhaps because they seem to be recoverable in general under the legal systems of most countries.

§11.31 Interest as Damages

While art. 78 provides that interest will be paid on sums in arrears, interest may also be a measure of damages suffered for delay in payment. The interest provided by art. 78 may not always adequately compensate because it is often paid at an official rate or under a calculation that does not provide full compensation for loss. Where that is the case, an injured party may wish to claim interest as damages under art. 74. For example, buyer's failure to pay may force seller to take a loan at a much higher rate of interest. If seller can prove causation and foreseeability, seller is entitled to recover the reasonable higher interest rate it paid. In *Shoes*, D App 19940114, seller recovered the interest it actually paid.

Recovering interest as damages requires that the injured party prove both causation and foreseeability. Recovering interest under art. 78 has no such requirement. Where the injured party has proof problems, it is better to claim under art. 78, even if it results in the recovery of less interest. Normally, one cannot recover interest under both provisions because that would be duplicative compensation. Where one seller could prove that the actual damages exceeded the amount payable under art. 78, the extra amount was awarded as damages. *Autumn textiles*, D Trial 19900424.

One way to avoid the need to prove causation and foreseeability is to specify the amount as liquidated damages. In *Wood flooring*, CHN Arb 20210311, the parties specified that late payment would subject the debtor to liquidated damages of .05% per day late. (This is the equivalent of slightly more than 18% annual interest.) The court awarded the liquidated damages, which was not trivial because the time from when payment was due to the arbitral award was more than 900 days, calling for a damages payment equal to more than 45% of the original payment due. The court evidently thought that this liquidated damages provision was the parties' amendment to art. 78, so it did not also award interest.

§11.32 Lost Volume

If seller has an inventory of goods or can easily produce more goods, he argues that his damages not only include the profit that would have been made on the breached contract, but also the profit he would have made on the substitute contract with which seller covers, because seller could have sold twice the quantity had the breach not occurred. This position has been endorsed by one court, *Jewelry*, A Sup. Ct. 20000428, and *CISG-AC 6*, though it is controversial. Against this, buyer argues that the sale might not be made even though seller proves that seller has excess inventory because the costs of making the sale might not be justified by the price obtained. Seller could rebut this argument by showing that seller did make the sale and that there was a profit on the sale made. There would be a profit on a subsequent sale because the market price will hold. It is also argued that seller might not make a subsequent sale because if the contract had been performed, buyer would have goods that she does not want and would take the subsequent sale from seller. This assumes that there is only one potential customer, and that buyer has the ability to outmarket seller in seller's market, both of which are unlikely. The better rule gives seller the profit from both sales as damages.

§11.33 Damages Not Based on Expectancy

Sometimes it is impossible to prove damages based on expectancy. This may be the case where the breach consists of reselling the product outside the territorial limits specified in the contract. It was certainly the case in *Pressure sensors*, S Arb 20070405, where buyer was found to have copied seller's source code in violation of a confidentiality agreement. No expectancy-based damage appears appropriate because the expectancy was that the source code would not be used. The arbitrator could have measured damages by a reasonable royalty for use of the code, which would have been what seller would have earned had a contract for the code been struck. The arbitrator instead opted for a disgorgement remedy, basing damages on buyer's profit on products using the code for a period before it was estimated that buyer would have developed its own code.

§11.34 Limiting Damages

The parties can modify any provision of CISG, including the articles on damages. They often do. Sometimes those modifications are effective, but care must always be taken in their drafting.

Most frequently, they eliminate the possibility of consequential damages, as they did in *Waterworks cooler*, A Sup. Ct. 20020114 and *American Mint*, US Trial. In the latter case, buyer's damages were limited to refund of the purchase price. Seller attempted to so limit damages in *Powdered milk*, D Sup. Ct. 20020109. The contract in *Ajax Tool*, US Trial, limited all remedies to defects discovered within 90 days, and to either repair or replacement at seller's option. However, summary judgment was denied so that the court could decide whether Can-Am had waived that limit by trying to repair defects discovered thereafter. There may be a clause fixing either the amount of damages or the way in which damages are computed. Another contract, after disclaiming all warranties, declared that seller would not be liable "for lost profits or for indirect, incidental consequential or commercial losses of any kind." *Norfolk Southern*, US Trial.

There is general agreement that once the parties alter CISG rules on remedies, the matter is not specifically governed by CISG.

Some commentators have suggested that the validity of damages remedies should be decided by weighing two CISG general principles—full compensation for damages against ability of the parties to make their own agreement. It is unclear how that weighing would result.

Courts have instead thought that limitation on damages was a matter of validity, specifically excluded from CISG by art. 4(a). *E.g., Milk packager*, SRB Arb 20080715; *Venison*, D App 19991028; *CISG-AC 10*. They used choice of law rules to select the appropriate law, then applied that law.

While some legal systems enforce contracts as written, most provide for some judicial control. Some legal systems only enforce such provisions if they are not manifestly excessive, or authorize the judge to reduce them to an amount that is not manifestly excessive. In *Milk packager*, SRB Arb 20080715, the disputed clause would not have been invalidated by Serbian law. German law invalidates clauses that provide lump-sum damages for delay in payment regardless of the length of the delay, *Venison*, D App 19991028, or that exclude all damages. *Vine wax*, D Sup. Ct. 19990324. United States law will not enforce provisions that deprive a party of all effective remedies, and will enforce liquidated damages clauses, but will not enforce penalties. A valid liquidated damages clause is where damages would be difficult to assess after the fact and the parties make a reasonable advance estimate of the damages. In dictum, *American Mint*, US Trial, opined that a liquidated damages clause would be valid under CISG. The payment of a fixed sum for delay in performance is likely to be held a penalty and invalid because not a serious estimate of the likely damage, which will vary with the length of the delay.

Application of domestic law does not mean that the result is the same as in a domestic case. Most domestic law provisions depend on the limitation being reasonable. What is reasonable may differ depending on whether the sale is domestic or international.

Whether the damages clause replaces or supplements CISG's provisions is an important one. The aggrieved party may contend that the liquidated damages provision in the contract does not fully compensate it for its losses, and it should also be able to use art. 74 to supplement the liquidated damages. Deciding that question involves construing the parties' intent, which begins (and sometimes ends) with the text of the contract.

D. Interest

§11.41 Interest in General

The specific provision on interest was a late addition to the CISG. Two factors probably made it seem necessary. The long tradition of opposition to usury in the Abrahamic religions, still a significant force in legal systems based on Islam, view the payment of some interest as a form of usury. Also, the extent to which interest might be available after a successful suit varied from country to country, and CISG prefers uniform rules.

Interest is due on any sum in arrears in addition to damages. Art. 78. That includes seller's obligation to repay sums received on contracts later avoided. Art. 84.

Interest is not conceived as damages. Damages are in a separate section II of CISG's chapter V; interest is in section III. If that were not enough, art. 78 is specific that interest is recoverable in addition to damages, indicating that interest is not viewed as damages. In practice, this means that a party claiming interest need not prove that he was harmed by not having the money on the due date.

§11.42 Examples Where Interest Is Due

The most common situation is the late payment of the purchase price. *Natural stone*, D Trial 20051102. A second common situation is failure by seller to repay the purchase price when the contract is avoided.

Interest is also due on amounts advanced by one party that are the obligation of the other. Buyer may pay customs duties and clearance charges that are the obligation of seller. *White crystal sugar*, Serbia Arb 20080123. Buyer may pay for parts needed for a cure, for which seller should reimburse. Art. 48(1).

Where seller prevailed on its claim and buyer prevailed on its counterclaim, the court held that each was entitled to interest on its claim because each was the prevailing party. However, neither the trial court nor the Third Circuit (in its affirmance) discussed the question in terms of CISG rather than U.S. law. *ECEM European Chemical 2*, US Trial.

Some situations calling for the payment of interest seem to be motivated by unjust enrichment, some are restitutionary, and some look like damages. *Chicago Prime Packers*, US Trial, suggests that nine different formulations have been used by courts to calculate the interest due.

In countries with slow judicial systems where interest rates are high, the obligation to pay interest can considerably raise the stakes of litigation. In the U.S., it is common for litigation that goes to the Court of Appeals to require five years from the time the suit is filed to be resolved, and suits are not usually filed on the day the payment was due. Arbitration is often not quicker. In *Caviar*, H Arb 19961210, 4.5 years passed before the arbitrators decided. In *Shenzen Synergy*, US Trial, it took almost four years from the time payment was due to award of judgment in a bench trial, and the interest due at a time of low interest was 20% of the judgment. It is not unusual for interest to exceed a quarter of the amount of damages. E.g., *PVC*, CH Trial 19991021, where the interest rate was not very high, but the delay to judgment was long. The champion delay I have found so far was *Computer graphic cards*, CDN Trial, where 20 years expired between the breach and the trial court's judgment.

§11.43 Sum in Arrears

For interest to be due, there must be a sum in arrears. Use of the word "sum" implies a monetary payment, so interest should not be due simply because nonmonetary performance is late. However, late performance is a breach that may result in damages. Failure to pay damages is a sum in arrears, so interest may end up being paid indirectly for late performance if it results in damages.

When is the sum in arrears? Take a typical case. Buyer refuses to accept delivery of an order of wire rod in October 2008 in a volatile market. Seller covers by selling the rod in November. Suit is brought in February 2010. In 2014, the trial court awards judgment for seller for the difference. The appeals court holds in 2015 that seller should have covered in October for a higher price than received in November, and awards judgment for the lesser amount. *Wire rod*, CH Sup. Ct. 20150402. This example suggests six different points from which the sum may be in arrears: the date of breach, the date of cover, the date when cover should have been effected, the date the suit was filed, the date of the lower court decision, or the date when the court decision becomes final.

It can be argued that there is no sum in arrears until a sum is fixed, either definitively or at least tentatively. Debtor claims that he cannot pay because he does not know how much to pay until creditor files suit, or perhaps until the trial court renders judgment. This position has been rejected. The sum need not be liquidated; the important question is the existence of the obligation to pay because, whether liquidated or not, the creditor suffers from the loss of the money due. *CISG-AC 14, PVC,* CH Trial 19991021, though *Vitamin C,* CHN Arb 19970818, seems to be to the contrary without explanation.

Interest on damages begins to accrue at the time of breach, even though the amount of the liability is unknown at the time. There are cases to the contrary, such as *Construction materials,* B App 20060424, holding that interest begins to accrue on the date the party receives the cover price, *Natural stone,* D Trial 20051102, suggesting that interest begins when the suit is filed, and *Sweet potatoes,* CHN Arb 19960314, saying without discussion that interest begins from the date the arbitral tribunal renders judgment. To minimize the interest, debtor can pay creditor an estimate, but at his own risk that creditor may become insolvent and unable to repay any overage if the amount owed turns out to be less than that which was paid. Indeed, the implication of accruing interest at the moment of breach is that if the debtor overpays the amount, the creditor must pay back the overage with interest from the date of payment.

§11.44 Rate, Compounding, and Currency

The controversy about interest has mostly concerned the rate at which it is to be paid. It is clear that CISG does not specify the rate. One should then consider whether the problem can be solved using general principles of CISG and, if not, use the choice of law rule of the forum.

Some cases have found a general principle of CISG to be full compensation for losses, which leads to using the rate at which the creditor would have needed to pay at the creditor's place of business to borrow the unpaid amount. *Metal sheets,* A Arb 19940615. Other courts suggest that a general principle of CISG is the prevention of unjust enrichment, so the appropriate interest rate is the rate in effect at debtor's place of business because debtor no doubt invested the money that should have been paid to creditor at his home base. *Natural stone,* D Trial 20051102. Another court chose the country with the lower rate. *VW Golf,* D Trial 20020822.

Most courts, usually without considering whether there is a general principle of CISG applicable, have used the applicable choice of law rule to determine the country whose law applies, and use that country's interest rules. Courts have variously chosen seller's law, *Chocolate,* R Arb 200/1994 19950425, forum law, *ECEM European Chemical 2,* US Trial, law designated by the parties' choice of law contained in one of the parties' standard terms, *Venison,* D App 19991028, law of the currency of payment, and one tribunal rested on so many diverse precedents that it is difficult to determine what the important one might be. *White crystal sugar*, Serbia Arb 20080123. One tribunal used the one-year London Inter Bank rate (LIBOR) on grounds that this was the rate generally used in Eurodollar settlements between operators in international trade, without presenting any evidence of this trade custom. *Steel bars*, ICC 6653, 19930326.

The United States has a special problem. Selecting U.S. law or the law of another country does not end the inquiry. If U.S. law is selected, the question then becomes whether federal or state law should apply. Many cases have not considered this problem and simply applied a law without discussing why. Of the courts that have recognized the problem, the consensus is that these cases, while often both federal question and diversity of citizenship cases, are closer to federal question cases, so federal law should apply, giving the judge great discretion. In *Shenzen Synergy*, US Trial, the court held for federal law, but thought that Texas law, where the court sat, gave appropriate guidance for the court's discretion. More appropriate was *Congelados* 2, US Trial, which, while incorrectly stating that the only source of jurisdiction was diversity, correctly held that interest should be determined under federal law rather than state law because the case more closely approximated a federal question case.

Selecting the law to determine the rate does not end the problem. There are many different rates of interest in most countries. There may be an official rate that is attached to judgments, though that may not exist in a country that does not tack interest onto judgments. There is the prime rate, for which few borrowers can qualify. Then there is the rate at which either the debtor or the creditor could have borrowed in its home country, best proven by the rate actually paid to borrow. *Italian Shoes*, D Trial 19961112. There is also what one might call the discouragement rate. That is a rate that is high enough to discourage the debtor from withholding payment. A debtor in need of money (who isn't?) can obtain it by withholding payment. This is better than going to a lending institution because you need not spend time completing a loan application, and there is no risk of the loan being refused. One tribunal adopted the median bank interest rate. *Chocolate*, R Arb 200/1994 19950425. One court noted that the interest rate for federal question cases is at the judge's discretion, then rejected the New York statutory rate of 9% as too high and the U.S. Treasury Bill rate of 0.5% as too low, and settled on the interest rate paid by delinquent income tax payers, which is the federal short-term rate plus three percentage points, the implication being that the rate would be recomputed as the federal short-term rate changed. *Shantou Real Lingerie*, US Trial.

Is the interest simple or compound? CISG does not specify. Again, there might be arguments as to whether a general principle of CISG applies, or whether choice of law rules point to the law of one country. *Construction materials*, B App 20060424, suggests that since CISG provides no guidance, creditor receives simple interest unless it proves that it should be compound, either because of trade custom, prior dealings of the parties, intent, or because debtor had to pay compound interest to secure replacement funds. *Shenzen Synergy*, US Trial, also opted for simple interest without explaining why.

Given all the uncertainties, a wise contracting party will provide the rate of interest and whether it is simple or compound in the contract to eliminate these uncertainties, as was done for the rate in *Construction materials*, B App 20060424.

It is generally agreed that the currency in which interest is to be calculated and paid is the currency in which the principal amount on which the interest is based is to be paid.

CHECKPOINTS

You should have learned that:

- No tribunal may grant either buyer or seller extra time to perform the contract. The parties may agree to extra time, and are encouraged to use the *nachfrist* procedure.
- Specific performance of the contract is an available remedy. There are few decided cases about it, as aggrieved parties usually prefer avoidance and damages.
- Both avoidance and price reduction are inconsistent with specific performance, so an aggrieved party who elects either remedy may not seek specific performance.
- Requesting a cure and granting extra time are both consistent with specific performance.
- A court need not order specific performance where it would not order it in a similar case under domestic law.
- Under U.S. law, specific performance is usually available only when the remedy at law is inadequate, usually because the goods are unique or it would be difficult for the aggrieved person to secure a substitute transaction.

- However, a U.S. court is likely to enforce an arbitral decision calling for specific performance.

- Damages may be awarded for all losses suffered as a result of contract breach, including lost profits.

- Damages are limited to those that the breacher ought to have foreseen as possible when making the contract. They do not include damages that the victim could have avoided by mitigation. Damages only include losses that are reasonably certain.

- Damages are intended to put the parties in the economic position they would have occupied had the contract been performed. In easy cases, that might only be the cost to repair the goods to be equal to what was promised, or the difference in value between what was promised and what was delivered.

- Damages may include seller's cost of reselling goods buyer has refused; buyer's liability to sub-buyers for malfunction of goods buyer has resold; or loss of buyer's resale profits.

- There are two special provisions for damages when the contract is avoided. When the aggrieved party reasonably covers, the aggrieved party may claim damages as the difference between the contract price and the cover price. When there is no cover, it is the difference between the contract price and the fair market value. The aggrieved party is not limited to these measures of damages.

- Even where there is no avoidance, parties have successfully used those damages measures.

- To be liable for damages, the breaching party must have been able to foresee the type of damages that would result from the breach by the time the contract was concluded. It is less clear that he must foresee the amount of those damages.

- Some cases have questioned whether resale of the goods by buyer is foreseeable.

- The aggrieved party is charged with mitigation, reducing the amount of damage caused by the breach as much as is commercially reasonable. In a declining market, an aggrieved buyer is charged as though he had found substitute goods within a reasonable time at the then-prevailing market price.

- The aggrieved party must even be willing to mitigate with the breacher, or with the aggrieved party's competitor.

- Damages for buyer's breach should be paid in the currency called for in the contract. Damages for seller's breach should normally be paid in buyer's currency. Some courts order damages paid in the currency of the court.

- Damages include general dispute resolution costs. They do not include attorney's fees. Whether attorney's fees of the prevailing party in the breach of contract action can be recovered depends on the domestic law of the forum. Attorney's fees incurred to defend suits resulting from the breach are included in damages.

- Damages include compensation for lost volume of sales.

- The parties may limit or modify their liability for damages, or provide for liquidated damages, to the extent that such a provision would be valid under domestic law.

- Interest is due on any sum in arrears. Alternatively, interest can be recovered as damages when it can be proven.

- Most courts hold that interest on damages begins to accrue at the time of breach, even though the amount of the liability is unknown at the time.

- Courts are in disagreement about whether interest is simple or compound and the rate of interest.

- Interest is paid in the currency in which the sum on which interest is calculated is paid.

CHAPTER 12

Procedure

ROADMAP

After reading this chapter, you should understand:

- The procedure in CISG cases is normally dictated by the law of the forum.
- CISG specifically places the burden of proof for excuse from paying damages due to an impediment on the person seeking the excuse.
- CISG does not speak specifically to the burden of proof in other situations.
- The party seeking recovery under a general rule has the burden of proving its elements, while a party seeking an exception to a general rule needs to prove the elements of the exception.
- The burden of proving nonconformity of goods is on the party alleging it.
- If the UN Limitations Convention applies, the statute of limitations is four years from delivery of the goods.
- If the UN Limitations Convention does not apply, the statute of limitations is determined by the choice of law rule of the forum, which usually points to forum law as procedural.

---

§12.01 Introduction

Usually, the procedure for resolving international contract disputes is not specifically prescribed by CISG. For the most part, procedural questions will be resolved according to the law of the forum. While this might provide an opportunity for forum shopping, it seems impractical to require a court to change its normal procedures because it is hearing an international contract case governed by CISG.

Two matters, however, require enhanced discussion. They are the burden of proof and the statute of limitations. The statute of limitations may be specified if countries have ratified CISG's companion convention on that point. Except in one case, CISG says nothing specific about the burden of proof.

Where a matter is not specified in CISG, the question then becomes whether it is a matter within the ambit of CISG that might be resolved using CISG's general principles. If not, it should be resolved using the law of the country to which choice of law principles point.

§12.02 Burden of Proof

Sometimes, CISG does specify the party with the burden of proof. A party is not liable for failure to perform "if he proves" certain elements. Art. 79(1). The burden of proof for excuse from paying damages is on the person seeking the excuse.

It is rare that CISG makes any reference to a burden of proof. For most provisions, CISG does not specifically assign the burden of proof. One court has held that CISG assigns the burden of proof on improper mitigation to the breacher based on the words "the party in breach may claim a reduction in damages…" *Reibacher Ind.*, US App. That seems less a specific allocation of the burden of proof than an application of the principle that one needs to claim mitigation in order to receive the benefit of it. The burden of proof might or might not follow. However, it seems like a correct decision under the principle below.

Whether burden of proof is generally covered by CISG, and what general principles of CISG might apply, is debated at length by commentators, but the cases tend to simply pronounce their results without justifying them. *Pizza cartons*, D Trial 20000413. It does not seem to matter whether the burden of proof is determined by CISG general principles or by domestic law, because the result is the same: the party advancing a proposition has the burden of proving its components. *Military shoe leather*, PL Sup. Ct. 20070511.

For instance, a party seeking damages has the burden of proving its entitlement to damages, and the amount of the damages. *Computer graphic cards*, CDN Trial. A party seeking to reduce the damages it must pay has the burden of proving that proper mitigation would have reduced its damages. That burden includes showing that any mitigation done by the aggrieved party was inadequate and demonstrating that there were other more favorable mitigations available that the aggrieved party unreasonably failed to use. *Iron molybdenum*, D App 19970228.

The rule that the party asserting something bears the burden of proof does not entirely answer the question. For instance, a breach is fundamental only if it substantially deprives a party of what he had expected to obtain under the contract and if such substantial deprivation was foreseeable. Substantial deprivation seems to be what the aggrieved party is asserting, but who is asserting foreseeability? *Coke*, ICC Arb 9187/1999 appears to assert that the party arguing that the consequences were not foreseeable is the one doing the asserting, but why is it not equally the responsibility of the party alleging fundamental breach to prove that it was foreseeable?

The distinction here seems to require the party seeking recovery under a general rule to prove the elements of that rule, while the party seeking exception must prove the elements of the exception. The problem with formulating the rule that way is that there is often no clear line between the rule and the exception. In the above example, is foreseeability part of the liability rule, or is nonforeseeability an exception?

§ 12.03 Burden of Proof on Conformity

In typical litigation, seller alleges that the goods conformed; buyer says they were nonconforming. Where seller sues buyer for the purchase price, seller normally establishes the existence of a contract and the delivery of the goods. Does seller need to prove that the goods conformed? If buyer sues for damages because the goods did not conform, does buyer need to prove the nonconformity?

One case held that the burden to prove nonconformity was on the person who asserted it, buyer, due to some unstated general principle of CISG, while discussing how similar that unstated general principle was to the UCC. The case is notable because the frozen meat passed from seller's supplier to buyer's customer without ever being in the possession of either party to the contract, and without either the supplier or the customer seriously examining the goods. *Chicago Prime Packers*, US App. One arbitrator refused to choose between the two theories, stating that both CISG and Dutch law put the burden of prov-ing nonconformity on a buyer resisting payment, *Rijn blend*, NL Arb 2319, 20021015, while another relied on both French law and "general principles of international trade." *Steel bars*, ICC 6653, 19930326.

Without explaining why, courts have held that the person alleging non-conformity has the burden of proving it, but need not prove the underlying technical reasons for the nonconformity. Where buyer alleged that seller's fab-ric did not satisfactorily take printing, proving the results of a test print was sufficient; buyer did not need to prove the science behind the failure to print. *Schmitz-Werke*, US App; *Laundry machine*, CH Sup. Ct. 20031113; *NZ mussels*, D Sup. Ct. 19950308.

Buyer seeking damages must not only prove nonconformity; she must also prove that she gave timely notice, and that the notice was sufficiently specific. *Vulcanized rubber*, I Trial 20000712. Buyer must retain enough of the goods that it can be determined whether the defect existed, and whether it was hid-den, which would extend the reasonable time within which buyer needs to give seller notice of nonconformity.

There is also the fact that many domestic legal systems place the burden of proof on the party who is likely to have superior knowledge of the facts that need to be established. CISG likewise tends to put the risk of loss on the party in possession or on the party who can best prove the loss.

§ 12.04 Burden of Proof on Derogation of CISG

Pizza cartons, D Trial 20000413, held that the burden of proof to establish that a rule of CISG did not apply is placed on the one who alleges it. Buyer alleged that normal CISG delivery rules did not apply because the parties had agreed on delivery to buyer's premises in Duisberg, but was unable to prove such an agreement.

§ 12.05 Statute of Limitations

There is general agreement that the statute of limitations is not a subject governed by CISG, either specifically or generally. In fact, there is a separate United Nations Convention that provides that actions must be brought within four years of delivery. *UN Limitations Conv.* arts. 8–12. It has only been ratified by 30 nations, a third of the number that have adhered to CISG, so its appli-cation is limited.

If the Limitations Convention does not apply, the question then becomes whether there is a general principle of CISG that applies. The existence of the Limitations Convention would argue against belief that the draftsmen intended a general principle to provide a statute of limitations.

If the Limitations Convention does not apply, conflict of laws rules generally point to the statute of limitations rule of the forum because that indicates the length of time after which the forum believes it cannot support a fair trial. Often this is simply justified on grounds that the forum follows its own procedural rules. This may create an opportunity for forum shopping if possible fora have limitations of different lengths. In *Steel*, CHN Arb 19971219, the Austrian statute was three years, the Chinese four. No forum shopping was possible because the contract contained an arbitration clause with a Chinese seat. The tribunal used the "closest connection" rule, and found that the statute of limitations has the closest connection to the place of arbitration, so used the longer Chinese statute.

§12.06 Weight of Evidence

CISG has no specific provisions on weighing evidence, nor does a general principle of CISG seem applicable. The rules of the forum on quantum of evidence required and its weighing apply. *Computer graphic cards*, CDN Trial.

CHECKPOINTS

You should have learned:

- The procedure in CISG cases is normally dictated by the law of the forum.
- CISG specifically places the burden of proof for excuse from paying damages due to an impediment on the person seeking the excuse.
- CISG does not speak specifically to the burden of proof in other situations.
- The party seeking recovery under a general rule has the burden of proving its elements, while a party seeking an exception to a general rule needs to prove the elements of the exception.
- The burden of proving nonconformity of goods is on the party alleging it.

- If the UN Limitations Convention applies, the statute of limitations is four years from delivery of the goods.
- If the UN Limitations Convention does not apply, the statute of limitations is determined by the choice of law rule of the forum, which usually points to forum law as procedural.

CHAPTER 13

Letters of Credit

ROADMAP

After reading this chapter, you should understand:

- The letter of credit is comparatively inexpensive and responds to seller's principal problem of not being paid, while being flexible enough to accommodate buyer's principal problem of paying but not receiving the goods ordered.

- Buyer asks her bank to issue an irrevocable letter of credit for the purchase price. Buyer's bank sends a communication to seller's bank promising to pay a fixed amount on presentation of named documents within a specified period. Seller's bank notifies seller that it has received the letter of credit. For payment, seller presents the specified documents to seller's bank and is paid. Seller's bank presents those documents to buyer's bank and is credited with the amount. Seller's bank pays seller.

- Buyer is only protected if one of the required documents is a certificate from a reputable inspector that the goods conform to the contract.

- The letter of credit transaction is not governed by CISG, but by domestic law and an international trade custom incorporated in the contract called Uniform Customs and Practices for Documentary Credit (UCP).

- The sales contract and the letter of credit are separate contracts. Breach of the sales contract is not a defense to a request for payment under the letter of credit.

- To compel payment, documents must strictly comply with the letter of credit. Strict compliance means that a reasonable bank examiner believes that the documents are genuine and refer to the same transaction in the manner called for by the letter of credit.

- Banks are usually insulated from liability in letter of credit transactions if they act in good faith.

- A court may temporarily enjoin the payment of a letter of credit if a material document is forged, materially fraudulent, or payment of the letter of credit would facilitate a material fraud by the beneficiary on the issuer or the applicant. An injunction will not issue unless the remedy at law is inadequate and buyer is likely to prevail at trial. A court will not enjoin payment to a holder in due course.

§13.01 Reasons for Use

Payment for international sales transactions is often by letter of credit. The letter of credit transaction is comparatively inexpensive, and responds to seller's principal problem, while being flexible enough to accommodate buyer's principal problem. Letters of credit typically cost under 2% of the face amount, which is less than most currency conversion charges or amounts taken by banks from merchants for credit card charges.

Seller's risk is that seller may not be paid, and may either lose control of the goods, or be unable to fully realize their value because they are located in a foreign country. Seller, when first dealing with a new international customer, is in a less advantageous position than when dealing domestically. Seller is more likely to have information about the creditworthiness and willingness to pay of a domestic customer. There are no currency conversion problems. To reduce seller's risk of nonpayment, the letter of credit transaction enlists two banks, and faith in documents. Here is how it works.

Buyer goes to buyer's bank and asks her bank to issue an irrevocable letter of credit. The letter of credit is a promise by buyer's bank that if it is presented specific documents by a set date, it will pay a fixed amount. Buyer's bank may require buyer to deposit the amount of the letter of credit with it, or may in essence make a loan to buyer of the amount on the letter of credit, with whatever interest and repayment terms are agreeable.

Seller, however, not only has little knowledge of buyer, but also has no relationship with buyer's bank. Seller has seller's regular bank. Buyer's bank sends the letter of credit to seller's bank, promising to pay the amount on the letter of credit against the documents required by it. Seller's bank in turn tells seller that if he gives it the required documents, the bank will deposit the indicated amount in seller's account. That is a promise that seller values because of his relationship with his bank and its apparent solvency.

Buyer's fear in this international sale is that she will not receive the goods that she has ordered. Nothing in the above assuages that fear. It can be minimized by the documents required. Those documents always include a commercial invoice and a document proving that something has been shipped and that permits buyer to collect the shipment. Required documents will include any documents, such as certificates of origin, that will enable customs to be cleared. Buyer should also require an inspection certificate from a reliable inspector certifying that the goods conform to the contract and are in good condition when the risk of loss passes.

The requirement of all these documents needs to be specified in the contract of sale, and will also be specified in the letter of credit.

Thus, the risk of two strangers dealing with each other is broken up into three trusted relationships: buyer trusts her bank and the inspector; buyer's bank and seller's bank deal with each other repeatedly and trust each other; and seller trusts his bank.

While this substantially reduces the risks on both sides, it does not eliminate them. Buyer remains at risk that the inspector might be bribed or negligent, or that the documents might be forged. Seller takes the risk that the people preparing the documents, who have probably not been to law school and speak a different language from that of the letter of credit, may give him documents that do not conform to the requirements of the letter of credit. However, the fact that letters of credit are available comparatively inexpensively testifies that the system works well most of the time.

§ 13.02 Law Governing Letters of Credit

There is not much law on the subject. The most comprehensive national law is Uniform Commercial Code (UCC) art. 5.

Not much law is needed, because most letters of credit specify that they are governed by the Uniform Customs and Practice for Documentary Credit (UCP), revised by the International Chamber of Commerce in Paris (ICC), and interpreted periodically by the ICC Banking Commission. Even when not specifically referred to in the letter of credit, courts sometimes apply the UCP where relevant as international trade custom. Where the UCP applies, it displaces contrary provisions of the UCC, so §5-108(b)'s seven-business-day limit for notification of dishonor is displaced by UCP art. 16d's five-business-day limit.

A fundamental principle of letter of credit law is that the letter of credit is a separate and independent contract from the underlying sales contract. One of the results is that CISG may apply to the sales contract, but it never governs the letter of credit because the letter of credit is not a sales contract.

§13.03 Conformity of Documents

The general rule is that the documents must strictly comply with the letter of credit. When documents conform, the bank must pay. When the documents do not conform, the bank may refuse to pay, but it may consult the applicant to ask for a waiver of the discrepancies. The bank has five business days to determine conformity and notify the presenter. If the bank refuses to pay, it must give a single notice to the person who presented the documents explaining the nonconformity and return the documents to the presenter. Otherwise, the bank must pay. Data in the documents do not necessarily make the documents nonconforming as long as the data is not inconsistent with the credit. UCP arts. 14a, b, d, e, 15, 16a, b, c, f.

The long-time leading case was *J.H. Rayner*, UK Trial, where the credit called for "Coromandel groundnuts," but the bills of lading were for "machine-shelled groundnut kernels." The bank refused payment. The presenter argued that anyone in the trade would know that these two descriptions were the same, but the court held that the bank was not obligated to know the terms used in every trade for which it issued letters of credit. But times change, and in *Voest-Alpine Trading*, US App, the court ordered payment despite seven alleged nonconformities. It read the UCP's consistency requirement to reject the mirror-image test in *J.H. Rayner*, and to call for a commonsense answer to the question of whether all the documents relate to the same transaction. It then held that various small errors, such as an incorrect letter of credit number or misspelling the name of the port or failing to stamp all copies of the packing list as originals would not have led the reasonable bank examiner to believe that they related to other transactions because those errors were nonsensical read literally. The exercise required by the *J.H. Rayner* court is mechanical; the *Voest-Alpine* court requires the bank examiner to exercise judgment. One of the reasons for the shift may be the general tendency to dispense with formalities, especially as these cases usually arise when there has been a price shift in the goods unfavorable to buyer between the signing of the contract and the presentation of the documents. The best statement of the current rule is that strict compliance means that a reasonable bank examiner believes that the documents are genuine and refer to the same transaction in the manner called for by the letter of credit. But even a one letter misspelling of a name on the bill of lading may justify refusal to pay where it is not an obvious mistake. *Bayenne*, US App.

§ 13.04 Responsibility of Banks

One reason the cost of letters of credit is so low is that the law highly favors banks. UCC § 5-116(b) provides that banks are governed by the law of the jurisdiction in which they are located. That means that a controversy between a bank and its customer is governed by the law of the bank's jurisdiction. That will often also be the customer's jurisdiction.

A bank's responsibility is to pay a letter of credit accompanied by conforming documents and to not pay it if conforming documents are not presented.

Banks are further insulated from liability when they "observe standard practice of financial institutions that regularly issue letters of credit," UCC § 5-108, and when they act in good faith, UCC § 5-109(a)(2). Banks are also not liable for transmission or translation errors. UCP art. 35.

Curiously, in a controversy between two banks, each bank is governed by the law of its jurisdiction. If the laws of the two jurisdictions do not agree on a crucial point in dispute, it is entirely possible that the controversy cannot be resolved because the two parties are governed by different laws. Because banks are repeat players with each other, most disputes between banks are solved by negotiation. But it is easy to imagine a conflict where seller's bank believes the documents comply and pays seller, while buyer's bank believes that they do not comply and refuses to reimburse seller's bank.

§ 13.05 Enjoining Payment of a Letter of Credit

While the sales contract and the letter of credit agreement are two separate and independent obligations, there is a tiny crack where they come together. The problem arises because there is often a long period between seller's delivery of the goods and buyer's receipt of them, at which time buyer may discover that she has not received what she was promised. Ordinarily, buyer is stuck with a breach of contract action. Buyer can ask her bank to refuse or delay payment on the letter of credit, but the bank is unlikely to risk liability when presented with apparently complying documents. The most buyer is likely to get from the bank is an agreement to delay a decision until the end of the five-business-day limit.

However, buyer may secure an injunction from a court preventing the payment of the letter of credit if a number of conditions are met. The injunction will not issue unless a material document is forged, materially fraudulent, or payment of the letter of credit would facilitate a material fraud by the beneficiary on the issuer or the applicant. If one of those applies, buyer also needs to prove that persons who may be affected by the lack of payment are adequately protected against loss, which probably means depositing the money in court; that normal requirements for an injunction are met, such as inadequacy of the remedy at law and the balance of hardships; that the person who will present the documents is not a protected person, such as a holder in due course; and that buyer is more likely than not to succeed in its claim of forgery or material fraud. Those are many requirements to fulfill in a very short period always under the threat that the seller will negotiate his rights under the letter of credit to a holder in due course before an injunction can issue. UCC §5-109(b).

The requirement that a material document be forged or materially fraudulent is perfectly consistent with the independence of the contract of sale from the letter of credit contract. The document is part of the letter of credit contract. Courts have further constricted the availability of an injunction by requiring that the beneficiary be involved in the forgery or fraud, or at least know of it. *Montrod*, UK App.

By contrast, the requirement that payment of the letter of credit would facilitate a material fraud by the beneficiary on the applicant blurs the distinction between the two contracts, and permits an injunction against paying the letter of credit based on fraud in the underlying contract. The difficulty is in distinguishing fraud from breach of contract. The leading case declared that fraud was not enough. It must be fraud that "so vitiated the entire transaction that the legitimate purposes of the independence of the issuer's obligation can no longer be served." *Mid-America Tire*, US App. The court held that this standard was met where seller, to induce buyer to purchase winter tires, told buyer that seller was the sole distributor for surplus Michelin tires and that it would make available a substantial quantity of summer tires at a significant discount, none of which was true. Seller knew that the summer tire deal was required for the sale of the winter tires, and also knew that the winter tires could not be imported into the U.S. The court noted that with a letter of credit, normally the remedy at law, damages, is adequate, but damages would be inadequate where seller was insolvent or likely to abscond with the funds, where the payment without receiving countervailing value might force buyer into bankruptcy, or where assessing damages would be speculative.

Even if all the above requirements are met, the claimant may be a protected party like a holder in due course. This may involve technical questions of negotiable instruments law, as demonstrated in *Banco de Santander*, UK App.

CHECKPOINTS

You should have learned that:

- The letter of credit is comparatively inexpensive and responds to seller's principal problem of not being paid, while being flexible enough to accommodate buyer's principal problem of paying but not receiving the goods ordered.

- Buyer asks her bank to issue an irrevocable letter of credit for the purchase price. Buyer's bank sends a communication to seller's bank promising to pay a fixed amount on presentation of named documents within a specified period. Seller's bank notifies seller that it has received the letter of credit. For payment, seller presents the specified documents to seller's bank and is paid. Seller's bank presents those documents to buyer's bank and is credited with the amount. Seller's bank pays seller.

- Buyer is only protected if one of the required documents is a certificate from a reputable inspector that the goods conform to the contract.

- The letter of credit transaction is not governed by CISG, but by domestic law and an international trade custom incorporated in the contract called Uniform Customs and Practices for Documentary Credit (UCP).

- The sales contract and the letter of credit are separate contracts. Breach of the sales contract is not a defense to a request for payment under the letter of credit.

- To compel payment, documents must strictly comply with the letter of credit. Strict compliance means that a reasonable bank examiner believes that the documents are genuine and refer to the same transaction in the manner called for by the letter of credit.

- Banks are usually insulated from liability in letter of credit transactions if they act in good faith.

- A court may temporarily enjoin the payment of a letter of credit if a material document is forged, materially fraudulent, or payment of the letter of credit would facilitate a material fraud by the beneficiary on the issuer or the applicant. An injunction will not issue unless the remedy at law is inadequate and buyer is likely to prevail at trial. A court will not enjoin payment to a holder in due course.

CHAPTER 14

U.S. Income Tax Considerations

ROADMAP

After reading this chapter, you should understand:

- Income tax considerations may influence whether a sale of goods takes place and are likely to influence its form.
- The U.S. taxes the worldwide income of its citizens, residents, and corporations.
- To relieve double taxation on foreign income that is taxed abroad, the U.S. grants a foreign tax credit for foreign income taxes paid.
- The foreign tax credit is limited to the percentage of U.S. income tax due that taxpayer's foreign source taxable income bears to taxpayer's total taxable income.
- Income from the manufacture and sale of goods is sourced at the place of manufacture.
- Income from the purchase and sale of goods is sourced at the place where title to the goods passes.
- By changing the place where delivery occurs, the parties can change income from the purchase and sale of goods from U.S. source to foreign source, thereby increasing taxpayer's potential foreign tax credit.
- Changing the source of income from U.S. source to foreign source may also be advantageous to a nonresident alien or foreign corporation.
- Tax treaties allocate taxing rights between the parties who sign the treaty. Generally, source countries may tax business income only if taxpayer has significant economic activity there. Investment income

is either exempt or lightly taxed in the source country, reserving most taxing rights to the residence country.

- In addition to the above, special rules apply when buyer and seller are related parties, either as parent and subsidiary, or as commonly owned entities. The first rule is that related parties will not be recognized as separate entities unless they have substantive business activities and are not lifeless facades.

- Sales between related parties must be at arm's length prices. For the sale of goods, an arm's length price may be determined by the most accurate of six methods: comparable uncontrolled price, resale price, cost-plus, comparable profits, profit split, or another reasonably persuasive method.

- In addition, certain income of controlled foreign corporations is taxed currently to its U.S. shareholders.

- A controlled foreign corporation is a non-U.S. corporation more than 50% of whose stock is owned by no more than five U.S. citizens, residents, or corporations, each of whom owns at least 10% of the corporation's stock.

- Foreign base company sales income is one form of a controlled foreign corporation's income that is taxed currently to its shareholders. Foreign base company sales income does not include income from the manufacture of goods by the corporation.

§ 14.01 Introduction

The fact that income taxes must be paid as a result of a sale of goods may occasionally determine whether the sale will take place. It will much more frequently affect the manner in which the sale occurs. Usually, buyer is not subject to income tax on the sale unless located in a country that taxes an advantageous purchase. The tax consequences of the sale are normally the concern of seller. However, buyer might be able to induce seller to share some of his tax savings if buyer agrees to restructure the transaction.

Recent statistics show that about 40% of U.S. import and export transactions are between parties who are related to each other, such as between a parent corporation and a subsidiary corporation, or between two entities owned beneficially by the same persons. One set of tax rules applies to transactions between independent parties. Those same rules, plus additional rules, apply to sales between related parties.

A. Sales between Unrelated Parties

§ 14.11 General U.S. Income Tax Rules for International Sales

A U.S. citizen, resident or corporation is subject to U.S. income tax on all income, regardless of where earned. They are taxed based on their status.

A foreign corporation or a nonresident alien pays U.S. income tax when it derives income from the U.S. It is taxed only on fixed and determinable annual and periodic income (FDAPI), certain gains from U.S. sources, and income effectively connected to a trade or business in the U.S. That requires rules to place income in each of those categories, and source rules to locate the income either within or outside the U.S. These taxpayers are taxed based on their activity, which is called source taxation.

Where the U.S. taxes income earned abroad based on status, double taxation may result if that income is also taxed in the country where it is earned. These cases where a domestic taxpayer has foreign income are "outbound transactions." Relief from double taxation is mostly provided by giving the taxpayer a credit for foreign income taxes paid. The taxpayer in theory pays an effective tax rate equal to either the foreign rate or the U.S. rate, whichever is greater. Achieving this is much easier said than done.

Taxation of foreign corporations and nonresident aliens, called "inbound transactions," pose different problems for the U.S. There are situations where the income's contact with the U.S. is so attenuated that the nuisance of the tax outweighs its imposition, even though the U.S. is the source of the income. That is distinguished from cases where the substantial economic penetration of the U.S. calls for U.S. tax. Relief of double taxation is left to the discretion of the foreign government that taxes this income on the basis of taxpayer's status.

Provisions for income from abroad or for foreign taxpayers are not an integral part of the system. One can best think of the U.S. system as having a base of provisions for purely domestic transactions and taxpayers. Overlying that system is a series of corrective rules that apply when the income or the taxpayer is foreign, those rules generally being designed to relieve double taxation and prevent avoidance of tax; overlying that system for residents of the roughly 40 foreign countries with which the U.S. has tax treaties are the rules embodied in the treaties that the taxpayer may elect if they are more favorable.

Adding foreign taxpayers and foreign income to the system creates significant administrative problems. These problems cover the gamut of the taxing system from audit to collection and presentation of proof to securing effective collection of the tax, once determined. These difficulties have resulted in special provisions that are beyond the scope of this book.

§14.12 Why Are Source Rules Important to Sales?

Source rules apply to both inbound and outbound transactions. There are only a few differences in the rules. Their application to the same transaction may benefit one taxpayer and disadvantage a related taxpayer, or one taxpayer may be both advantaged and disadvantaged by the same rule in different transactions.

Source rules are important for two reasons. They limit the ability of the U.S. to tax foreign corporations and nonresident aliens (foreign taxpayers). They are also important to U.S. persons with foreign income because they form the basis for computing the limitation on the foreign tax credit. In both cases, taxpayers try to increase their foreign source income and decrease their foreign source deductions on the assumption, generally true before 2018, that U.S. income tax will exceed foreign tax.

§14.13 The Foreign Tax Credit

The foreign tax credit is the primary U.S. device for relieving double taxation. A U.S. person can credit foreign income taxes paid up to the amount of his U.S. tax on his foreign source income.

A system where any French income tax would be credited against U.S. tax would make the taxpayer indifferent to the amount of French taxes paid as long as they did not exceed the U.S. tax. Such a system would enrich France at the expense of the U.S. To avoid this, a limit was placed on the foreign tax credit to assure that the credit only offset U.S. tax on foreign source income. Also, many taxpayers have income from numerous jurisdictions, some of which tax different kinds of income, like business income, personal service income, or investment income, at differing rates. Taxpayers tried to blend their income so the foreign tax credit from high tax income would soak up the limitation otherwise unused because some income is minimally taxed by the foreign country, often because of limits in income tax treaties.

The device that prevents the credit of foreign tax paid on one form of income against U.S. tax on another form of income is the foreign tax credit limitation. This is a simple concept with complicated execution. The maximum foreign tax that could be credited was the U.S. tax multiplied by a fraction: the numerator is foreign source income and the denominator is total income. The U.S. tax is deemed ratably applied to all income. Assume foreign income of $100, foreign taxes of $33, and U.S. income of $200. The tentative U.S. tax on $300 at 21% is $63. The foreign income tax paid is $33, but the limitation is $21: U.S. tax $63 x foreign source income $100/total income $300, so taxpayer pays $33 to the foreign state and $42 ($63–$21) to the US

This results in foreign tax of $12 that cannot be credited.

But suppose taxpayer can shift $100 of the U.S. source income to a foreign country without paying additional foreign tax. After the shift, the result is no change in initial U.S. tax liability, no change in foreign tax, but taxpayer now has two-thirds of his income from foreign sources ($200/$300). The foreign tax credit limitation is now $42, so all of the $33 foreign tax paid can be credited. Taxpayer pays $33 to the foreign state plus $21 ($63–$42) to the U.S.

In reality, the situation is much more complicated, but that explains enough for our purposes. The point is that seller usually wants to turn as much U.S. source income into foreign source income as he can without incurring significantly more foreign income tax. To do that, he uses the source rules.

§14.14 Source Rules for the Sale of Goods

Two different provisions determine source rules. One is for goods made by the taxpayer; the other is for goods taxpayer buys and sells.

Income from the manufacture and sale of goods made by seller is sourced where the goods are made. Goods are made where the assets owned by taxpayer used to make the goods are located. If taxpayer's only manufacturing plant is in the U.S., all income from selling goods made there would be from U.S. sources. This encourages U.S. manufacturers to locate their plants in low-tax foreign countries. If making the goods requires skills that are only available in the U.S., it encourages the manufacturer to place the steps it can offshore. In some industries, preparation of the goods is done in the U.S., and assembly is done abroad. If there are production assets both in the U.S. and abroad, the rule encourages manufacturers to use leased plant and intellectual property in the U.S., and owned assets abroad, because only owned assets count in making the allocation. *26 U.S.C. §863(b), 26 C.F.R. §§1.863-1(b), 1.863-3(c).*

For the trader who buys and sells goods, the source is where the sale takes place. *26 U.S.C. §§861(a)(6), 862(a)(6).* "A sale of personal property is consummated at the time when, and the place where, the rights, title and interest of the seller in the property are transferred to the buyer." *26 C.F.R. §1.861-7(c).* That means that the parties to the sales contract can change the tax source of resale income by contract. Specifically, by changing the selection of the incoterm used from fob (free on board) or cif (cost insurance freight) to ddu (delivered duty unpaid) or ddp (delivered duty paid) the parties can change the source of sales income from U.S. source to foreign source.

The regulation adds that when the place of risk passage is arranged primarily for tax avoidance purposes, a multifactor test will be used. Consequently, in arranging the passage of risk, seller should be prepared to present good business reasons for the choice of the place where rights pass. In *Liggett Group*, US Trial, taxpayer bought J&B Scotch in London fob and resold it to American wholesalers fob UK. In fact, the whiskey was delivered directly by J&B to the ships designated by taxpayer's customers without being touched by taxpayer because taxpayer had no employees in the UK. For reasons unknown, IRS stipulated that the sales format was not arranged primarily for tax avoidance purposes, and the court confirmed that taxpayer's income from these sales was sourced outside the U.S. It mentioned in passing valid business reasons for the arrangement where customers directed the whiskey to bonded warehouses. Customers could time the payment of customs and excise taxes by deciding when to withdraw the whiskey from the bonded warehouses, yet had the whiskey where it could be accessed quickly; and by arranging its own import, it avoided handling charges that otherwise would have been imposed by taxpayer. The procedure reduced taxpayer's overhead and simplified its operations because it did not need to insure the whiskey or pay freight or storage charges, and that permitted taxpayer to charge lower prices (though there was no evidence that as J&B's exclusive U.S. dealer, it ever did charge lower prices).

§14.15 The Role of Income Tax Treaties

Useful though this was, it would not have been undertaken had it exposed Liggett to the much higher income taxes prevailing at the time in the UK. Income tax treaties allocate taxing jurisdiction between most of the world's major trading partners. Generally, the country that is the source of the income receives the first right to tax, and the residence country is left to provide relief from double taxation. That first right to tax at source is limited to situations where taxpayer has sufficient economic penetration of the host country to justify the trouble. Standard provisions in U.S. income tax treaties say that business profits are taxable in a country only if the person earning the income has a permanent establishment there. A permanent establishment means a fixed place of business through which the business of an enterprise is carried on, such as an office, factory, mine, or a dependent agent, none of which Liggett had in England. *Convention US-UK.* As a result, Liggett paid no English income tax on these sales.

B. Controlled Sales

§ 14.21 Special Tax Provisions for Controlled Sales

Congress has constructed a series of special tax provisions applicable to transactions between related entities. They include rules relating to transfer pricing, controlled foreign corporation inclusions, export tax benefits, foreign investment companies, passive foreign investment companies, foreign personal holding companies, international boycotts, and foreign trusts. Each area is much too complicated to be treated in depth in a book on international sales contracts. Here is a small taste of the sorts of rules encountered in controlled sales on transfer pricing, with the warning that there is much more detail with which counsel should be concerned.

To illustrate, consider this problem adapted from material prepared by the late David Tillinghast, Assistant Secretary of the Treasury. Your client is CleanAir, a U.S. corporation that has successfully installed pollution monitoring and scrubbing equipment in U.S. industries. It contemplates entering the European market by establishing a wholly owned subsidiary in a European country. Its main competitive asset is the know-how of its staff in combining its monitors, scrubbers, and bought parts with its clients' manufacturing processes. The sub will sell pollution control systems to its European customers consisting of scrubbers made in the U.S., monitors assembled in Europe whose component parts are sold to it by CleanAir, and numerous other parts that the sub will buy on the open market. The monitors will be assembled with the help of specialized machinery to be built and sold to the sub by CleanAir. The assembled monitors will also be sold to unrelated parties in Europe. CleanAir currently sells the scrubbers wholesale in the U.S. It does not sell the monitors. CleanAir will furnish the sub with an extensive staff in both production and marketing, as well as a chief executive, though it will try to train and hire Europeans for those jobs as quickly as possible. It estimates that the subsidiary will need about $8 million for a plant and $4 million for working capital for three years. CleanAir's sub can borrow $6 million from European banks, repayable in years 4–7, and $4 million from CleanAir's U.S. bank, repayable in 10 years, both with CleanAir's guarantee. It intends to supply the other $2 million from its own funds.

§14.22 Existence of the Foreign Corporation

The first hurdle CleanAir might face is to establish that the foreign subsidiary exists. If it is disregarded by the tax authorities, its income belongs to its parent and is taxed by the U.S. as earned. The question is whether the corporation is a viable business concern or a lifeless facade. When a wealthy Texas oil executive established a Swiss corporation that dealt in working interests in oil and gas leases that someone else worked, the court decided that it was a viable business concern even though everything it did could be (and probably was) done by its Swiss lawyer without leaving his office. It involved buying and selling oil interests, paying obligations, signing contracts, and maintaining bank accounts and books separate from its shareholder. *Perry R. Bass*, US Trial. Compared to that, CleanAir's sub will have a great deal of activity.

§14.23 Transfer Pricing—General Rule

Even if CleanAir's European subsidiary exists, all of its income may be taxed to its parent. When related parties deal with each other, the tax consequences should reflect reality and not permit the enterprise to arrange its affairs so that it pays the least amount of income tax. The solution has been the arm's length price. A transaction between related parties can be revalued at the price at which two unrelated parties would have engaged in the same transaction. Easy to say, not so easy to do. *26 U.S.C. §482* gives broad discretion to IRS to "...allocate gross income, deductions, credits or allowances between or among such [related parties if he determines that such] allocation is necessary in order ...clearly to reflect the income of any such [related parties]."

All the transactions between CleanAir and its subsidiary invoke transfer pricing problems. We will not deal with the problems related to the provision of employees, capital, the corporate name, the loan guarantee, or the intellectual property—only the sale of the scrubbers, monitor parts and the specialized manufacturing equipment, because they are "goods."

§14.24 Transfer Pricing for the Sale of Tangible Personal Property

26 C.F.R. §1.482-3 states that to determine an arm's length charge, one should examine six pricing methods and determine which is the best (most accurate) method. Those methods are comparable uncontrolled price, resale price, cost plus, comparable profits, profit split, and unspecified methods.

§14.25 Transfer Pricing—Comparable Uncontrolled Price

The comparable uncontrolled price method asks what price prevails for the same goods under the same market conditions between unrelated parties. Taking our three products, CleanAir sells the scrubbers to uncontrolled buyers, but not the monitor parts or the manufacturing equipment. So the scrubbers might use the comparable uncontrolled price method, especially since the product is identical. But is the market identical, or even comparable? U.S. sales are to wholesalers, whereas the sub will be an installer. Are the quantities sold similar? Is the competitive market in the U.S. similar to the European market? Are the terms of the sales comparable?

If there are differences, the comparable uncontrolled price method may still be the best method if those differences can be reliably accounted for by adjusting the price.

There are some inherent differences between uncontrolled sales and controlled sales that need not be accounted for, as least not yet. These are costs and risks that exist in uncontrolled sales, but do not exist in sales to controlled entities. One is that seller need not expend money on advertising or other marketing costs. A second is that unless the related party is in financial trouble, there is no need for a reserve for bad debts or an allowance for attorney's fees to collect the purchase price, because the related party will pay. A third is that whenever one sells a product, one runs the risk that the buyer will reverse engineer it and begin producing the product itself, even though its production may involve patents. That risk does not exist with sales to a controlled entity.

§ 14.26 Transfer Pricing—Resale Price Method

The resale price method is most useful when one party sells goods to a related party, who resells the goods without significant change to an unrelated party. Minor assembly is not considered to be significant change. One works back from the price at which the goods are resold to an unrelated party by subtracting from it an appropriate markup.

It appears that the monitor parts qualify because the completed monitor is not significantly changed from the part sold by CleanAir. One would need to make adjustments for the additional parts, labor, and machinery use. Is the resale otherwise comparable to the purchase? It appears that the purchase is in bulk. Some of the goods are used for clients, others are sold to unrelated parties, probably in much smaller quantities.

Once appropriate adjustments are made, how does one determine the appropriate markup? Profit margins of specific products are not usually made public by companies. The U.S. Department of Commerce collects a great deal of information about businesses, and may even publish average data about profit margins, but those averages may conceal significant differences.

§ 14.27 Transfer Pricing—Cost Plus

The machinery to be sold by CleanAir to its sub cannot be valued using comparable uncontrolled sales, because there are no sales. It also cannot use resale price, because there is no resale. The subsidiary will use the machinery in its manufacturing process. The machinery sale seems amenable to the cost plus method. This method takes seller's cost of buying or producing the item and adds to it an appropriate markup for what seller adds to the goods.

One might make the same comments about the difficulty of determining profit margins here as for the resale profits method.

§ 14.28 Transfer Pricing—Comparable Profits

The comparable profit method does not look at the price of the goods sold. Instead, it looks at the profit made on similar goods sold by similar companies to unrelated parties. It considers such financial figures as rate of return on capital employed, ratio between profit and cost, or ratio between profit and sales revenue. Again, one of the problems with this method is obtaining reliable data about unrelated sales at the level of individual products, especially when those products are unique.

§14.29 Transfer Pricing—Profit Split

The profit split method begins with the total profit achieved on the transaction by the related parties. It asks whether the way that profit has been divided between the related entities reflects the relative economic contributions of the entities. As this information is not likely to be available at the individual product level, it uses data for the most narrowly defined business activity that includes the related transactions. The advantage of this method is that the data needed is available to the enterprise.

§14.30 Other Methods

Any other method that is reasonably persuasive might be used. For instance, when a similar offer is received from an unrelated third party, that might be evidence of an arm's length price.

§14.31 Controlled Foreign Corporations in General

Because a foreign corporation is not taxed on its income from foreign sources, and a U.S. person is only taxed on income from a foreign corporation when received, many U.S. businesses were using foreign related corporations as banks to finance operations outside the U.S. and paying no U.S. income tax on the earnings of those foreign corporations. Treasury proposed to tax the earnings of controlled foreign corporations as it was earned. Congress agreed, but only by half.

A controlled foreign corporation is a foreign corporation more than half of whose stock is owned directly or indirectly by U.S. persons, each of whom owns at least 10% of the corporation's stock. *26 U.S.C. §§951, 957.*

The compromise to which Congress agreed was to tax currently income for which it thought the use of a foreign corporation was unnecessary, which it called subpart F income. It lumped into that category most investment income, and some income from active businesses where related parties were involved. The income with which we are concerned is foreign base company sales income.

§14.32 Foreign Base Company Sales Income

Foreign base company sales income (FBCSI) is subpart F income that will be taxed currently to the U.S. shareholders of a controlled foreign corporation (CFC).

FBCSI begins as income from sales involving related parties. The CFC may be either buyer or seller or both. Also, the goods must be used and made outside the country in which the corporation is incorporated. So if CleanAir establishes a CFC in Switzerland and the CFC sells pollution control systems in Switzerland, that is not FBCSI. That is because there is a good business reason to establish a subsidiary corporation in the country in which it sells goods. Likewise if the CFC is set up in the country where the goods are made.

In addition, if the corporation itself substantially transforms the goods, its income is not FBCSI, presumably because the company is engaging in substantial business activity. *26 U.S.C. §954.* Regulations provide a safe harbor, that the goods are substantially transformed if the conversion costs exceed 20% of the total cost of the goods. Even if the 20% test is not met, one can still argue that what the corporation did was substantial transformation. Taxpayer did just that in *Dave Fischbein*, US Trial, where taxpayer's controlled foreign corporation used 283 parts mostly bought from taxpayer to put together its bag-closing machinery in 58 steps over six hours. While the first task in most litigation is to keep the judge awake, the prime goal in this case was to put the judge to sleep. By going into excruciating detail about each part used and each step in the process, the judge would be convinced that the totality of the foreign corporation's work was substantial transformation. Counsel succeeded.

There is much more to FBCSI and all the above tax provisions. This book only presents a taste of what a skilled international tax lawyer can do.

CHECKPOINTS

You should have learned that:

- Income tax considerations may influence whether a sale of goods takes place and is likely to influence its form.
- The U.S. taxes the worldwide income of its citizens, residents, and corporations.

- To relieve double taxation on foreign income that is taxed abroad, the U.S. grants a foreign tax credit for foreign income taxes paid.

- The foreign tax credit is limited to the percentage of U.S. income tax due that taxpayer's foreign source taxable income bears to taxpayer's total taxable income.

- Income from the manufacture and sale of goods is sourced at the place of manufacture.

- Income from the purchase and sale of goods is sourced at the place where title to the goods passes.

- By changing the place where delivery occurs, the parties can change income from the purchase and sale of goods from U.S. source to foreign source, thereby increasing taxpayer's potential foreign tax credit.

- Changing the source of income from U.S. source to foreign source may also be advantageous to a nonresident alien or foreign corporation.

- Tax treaties allocate taxing rights between the parties who sign the treaty. Generally, source countries may tax business income only if taxpayer has significant economic activity there. Investment income is either exempt or lightly taxed in the source country, reserving most taxing rights to the residence country.

- In addition to the above, special rules apply when buyer and seller are related parties, either as parent and subsidiary or as commonly owned entities. The first rule is that related parties will not be recognized as separate entities unless they have substantive business activities and are not lifeless facades.

- Sales between related parties must be at arm's length prices. For the sale of goods, an arm's length price may be determined by the most accurate of six methods: comparable uncontrolled price, resale price, cost-plus, comparable profits, profit split, or another reasonably persuasive method.

- In addition, certain income of controlled foreign corporations is taxed currently to its U.S. shareholders.

- A controlled foreign corporation is a non-U.S. corporation more than 50% of whose stock is owned by no more than five U.S. citizens, residents, or corporations, each of whom owns at least 10% of the corporation's stock.

- Foreign base company sales income is one form of a controlled foreign corporation's income that is taxed currently to its shareholders. Foreign base company sales income does not include income from the manufacture of goods by the corporation.

United Nations Convention on Contracts for the International Sale of Goods (1980)

[On 8/1/2022, the following 95 countries are CISG Contracting States: Albania, Argentina, Armenia, Australia, Austria, Azerbaijan, Bahrain, Belarus, Belgium, Benin, Bosnia & Herzegovina, Brazil, Bulgaria, Burundi, Cameroon, Canada, Chile, China, Colombia, Congo, Costa Rica, Croatia, Cuba, Cyprus, Czechia, Denmark, Dominican Republic, Ecuador, Egypt, El Salvador, Estonia, Fiji, Finland, France, Gabon, Georgia, Germany, Ghana, Greece, Guinea, Guatemala, Guyana, Honduras, Hungary, Iceland, Iraq, Israel, Italy, Japan, Korea (both), Kyrgyzstan, Lao, Latvia, Lebanon, Lesotho, Liberia, Liechtenstein, Lithuania, Luxembourg, Macedonia, Madagascar, Mauritania, Mexico, Moldova, Mongolia, Montenegro, Netherlands, New Zealand, Norway, Palestine, Paraguay, Peru, Poland, Portugal, Romania, Russian Federation, St. Vincent & the Grenadines, San Marino, Serbia, Singapore, Slovakia, Slovenia, Spain, Sweden, Switzerland, Syria, Turkey, Turkmenistan, Uganda, Ukraine, U.S.A., Uruguay, Uzbekistan, Viet Nam and Zambia. In the United States, CISG has been considered a self-executing treaty, so no federal legislation was enacted to put it in force.]

THE STATES PARTIES TO THIS CONVENTION

BEARING IN MIND the broad objectives in the resolutions adopted by the sixth special session of the General Assembly of the United Nations on the establishment of a New International Economic Order,

CONSIDERING that the development of international trade on the basis of equality and mutual benefit is an important element in promoting friendly relations among States,

BEING OF THE OPINION that the adoption of uniform rules which govern contracts for the international sale of goods and take into account the different social, economic and legal systems would contribute to the removal of legal barriers in international trade and promote the development of international trade,

HAVE AGREED as follows:

PART I. SPHERE OF APPLICATION AND GENERAL PROVISIONS

CHAPTER I. SPHERE OF APPLICATION

Article 1 (1) This Convention applies to contracts of sale of goods between parties whose places of business are in different States:

(a) when the States are Contracting States; or

(b) when the rules of private international law lead to the application of the law of a Contracting State.

(2) The fact that the parties have their places of business in different States is to be disregarded whenever this fact does not appear either from the contract or from any dealings between, or from information disclosed by, the parties at any time before or at the conclusion of the contract.

(3) Neither the nationality of the parties nor the civil or commercial character of the parties or of the contract is to be taken into consideration in determining the application of this Convention.

Article 2 This Convention does not apply to sales:

(a) of goods bought for personal, family or household use, unless the seller, at any time before or at the conclusion of the contract, neither knew nor ought to have known that the goods were bought for any such use;

(b) by auction;

(c) on execution or otherwise by authority of law;

(d) of stocks, shares, investment securities, negotiable instruments or money;

(e) of ships, vessels, hovercraft or aircraft;

(f) of electricity.

Article 3 (1) Contracts for the supply of goods to be manufactured or produced are to be considered sales unless the party who orders the goods undertakes to supply a substantial part of the materials necessary for such manufacture or production.

(2) This Convention does not apply to contracts in which the preponderant part of the obligations of the party who furnishes the goods consists in the supply of labour or other services.

Article 4 This Convention governs only the formation of the contract of sale and the rights and obligations of the seller and the buyer arising from such a contract. In particular, except as otherwise expressly provided in this Convention, it is not concerned with:

(a) the validity of the contract or of any of its provisions or of any usage;

(b) the effect which the contract may have on the property in the goods sold.

Article 5 This Convention does not apply to the liability of the seller for death or personal injury caused by the goods to any person.

Article 6 The parties may exclude the application of this Convention or, subject to article 12, derogate from or vary the effect of any of its provisions.

CHAPTER II. GENERAL PROVISIONS

Article 7 (1) In the interpretation of this Convention, regard is to be had to its international character and to the need to promote uniformity in its application and the observance of good faith in international trade.

(2) Questions concerning matters governed by this Convention which are not expressly settled in it are to be settled in conformity with the general principles on which it is based or, in the absence of such principles, in conformity with the law applicable by virtue of the rules of private international law.

Article 8 (1) For the purposes of this Convention statements made by and other conduct of a party are to be interpreted according to his intent where the other party knew or could not have been unaware what that intent was.

(2) If the preceding paragraph is not applicable, statements made by and other conduct of a party are to be interpreted according to the understanding that a reasonable person of the same kind as the other party would have had in the same circumstances.

(3) In determining the intent of a party or the understanding a reasonable person would have had, due consideration is to be given to all relevant circumstances of the case including the negotiations, any practices which the parties have established between themselves, usages and any subsequent conduct of the parties.

Article 9 (1) The parties are bound by any usage to which they have agreed and by any practices which they have established between themselves.

(2) The parties are considered, unless otherwise agreed, to have impliedly made applicable to their contract or its formation a usage of which the parties knew or ought to have known and which in international trade is widely known to, and regularly observed by, parties to contracts of the type involved in the particular trade concerned.

Article 10 For the purposes of this Convention:

(a) if a party has more than one place of business, the place of business is that which has the closest relationship to the contract and its performance, having regard to the circumstances known to or contemplated by the parties at any time before or at the conclusion of the contract;

(b) if a party does not have a place of business, reference is to be made to his habitual residence.

Article 11 A contract of sale need not be concluded in or evidenced by writing and is not subject to any other requirement as to form. It may be proved by any means, including witnesses.

Article 12 Any provision of article 11, article 29 or Part II of this Convention that allows a contract of sale or its modification or termination by agreement or any offer, acceptance or other indication of intention to be made in any form other than in writing does not apply where any party has his place of business in a Contracting State which has made a declaration under article 96 of this Convention. The parties may not derogate from or vary the effect of this article.

Article 13 For the purposes of this Convention "writing" includes telegram and telex.

PART II. FORMATION OF THE CONTRACT

Article 14 (1) A proposal for concluding a contract addressed to one or more specific persons constitutes an offer if it is sufficiently definite and indicates the intention of the offeror to be bound in case of acceptance. A proposal is sufficiently definite if it indicates the goods and expressly or implicitly fixes or makes provision for determining the quantity and the price.

(2) A proposal other than one addressed to one or more specific persons is to be considered merely as an invitation to make offers, unless the contrary is clearly indicated by the person making the proposal.

Article 15 (1) An offer becomes effective when it reaches the offeree.

(2) An offer, even if it is irrevocable, may be withdrawn if the withdrawal reaches the offeree before or at the same time as the offer.

Article 16 (1) Until a contract is concluded an offer may be revoked if the revocation reaches the offeree before he has dispatched an acceptance.

(2) However, an offer cannot be revoked:

(a) if it indicates, whether by stating a fixed time for acceptance or otherwise, that it is irrevocable; or

(b) if it was reasonable for the offeree to rely on the offer as being irrevocable and the offeree has acted in reliance on the offer.

Article 17 An offer, even if it is irrevocable, is terminated when a rejection reaches the offeror.

Article 18 (1) A statement made by or other conduct of the offeree indicating assent to an offer is an acceptance. Silence or inactivity does not in itself amount to acceptance.

(2) An acceptance of an offer becomes effective at the moment the indication of assent reaches the offeror. An acceptance is not effective if the indication of assent does not reach the offeror within the time he has fixed or, if no time is fixed, within a reasonable time, due account being taken of the circumstances of the transaction, including the rapidity of the means of communication employed by the offeror. An oral offer must be accepted immediately unless the circumstances indicate otherwise.

(3) However, if, by virtue of the offer or as a result of practices which the parties have established between themselves or of usage, the offeree may indicate assent by performing an act, such as one relating to the dispatch of the goods or payment of the price, without notice to the offeror, the acceptance is effective at the moment the act is performed, provided that the act is performed within the period of time laid down in the preceding paragraph.

Article 19 (1) A reply to an offer which purports to be an acceptance but contains additions, limitations or other modifications is a rejection of the offer and constitutes a counter-offer.

(2) However, a reply to an offer which purports to be an acceptance but contains additional or different terms which do not materially alter the terms of the offer constitutes an acceptance, unless the offeror, without undue delay, objects orally to the discrepancy or dispatches a notice to that effect. If he does not so object, the terms of the contract are the terms of the offer with the modifications contained in the acceptance.

(3) Additional or different terms relating, among other things, to the price, payment, quality and quantity of the goods, place and time of delivery, extent

of one party's liability to the other or the settlement of disputes are considered to alter the terms of the offer materially.

Article 20 (1) A period of time for acceptance fixed by the offeror in a telegram or a letter begins to run from the moment the telegram is handed in for dispatch or from the date shown on the letter or, if no such date is shown, from the date shown on the envelope. A period of time for acceptance fixed by the offeror by telephone, telex or other means of instantaneous communication, begins to run from the moment that the offer reaches the offeree.

(2) Official holidays or non-business days occurring during the period for acceptance are included in calculating the period. However, if a notice of acceptance cannot be delivered at the address of the offeror on the last day of the period because that day falls on an official holiday or a non-business day at the place of business of the offeror, the period is extended until the first business day which follows.

Article 21 (1) A late acceptance is nevertheless effective as an acceptance if without delay the offeror orally so informs the offeree or dispatches a notice to that effect.

(2) If a letter or other writing containing a late acceptance shows that it has been sent in such circumstances that if its transmission had been normal it would have reached the offeror in due time, the late acceptance is effective as an acceptance unless, without delay, the offeror orally informs the offeree that he considers his offer as having lapsed or dispatches a notice to that effect.

Article 22 An acceptance may be withdrawn if the withdrawal reaches the offeror before or at the same time as the acceptance would have become effective.

Article 23 A contract is concluded at the moment when an acceptance of an offer becomes effective in accordance with the provisions of this Convention.

Article 24 For the purposes of this Part of the Convention, an offer, declaration of acceptance or any other indication of intention "reaches" the addressee when it is made orally to him or delivered by any other means to him personally to his place of business or mailing address or, if he does not have a place of business or mailing address, to his habitual residence.

PART III. SALE OF GOODS
CHAPTER 1. GENERAL PROVISIONS

Article 25 A breach of contract committed by one of the parties is fundamental if it results in such detriment to the other party as substantially to deprive him of what he is entitled to expect under the contract, unless the party in breach did not foresee and a reasonable person of the same kind in the same circumstances would not have foreseen such a result.

Article 26 A declaration of avoidance of the contract is effective only if made by notice to the other party.

Article 27 Unless otherwise expressly provided in this Part of the Convention, if any notice, request or other communication is given or made by a party in accordance with this Part and by means appropriate in the circumstances, a delay or error in the transmission of the communication or its failure to arrive does not deprive that party of the right to rely on the communication.

Article 28 If, in accordance with the provisions of this Convention, one party is entitled to require performance of any obligation by the other party, a court is not bound to enter a judgment for specific performance unless the court would do so under its own law in respect of similar contracts of sale not governed by this Convention.

Article 29 (1) A contract may be modified or terminated by the mere agreement of the parties.

(2) A contract in writing which contains a provision requiring any modification or termination by agreement to be in writing may not be otherwise modified or terminated by agreement. However, a party may be precluded by his conduct from asserting such a provision to the extent that the other party has relied on that conduct.

CHAPTER II. OBLIGATIONS OF THE SELLER

Article 30 The seller must deliver the goods, hand over any documents relating to them and transfer the property in the goods, as required by the contract and this Convention.

Section I. Delivery of the Goods and Handing Over of Documents

Article 31 If the seller is not bound to deliver the goods at any other particular place, his obligation to deliver consists:

(a) if the contract of sale involves carriage of the goods—in handing the goods over to the first carrier for transmission to the buyer;

(b) if, in cases not within the preceding subparagraph, the contract relates to specific goods, or unidentified goods to be drawn from a specific stock or to be manufactured or produced, and at the time of the conclusion of the contract the parties knew that the goods were at, or were to be manufactured or produced at, a particular place—in placing the goods at the buyer's disposal at that place;

(c) in other cases—in placing the goods at the buyer's disposal at the place where the seller had his place of business at the time of the conclusion of the contract.

Article 32 (1) If the seller, in accordance with the contract or this Convention, hands the goods over to a carrier and if the goods are not clearly identified to the contract by markings on the goods, by shipping documents or otherwise, the seller must give the buyer notice of the consignment specifying the goods.

(2) If the seller is bound to arrange for carriage of the goods, he must make such contracts as are necessary for carriage to the place fixed by means of transportation appropriate in the circumstances and according to the usual terms for such transportation.

(3) If the seller is not bound to effect insurance in respect of the carriage of the goods, he must, at the buyer's request, provide him with all available information necessary to enable him to effect such insurance.

Article 33 The seller must deliver the goods:

(a) if a date is fixed by or determinable from the contract, on that date;

(b) if a period of time is fixed by or determinable from the contract, at any time within that period unless circumstances indicate that the buyer is to choose a date; or

(c) in any other case, within a reasonable time after the conclusion of the contract.

Article 34 If the seller is bound to hand over documents relating to the goods, he must hand them over at the time and place and in the form required by the contract. If the seller has handed over documents before that time, he may, up to that time, cure any lack of conformity in the documents, if the exercise of this right does not cause the buyer unreasonable inconvenience or unreasonable expense. However, the buyer retains any right to claim damages as provided for in this Convention.

Section II. Conformity of the Goods and Third Party Claims

Article 35 (1) The seller must deliver goods which are of the quantity, quality and description required by the contract and which are contained or packaged in the manner required by the contract.

(2) Except where the parties have agreed otherwise, the goods do not conform with the contract unless they:

(a) are fit for the purposes for which goods of the same description would ordinarily be used;

(b) are fit for any particular purpose expressly or impliedly made known to the seller at the time of the conclusion of the contract, except where the circumstances show that the buyer did not rely, or that it was unreasonable for him to rely, on the seller's skill and judgement;

(c) possess the qualities of goods which the seller has held out to the buyer as a sample or model;

(d) are contained or packaged in the manner usual for such goods or, where there is no such manner, in a manner adequate to preserve and protect the goods.

(3) The seller is not liable under subparagraphs (a) to (d) of the preceding paragraph for any lack of conformity of the goods if at the time of the conclusion of the contract the buyer knew or could not have been unaware of such lack of conformity.

Article 36 (1) The seller is liable in accordance with the contract and this Convention for any lack of conformity which exists at the time when the risk passes to the buyer, even though the lack of conformity becomes apparent only after that time.

(2) The seller is also liable for any lack of conformity which occurs after the time indicated in the preceding paragraph and which is due to a breach of any of his obligations, including a breach of any guarantee that for a period of time the goods will remain fit for their ordinary purpose or for some particular purpose or will retain specified qualities or characteristics.

Article 37 If the seller has delivered goods before the date for delivery, he may, up to that date, deliver any missing part or make up any deficiency in the quantity of the goods delivered, or deliver goods in replacement of any non-conforming goods delivered or remedy any lack of conformity in the goods delivered, provided that the exercise of this right does not cause the buyer unreasonable inconvenience or unreasonable expense. However, the buyer retains any right to claim damages as provided for in this Convention.

Article 38 (1) The buyer must examine the goods, or cause them to be examined, within as short a period as is practicable in the circumstances.

(2) If the contract involves carriage of the goods, examination may be deferred until after the goods have arrived at their destination.

(3) If the goods are redirected in transit or redispatched by the buyer without a reasonable opportunity for examination by him and at the time of the conclusion of the contract the seller knew or ought to have known of the possibility of such redirection or redispatch, examination may be deferred until after the goods have arrived at the new destination.

Article 39 (1) The buyer loses the right to rely on a lack of conformity of the goods if he does not give notice to the seller specifying the nature of the lack of conformity within a reasonable time after he has discovered it or ought to have discovered it.

(2) In any event, the buyer loses the right to rely on a lack of conformity of the goods if he does not give the seller notice thereof at the latest within a period of two years from the date on which the goods were actually handed over to the buyer, unless this time-limit is inconsistent with a contractual period of guarantee.

Article 40 The seller is not entitled to rely on the provisions of articles 38 and 39 if the lack of conformity relates to facts of which he knew or could not have been unaware and which he did not disclose to the buyer.

Article 41 The seller must deliver goods which are free from any right or claim of a third party, unless the buyer agreed to take the goods subject to that right or claim. However, if such right or claim is based on industrial property or other intellectual property, the seller's obligation is governed by article 42.

Article 42 (1) The seller must deliver goods which are free from any right or claim of a third party based on industrial property or other intellectual property, of which at the time of the conclusion of the contract the seller knew or could not have been unaware, provided that the right or claim is based on industrial property or other intellectual property:

(a) under the law of the State where the goods will be resold or otherwise used, if it was contemplated by the parties at the time of the conclusion of the contract that the goods would be resold or otherwise used in that State; or

(b) in any other case, under the law of the State where the buyer has his place of business.

(2) The obligation of the seller under the preceding paragraph does not extend to cases where:

(a) at the time of the conclusion of the contract the buyer knew or could not have been unaware of the right or claim; or

(b) the right or claim results from the seller's compliance with technical drawings, designs, formulae or other such specifications furnished by the buyer.

Article 43 (1) The buyer loses the right to rely on the provisions of article 41 or article 42 if he does not give notice to the seller specifying the nature of the right or claim of the third party within a reasonable time after he has become aware or ought to have become aware of the right or claim.

(2) The seller is not entitled to rely on the provisions of the preceding paragraph if he knew of the right or claim of the third party and the nature of it.

Article 44 Notwithstanding the provisions of paragraph (1) of article 39 and paragraph (1) of article 43, the buyer may reduce the price in accordance with article 50 or claim damages, except for loss of profit, if he has a reasonable excuse for his failure to give the required notice.

Section III. Remedies for Breach of Contract by the Seller

Article 45 (1) If the seller fails to perform any of his obligations under the contract or this Convention, the buyer may:

(a) exercise the rights provided in articles 46 to 52;

(b) claim damages as provided in articles 74 to 77.

(2) The buyer is not deprived of any right he may have to claim damages by exercising his right to other remedies.

(3) No period of grace may be granted to the seller by a court or arbitral tribunal when the buyer resorts to a remedy for breach of contract.

Article 46 (1) The buyer may require performance by the seller of his obligations unless the buyer has resorted to a remedy which is inconsistent with this requirement.

(2) If the goods do not conform with the contract, the buyer may require delivery of substitute goods only if the lack of conformity constitutes a fundamental breach of contract and a request for substitute goods is made either in conjunction with notice given under article 39 or within a reasonable time thereafter.

(3) If the goods do not conform with the contract, the buyer may require the seller to remedy the lack of conformity by repair, unless this is unreasonable having regard to all the circumstances. A request for repair must be made either in conjunction with notice given under article 39 or within a reasonable time thereafter.

Article 47 (1) The buyer may fix an additional period of time of reasonable length for performance by the seller of his obligations.

(2) Unless the buyer has received notice from the seller that he will not perform within the period so fixed, the buyer may not, during that period, resort to any remedy for breach of contract. However, the buyer is not deprived thereby of any right he may have to claim damages for delay in performance.

Article 48 (1) Subject to article 49, the seller may, even after the date for delivery, remedy at his own expense any failure to perform his obligations, if he can do so without unreasonable delay and without causing the buyer unreasonable inconvenience or uncertainty of reimbursement by the seller of expenses advanced by the buyer. However, the buyer retains any right to claim damages as provided for in this Convention.

(2) If the seller requests the buyer to make known whether he will accept performance and the buyer does not comply with the request within a reasonable time, the seller may perform within the time indicated in his request. The buyer may not, during that period of time, resort to any remedy which is inconsistent with performance by the seller.

(3) A notice by the seller that he will perform within a specified period of time is assumed to include a request, under the preceding paragraph, that the buyer make known his decision.

(4) A request or notice by the seller under paragraph (2) or (3) of this article is not effective unless received by the buyer.

Article 49 (1) The buyer may declare the contract avoided:

(a) if the failure by the seller to perform any of his obligations under the contract or this Convention amounts to a fundamental breach of contract; or

(b) in case of non-delivery, if the seller does not deliver the goods within the additional period of time fixed by the buyer in accordance with paragraph (1) of article 47 or declares that he will not deliver within the period so fixed.

(2) However, in cases where the seller has delivered the goods, the buyer loses the right to declare the contract avoided unless he does so:

(a) in respect of late delivery, within a reasonable time after he has become aware that delivery has been made;

(b) in respect of any breach other than late delivery, within a reasonable time:

(i) after he knew or ought to have known of the breach;

(ii) after the expiration of any additional period of time fixed by the buyer in accordance with paragraph (1) of article 47, or after the seller has declared that he will not perform his obligations within such an additional period; or

(iii) after the expiration of any additional period of time indicated by the seller in accordance with paragraph (2) of article 48, or after the buyer has declared that he will not accept performance.

Article 50 If the goods do not conform with the contract and whether or not the price has already been paid, the buyer may reduce the price in the same proportion as the value that the goods actually delivered had at the time of the delivery bears to the value that conforming goods would have had at that time. However, if the seller remedies any failure to perform his obligations in accordance with article 37 or article 48 or if the buyer refuses to accept performance by the seller in accordance with those articles, the buyer may not reduce the price.

Article 51 (1) If the seller delivers only a part of the goods or if only a part of the goods delivered is in conformity with the contract, articles 46 to 50 apply in respect of the part which is missing or which does not conform.

(2) The buyer may declare the contract avoided in its entirety only if the failure to make delivery completely or in conformity with the contract amounts to a fundamental breach of the contract.

Article 52 (1) If the seller delivers the goods before the date fixed, the buyer may take delivery or refuse to take delivery.

(2) If the seller delivers a quantity of goods greater than that provided for in the contract, the buyer may take delivery or refuse to take delivery of the excess quantity. If the buyer takes delivery of all or part of the excess quantity, he must pay for it at the contract rate.

CHAPTER III. OBLIGATIONS OF THE BUYER

Article 53 The buyer must pay the price for the goods and take delivery of them as required by the contract and this Convention.

Section I. Payment of the Price

Article 54 The buyer's obligation to pay the price includes taking such steps and complying with such formalities as may be required under the contract or any laws and regulations to enable payment to be made.

Article 55 Where a contract has been validly concluded but does not expressly or implicitly fix or make provision for determining the price, the parties are considered, in the absence of any indication to the contrary, to have impliedly made reference to the price generally charged at the time of the conclusion of the contract for such goods sold under comparable circumstances in the trade concerned.

Article 56 If the price is fixed according to the weight of the goods, in case of doubt it is to be determined by the net weight.

Article 57 (1) If the buyer is not bound to pay the price at any other particular place, he must pay it to the seller:

(a) at the seller's place of business; or

(b) if the payment is to be made against the handing over of the goods or of documents, at the place where the handing over takes place.

(2) The seller must bear any increase in the expenses incidental to payment which is caused by a change in his place of business subsequent to the conclusion of the contract.

Article 58 (1) If the buyer is not bound to pay the price at any other specific time, he must pay it when the seller places either the goods or documents controlling their disposition at the buyer's disposal in accordance with the contract and this Convention. The seller may make such payment a condition for handing over the goods or documents.

(2) If the contract involves carriage of the goods, the seller may dispatch the goods on terms whereby the goods, or documents controlling their disposition, will not be handed over to the buyer except against payment of the price.

(3) The buyer is not bound to pay the price until he has had an opportunity to examine the goods, unless the procedures for delivery or payment agreed upon by the parties are inconsistent with his having such an opportunity.

Article 59 The buyer must pay the price on the date fixed by or determinable from the contract and this Convention without the need for any request or compliance with any formality on the part of the seller.

Section II. Taking delivery

Article 60 The buyer's obligation to take delivery consists:

(a) in doing all the acts which could reasonably be expected of him in order to enable the seller to make delivery; and

(b) in taking over the goods.

Section III. Remedies for Breach of Contract by the Buyer

Article 61 (1) If the buyer fails to perform any of his obligations under the contract or this Convention, the seller may:

(a) exercise the rights provided in articles 62 to 65;

(b) claim damages as provided in articles 74 to 77.

(2) The seller is not deprived of any right he may have to claim damages by exercising his right to other remedies.

(3) No period of grace may be granted to the buyer by a court or arbitral tribunal when the seller resorts to a remedy for breach of contract.

Article 62 The seller may require the buyer to pay the price, take delivery or perform his other obligations, unless the seller has resorted to a remedy which is inconsistent with this requirement.

Article 63 (1) The seller may fix an additional period of time of reasonable length for performance by the buyer of his obligations.

(2) Unless the seller has received notice from the buyer that he will not perform within the period so fixed, the seller may not, during that period, resort to any remedy for breach of contract. However, the seller is not deprived thereby of any right he may have to claim damages for delay in performance.

Article 64 (1) The seller may declare the contract avoided:

(a) if the failure by the buyer to perform any of his obligations under the contract or this Convention amounts to a fundamental breach of contract; or

(b) if the buyer does not, within the additional period of time fixed by the seller in accordance with paragraph (1) of article 63, perform his obligation to pay the price or take delivery of the goods, or if he declares that he will not do so within the period so fixed.

(2) However, in cases where the buyer has paid the price, the seller loses the right to declare the contract avoided unless he does so:

(a) in respect of late performance by the buyer, before the seller has become aware that performance has been rendered; or

(b) in respect of any breach other than late performance by the buyer, within a reasonable time:

(i) after the seller knew or ought to have known of the breach; or

(ii) after the expiration of any additional period of time fixed by the seller in accordance with paragraph (1) of article 63, or after the buyer has declared that he will not perform his obligations within such an additional period.

Article 65 (1) If under the contract the buyer is to specify the form, measurement or other features of the goods and he fails to make such specification either on the date agreed upon or within a reasonable time after receipt of a request from the seller, the seller may, without prejudice to any other rights he may have, make the specification himself in accordance with the requirements of the buyer that may be known to him.

(2) If the seller makes the specification himself, he must inform the buyer of the details thereof and must fix a reasonable time within which the buyer may make a different specification. If, after receipt of such a communication, the buyer fails to do so within the time fixed, the specification made by the seller is binding.

CHAPTER IV. PASSING OF RISK

Article 66 Loss of or damage to the goods after the risk has passed to the buyer does not discharge him from his obligation to pay the price, unless the loss or damage is due to an act or omission of the seller.

Article 67 (1) If the contract of sale involves carriage of the goods and the seller is not bound to hand them over at a particular place, the risk passes to the buyer when the goods are handed over to the first carrier for transmission to the buyer in accordance with the contract of sale. If the seller is bound to hand the goods over to a carrier at a particular place, the risk does not pass to the buyer until the goods are handed over to the carrier at that place. The fact that the seller is authorized to retain documents controlling the disposition of the goods does not affect the passage of the risk.

(2) Nevertheless, the risk does not pass to the buyer until the goods are clearly identified to the contract, whether by markings on the goods, by shipping documents, by notice given to the buyer or otherwise.

Article 68 The risk in respect of goods sold in transit passes to the buyer from the time of the conclusion of the contract. However, if the circumstances so indicate, the risk is assumed by the buyer from the time the goods were handed over to the carrier who issued the documents embodying the contract of carriage. Nevertheless, if at the time of the conclusion of the contract of sale the seller knew or ought to have known that the goods had been lost or damaged and did not disclose this to the buyer, the loss or damage is at the risk of the seller.

Article 69 (1) In cases not within articles 67 and 68, the risk passes to the buyer when he takes over the goods or, if he does not do so in due time, from the time when the goods are placed at his disposal and he commits a breach of contract by failing to take delivery.

(2) However, if the buyer is bound to take over the goods at a place other than a place of business of the seller, the risk passes when delivery is due and the buyer is aware of the fact that the goods are placed at his disposal at that place.

(3) If the contract relates to goods not then identified, the goods are considered not to be placed at the disposal of the buyer until they are clearly identified to the contract.

Article 70 If the seller had committed a fundamental breach of contract, articles 67, 68 and 69 do not impair the remedies available to the buyer on account of the breach.

CHAPTER V. PROVISIONS COMMON TO THE OBLIGATIONS OF THE SELLER AND OF THE BUYER
Section I. Anticipatory Breach and Instalment Contracts

Article 71 (1) A party may suspend the performance of his obligations if, after the conclusion of the contract, it becomes apparent that the other party will not perform a substantial part of his obligations as a result of:

(a) a serious deficiency in his ability to perform or in his creditworthiness; or

(b) his conduct in preparing to perform or in performing the contract.

(2) If the seller has already dispatched the goods before the grounds described in the preceding paragraph become evident, he may prevent the handing over of the goods to the buyer even though the buyer holds a document which entitles him to obtain them. The present paragraph relates only to the rights in the goods as between the buyer and the seller.

(3) A party suspending performance, whether before or after dispatch of the goods, must immediately give notice of the suspension to the other party and must continue with performance if the other party provides adequate assurance of his performance.

Article 72 (1) If prior to the date for performance of the contract it is clear that one of the parties will commit a fundamental breach of contract, the other party may declare the contract avoided.

(2) If time allows, the party intending to declare the contract avoided must give reasonable notice to the other party in order to permit him to provide adequate assurance of his performance.

(3) The requirements of the preceding paragraph do not apply if the other party has declared that he will not perform his obligations.

Article 73 (1) In the case of a contract for delivery of goods by instalments, if the failure of one party to perform any of his obligations in respect of any instalment constitutes a fundamental breach of contract with respect to that instalment, the other party may declare the contract avoided with respect to that instalment.

(2) If one party's failure to perform any of his obligations in respect of any instalment gives the other party good grounds to conclude that a fundamental breach of contract will occur with respect to future installments, he may declare the contract avoided for the future, provided that he does so within a reasonable time.

(3) A buyer who declares the contract avoided in respect of any delivery may, at the same time, declare it avoided in respect of deliveries already made or of future deliveries if, by reason of their interdependence, those deliveries could not be used for the purpose contemplated by the parties at the time of the conclusion of the contract.

Section II. Damages

Article 74 Damages for breach of contract by one party consist of a sum equal to the loss, including loss of profit, suffered by the other party as a consequence of the breach. Such damages may not exceed the loss which the party in breach foresaw or ought to have foreseen at the time of the conclusion of the contract, in the light of the facts and matters of which he then knew or ought to have known, as a possible consequence of the breach of contract.

Article 75 If the contract is avoided and if, in a reasonable manner and within a reasonable time after avoidance, the buyer has bought goods in replacement or the seller has resold the goods, the party claiming damages may recover the difference between the contract price and the price in the substitute transaction as well as any further damages recoverable under article 74.

Article 76 (1) If the contract is avoided and there is a current price for the goods, the party claiming damages may, if he has not made a purchase or resale under article 75, recover the difference between the price fixed by the contract and the current price at the time of avoidance as well as any further damages recoverable under article 74. If, however, the party claiming damages has avoided the contract after taking over the goods, the current price at the time of such taking over shall be applied instead of the current price at the time of avoidance.

(2) For the purpose of the preceding paragraph, the current price is the price prevailing at the place where delivery of the goods should have been made or, if there is no current price at that place, the price at such other place as serves as a reasonable substitute, making due allowance for differences in the cost of transporting the goods.

Article 77 A party who relies on a breach of contract must take such measures as are reasonable in the circumstances to mitigate the loss, including loss of profit, resulting from the breach. If he fails to take such measures, the party in breach may claim a reduction in the damages in the amount by which the loss should have been mitigated.

Section III. Interest

Article 78 If a party fails to pay the price or any other sum that is in arrears, the other party is entitled to interest on it, without prejudice to any claim for damages recoverable under article 74.

Section IV. Exemptions

Article 79 (1) A party is not liable for a failure to perform any of his obligations if he proves that the failure was due to an impediment beyond his control and that he could not reasonably be expected to have taken the impediment into account at the time of the conclusion of the contract or to have avoided or overcome it or its consequences.

(2) If the party's failure is due to the failure by a third person whom he has engaged to perform the whole or a part of the contract, that party is exempt from liability only if:

(a) he is exempt under the preceding paragraph; and

(b) the person whom he has so engaged would be so exempt if the provisions of that paragraph were applied to him.

(3) The exemption provided by this article has effect for the period during which the impediment exists.

(4) The party who fails to perform must give notice to the other party of the impediment and its effects on his ability to perform. If the notice is not received by the other party within a reasonable time after the party who fails to perform knew or ought to have known of the impediment, he is liable for damages resulting from such non-receipt.

(5) Nothing in this article prevents either party from exercising any right other than to claim damages under this Convention.

Article 80 A party may not rely on a failure of the other party to perform, to the extent that such failure was caused by the first party's act or omission.

Section V. Effects of Avoidance

Article 81 (1) Avoidance of the contract releases both parties from their obligations under it, subject to any damages which may be due. Avoidance does not affect any provision of the contract for the settlement of disputes or any other provision of the contract governing the rights and obligations of the parties consequent upon the avoidance of the contract.

(2) A party who has performed the contract either wholly or in part may claim restitution from the other party of whatever the first party has supplied or paid under the contract. If both parties are bound to make restitution, they must do so concurrently.

Article 82 (1) The buyer loses the right to declare the contract avoided or to require the seller to deliver substitute goods if it is impossible for him to make restitution of the goods substantially in the condition in which he received them.

(2) The preceding paragraph does not apply:

(a) if the impossibility of making restitution of the goods or of making restitution of the goods substantially in the condition in which the buyer received them is not due to his act or omission;

(b) if the goods or part of the goods have perished or deteriorated as a result of the examination provided for in article 38; or

(c) if the goods or part of the goods have been sold in the normal course of business or have been consumed or transformed by the buyer in the course of normal use before he discovered or ought to have discovered the lack of conformity.

Article 83 A buyer who has lost the right to declare the contract avoided or to require the seller to deliver substitute goods in accordance with article 82 retains all other remedies under the contract and this Convention.

Article 84 (1) If the seller is bound to refund the price, he must also pay interest on it, from the date on which the price was paid.

(2) The buyer must account to the seller for all benefits which he has derived from the goods or part of them:

(a) if he must make restitution of the goods or part of them; or

(b) if it is impossible for him to make restitution of all or part of the goods or to make restitution of all or part of the goods substantially in the condition in which he received them, but he has nevertheless declared the contract avoided or required the seller to deliver substitute goods.

Section VI. Preservation of the goods

Article 85 If the buyer is in delay in taking delivery of the goods or, where payment of the price and delivery of the goods are to be made concurrently, if he fails to pay the price, and the seller is either in possession of the goods or otherwise able to control their disposition, the seller must take such steps as are reasonable in the circumstances to preserve them. He is entitled to retain them until he has been reimbursed his reasonable expenses by the buyer.

Article 86 (1) If the buyer has received the goods and intends to exercise any right under the contract or this Convention to reject them, he must take such steps to preserve them as are reasonable in the circumstances. He is entitled to retain them until he has been reimbursed his reasonable expenses by the seller.

(2) If goods dispatched to the buyer have been placed at his disposal at their destination and he exercises the right to reject them, he must take possession of them on behalf of the seller, provided that this can be done without payment of the price and without unreasonable inconvenience or unreasonable

expense. This provision does not apply if the seller or a person authorized to take charge of the goods on his behalf is present at the destination. If the buyer takes possession of the goods under this paragraph, his rights and obligations are governed by the preceding paragraph.

Article 87 A party who is bound to take steps to preserve the goods may deposit them in a warehouse of a third person at the expense of the other party provided that the expense incurred is not unreasonable.

Article 88 (1) A party who is bound to preserve the goods in accordance with article 85 or 86 may sell them by any appropriate means if there has been an unreasonable delay by the other party in taking possession of the goods or in taking them back or in paying the price or the cost of preservation, provided that reasonable notice of the intention to sell has been given to the other party.

(2) If the goods are subject to rapid deterioration or their preservation would involve unreasonable expense, a party who is bound to preserve the goods in accordance with article 85 or 86 must take reasonable measures to sell them. To the extent possible he must give notice to the other party of his intention to sell.

(3) A party selling the goods has the right to retain out of the proceeds of sale an amount equal to the reasonable expenses of preserving the goods and of selling them. He must account to the other party for the balance.

PART IV. FINAL PROVISIONS

Article 89 The Secretary-General of the United Nations is hereby designated as the depositary for this Convention.

Article 90 This Convention does not prevail over any international agreement which has already been or may be entered into and which contains provisions concerning the matters governed by this Convention, provided that the parties have their places of business in States parties to such agreement.

Article 91 (1) This Convention is open for signature at the concluding meeting of the United Nations Conference on Contracts for the International Sale of Goods and will remain open for signature by all States at the Headquarters of the United Nations, New York until 30 September 1981.

(2) This Convention is subject to ratification, acceptance or approval by the signatory States.

(3) This Convention is open for accession by all States which are not signatory States as from the date it is open for signature.

(4) Instruments of ratification, acceptance, approval and accession are to be deposited with the Secretary-General of the United Nations.

Article 92 (1) A Contracting State may declare at the time of signature, ratification, acceptance, approval or accession that it will not be bound by Part II of this Convention or that it will not be bound by Part III of this Convention.

(2) A Contracting State which makes a declaration in accordance with the preceding paragraph in respect of Part II or Part III of this Convention is not to be considered a Contracting State within paragraph (1) of article 1 of this Convention in respect of matters governed by the Part to which the declaration applies.

Article 93 (1) If a Contracting State has two or more territorial units in which, according to its constitution, different systems of law are applicable in relation to the matters dealt with in this Convention, it may, at the time of signature, ratification, acceptance, approval or accession, declare that this Convention is to extend to all its territorial units or only to one or more of them, and may amend its declaration by submitting another declaration at any time.

(2) These declarations are to be notified to the depositary and are to state expressly the territorial units to which the Convention extends.

(3) If, by virtue of a declaration under this article, this Convention extends to one or more but not all of the territorial units of a Contracting State, and if the place of business of a party is located in that State, this place of business, for the purposes of this Convention, is considered not to be in a Contracting State, unless it is in a territorial unit to which the Convention extends.

(4) If a Contracting State makes no declaration under paragraph (1) of this article, the Convention is to extend to all territorial units of that State.

Article 94 (1) Two or more Contracting States which have the same or closely related legal rules on matters governed by this Convention may at any time declare that the Convention is not to apply to contracts of sale or to their formation where the parties have their places of business in those States. Such declarations may be made jointly or by reciprocal unilateral declarations.

(2) A Contracting State which has the same or closely related legal rules on matters governed by this Convention as one or more non-Contracting States may at any time declare that the Convention is not to apply to contracts of sale or to their formation where the parties have their places of business in those States.

(3) If a State which is the object of a declaration under the preceding paragraph subsequently becomes a Contracting State, the declaration made will, as from the date on which the Convention enters into force in respect of the new

Contracting State, have the effect of a declaration made under paragraph (1), provided that the new Contracting State joins in such declaration or makes a reciprocal unilateral declaration.

Article 95 Any State may declare at the time of the deposit of its instrument of ratification, acceptance, approval or accession that it will not be bound by subparagraph (1)(b) of article 1 of this Convention.

Article 96 A Contracting State whose legislation requires contracts of sale to be concluded in or evidenced by writing may at any time make a declaration in accordance with article 12 that any provision of article 11, article 29, or Part II of this Convention, that allows a contract of sale or its modification or termination by agreement or any offer, acceptance, or other indication of intention to be made in any form other than in writing, does not apply where any party has his place of business in that State.

Article 97 (1) Declarations made under this Convention at the time of signature are subject to confirmation upon ratification, acceptance or approval,

(2) Declarations and confirmations of declarations are to be in writing and be formally notified to the depositary.

(3) A declaration takes effect simultaneously with the entry into force of this Convention in respect of the State concerned. However, a declaration of which the depositary receives formal notification after such entry into force takes effect on the first day of the month following the expiration of six months after the date of its receipt by the depositary. Reciprocal unilateral declarations under article 94 take effect on the first day of the month following the expiration of six months after the receipt of the latest declaration by the depositary.

(4) Any State which makes a declaration under this Convention may withdraw it at any time by a formal notification in writing addressed to the depositary. Such withdrawal is to take effect on the first day of the month following the expiration of six months after the date of the receipt of the notification by the depositary.

(5) A withdrawal of a declaration made under article 94 renders inoperative, as from the date on which the withdrawal takes effect, any reciprocal declaration made by another State under that article.

Article 98 No reservations are permitted except those expressly authorized in this Convention.

Article 99 (1) This Convention enters into force, subject to the provisions of paragraph (6) of this article, on the first day of the month following the expiration of twelve months after the date of deposit of the tenth instrument of ratification, acceptance, approval or accession, including an instrument which contains a declaration made under article 92.

(2) When a State ratifies, accepts, approves or accedes to this Convention after the deposit of the tenth instrument of ratification, acceptance, approval or accession, this Convention, with the exception of the Part excluded, enters into force in respect of that State, subject to the provisions of paragraph (6) of this article, on the first day of the month following the expiration of twelve months after the date of the deposit of its instrument of ratification, acceptance, approval or accession.

(3) A State which ratifies, accepts, approves or accedes to this Convention and is a party to either or both the Convention relating to a Uniform Law on the Formation of Contracts for the International Sale of Goods done at The Hague on 1 July 1964 (1964 Hague Formation Convention) and the Convention relating to a Uniform Law on the International Sale of Goods done at The Hague on 1 July 1964 (1964 Hague Sales Convention) shall at the same time denounce, as the case may be, either or both the 1964 Hague Sales Convention and the 1964 Hague Formation Convention by notifying the Government of the Netherlands to that effect.

(4) A State party to the 1964 Hague Sales Convention which ratifies, accepts, approves or accedes to the present Convention and declares or has declared under article 92 that it will not be bound by Part II of this Convention shall at the time of ratification, acceptance, approval or accession denounce the 1964 Hague Sales Convention by notifying the Government of the Netherlands to that effect.

(5) A State party to the 1964 Hague Formation Convention which ratifies, accepts, approves or accedes to the present Convention and declares or has declared under article 92 that it will not be bound by Part III of this Convention shall at the time of ratification, acceptance, approval or accession denounce the 1964 Hague Formation Convention by notifying the Government of the Netherlands to that effect.

(6) For the purpose of this article, ratifications, acceptances, approvals and accessions in respect of this Convention by States parties to the 1964 Hague Formation Convention or to the 1964 Hague Sales Convention shall not be effective until such denunciations as may be required on the part of those States in respect of the latter two Conventions have themselves become effective. The depositary of this Convention shall consult with the Government of the Netherlands, as the depositary of the 1964 Conventions, so as to ensure necessary co-ordination in this respect.

Article 100 (1) This Convention applies to the formation of a contract only when the proposal for concluding the contract is made on or after the date when the Convention enters into force in respect of the Contracting States referred to in subparagraph (1)(a) or the Contracting State referred to in subparagraph (1)(b) of article 1.

(2) This Convention applies only to contracts concluded on or after the date when the Convention enters into force in respect of the Contracting States referred to in subparagraph (1)(a) or the Contracting State referred to in subparagraph (1)(b) of article 1.

Article 101 (1) A Contracting State may denounce this Convention, or Part II or Part III of the Convention, by a formal notification in writing addressed to the depositary.

(2) The denunciation takes effect on the first day of the month following the expiration of twelve months after the notification is received by the depositary. Where a longer period for the denunciation to take effect is specified in the notification, the denunciation takes effect upon the expiration of such longer period after the notification is received by the depositary.

DONE at Vienna, this day of eleventh day of April, one thousand nine hundred and eighty, in a single original, of which the Arabia, Chinese, English, French, Russian and Spanish texts are equally authentic.

IN WITNESS WHEREOF the undersigned plenipotentiaries, being duly authorized by their respective Governments, have signed this Convention.

Mastering International Sales Law Checklist

CHAPTER 1 Introduction to International Sales Law

☐ Enterprises make contracts for future performance to reduce their risks.

☐ Every risk reduction has a cost and foregoes an opportunity. The contract is evidence that the enterprise values the risk reduction more than the opportunity and believes the cost is reasonable.

☐ Seller and buyer may have a variety of identities and purposes. They may be individuals, partnerships, corporations, or any type of entity allowed by domestic law. The manufacturer needs to buy raw materials and sell finished goods. Buyer may be a manufacturer who will further change the goods, a wholesaler, a retailer, or a trader who has found an advantageous purchase and hopes to quickly arrange a profitable sale.

☐ The transaction may be a casual sale, but more frequently will be part of a relationship where the parties have dealt together for years.

☐ The parties may be dealing at arm's length or they may be companies related to each other by common ownership.

☐ The contract price may be huge, middling, or small.

☐ The contract may be a few words spoken by phone, or a book.

☐ Most contracts consist of standard forms drafted by lawyers for seller and buyer with negotiable terms to be filled in. Standard forms are used for valid business reasons, but are probably more important to seller as a way of controlling seller's sales agents.

☐ The subject matter of the contract, the goods, may be fungible goods like commodities or unique goods like artwork, but will most frequently be in between—goods that are neither unique nor primary goods.

☐ International sales present more risks than domestic sales. The parties are less likely to have information about each other. Seller's main risk is that he will deliver the goods but not be paid. Buyer's main risk is that he will pay but not receive the goods ordered. The irrevocable letter of credit requiring an inspection certificate is a way both parties can reduce their main risks.

☐ If a dispute arises that cannot be resolved by negotiation, the forum in which the dispute will be resolved may significantly affect the results. Wise parties choose a forum for dispute resolution in the contract.

☐ Different countries apply different choice of law rules, and will also have different substantive law rules. Choosing applicable law may reduce costs and lead to a more favorable outcome.

☐ One solution has been to promote uniform choice of law rules. A second has been to promote harmonization of domestic law rules for international contracts. A third has been to adopt standard contracts in industries. None has been very successful. The Convention on Contracts for the International Sale of Goods (CISG) is an attempt at an international *lex mercatoria* for the sale of goods.

☐ A lawyer's duty is to exercise the legal knowledge, skill, thoroughness, and preparation reasonably necessary for the representation. This requires a thorough knowledge of CISG and the ways in which it differs from domestic law.

☐ CISG is United States law.

CHAPTER 2 Interpretation

☐ In interpreting CISG, it is important to know differences in law drafting and interpretation between common law and civil law countries.

☐ Civil law statutes are short and general. They leave much room for "the appreciation of the judge."

☐ In interpreting statutes, civil law states use general principles to supply content for more specific provisions.

☐ A prime source of law is the writing of distinguished professors in civil law systems.

☐ Civil law systems do not consider previous judicial opinions sources of law.

☐ If previous judicial opinions are considered, no distinction is made there between holding and dictum.

☐ CISG specifies that its international character is to be considered in its interpretation. This calls for consideration of different business practices as well as different legal systems.

☐ CISG calls for uniformity of its interpretation across national boundaries. Difficult because of lack of resources, this nonetheless requires courts to consider interpretations made in other countries.

☐ CISG asks that in choosing between interpretations of it, consideration be given to whether one interpretation will be more conducive to encouraging good faith in international sales.

☐ CISG states that where a matter is not specifically dictated by CISG, but is generally covered by it, the matter should be decided by general principles of CISG. There is much disagreement on the substance of those general principles.

☐ When there is no specific CISG provision and no general principle of CISG can resolve the case, recourse should be had to the domestic law chosen by the parties or by the choice of law principles of the forum.

☐ CISG also contains rules for determining the intent of the parties to the contract. Intent can be gleaned from the parties' statements or actions, from their prior dealings, or from trade custom.

☐ The subjective intent of a party's words or conduct will govern if the other party should have understood them.

☐ If there is no reason for the other party to understand words or conduct, they will be interpreted objectively in accord with what a reasonable person in the position of the other party would have understood, considering all the facts and circumstances surrounding the case.

☐ This broad scope for evidence of intent means that the U.S. parol evidence rule often cannot be invoked to limit the introduction of evidence of intent. Parties can invoke the parol evidence rule if they make that clear in their contract.

☐ In the absence of evidence to the contrary, the parties are assumed to incorporate any customs in the international trade in the goods involved into their contract. This requires proof both of the custom and of the fact that it is widely known and observed in the particular international trade.

☐ Dealings of the parties from prior similar contracts can be used to determine their intent on this contract. The prior dealings must be consistent, relevant to the question at hand, and under similar circumstances.

☐ Dealings of the parties in administering the contract in dispute may also provide evidence of the contract's meaning.

☐ In a conflict between trade custom and dealings of the parties, dealings of the parties should prevail as more accurately demonstrating the intent of the parties.

CHAPTER 3 Policies Behind CISG

☐ CISG establishes default rules. Those rules are most successful when they anticipate the rules that the parties would have written for themselves had they possessed perfect foresight, enough time, and unlimited resources.

☐ The parties, with a few exceptions, can change these rules.

☐ The rules the parties would have negotiated usually involved keeping costs low, reducing the opportunity for strategic behavior, and fundamental fairness.

☐ Costs can be kept low by assigning responsibility to the person in the best position to fulfill those responsibilities. That will usually be either the person in possession, the person with the greater knowledge, or the person who can do what is required at the least cost.

☐ Requiring prompt notice of matters amiss in the relationship is one way in which strategic behavior is reduced.

CHAPTER 4 Scope

☐ CISG applies to some, but not all, international contracts for the sale of goods. CISG's terms are used to determine whether it applies.

☐ Technically, CISG is a contract between states, obliging the courts of signatory states to apply it when appropriate. In fact, it is often applied when appropriate by non-signatory states and by arbitral tribunals.

☐ CISG applies to contracts for the sale of goods between parties who have their places of business in different states, and either: (1) those states are both contracting states or (2) the applicable choice of law rule points to the law of a contracting state, and the forum state has not opted out of that provision.

☐ CISG does not apply if the actual internationality of the contract is not apparent to both parties by the time the contract is concluded.

☐ An agent for an undisclosed principal should be considered a party.

☐ Where a party has more than one place of business, the place of business that has the closest connection to the contract and its performance is the place used.

☐ A party must do business at a place for more than a limited time to qualify it as a place of business.

☐ A place of business may be a branch, or may be separately organized.

☐ An agent may or may not be a place of business of the principal.

☐ A sale obligates seller to deliver and transfer property in goods or documents and buyer must pay the price and take delivery. Whether a sale has taken place depends on the substance of the transaction, not its form.

☐ A sale includes a barter.

☐ In the absence of other evidence, there is no sale between a consignor and his consignee.

☐ A sale may take place within a framework agreement such as a distribution, exclusive supply, or requirements contract if the goods and quantity are identifiable. A framework agreement without such specification is not governed by CISG.

- [ ] CISG does not define goods. Anything that is physically deliverable may qualify as goods. Land or buildings do not qualify unless the contract calls for the buildings to be delivered.

- [ ] Some goods are not governed by CISG. They include investment securities, negotiable instruments, money, ships, aircraft, or electricity.

- [ ] The provision of services is not the sale of goods, but the sale of goods often involves ancillary services. A contract is governed by CISG unless the value of the services provided exceeds the value of the goods, considering that the cost of labor and other services required to produce goods are not counted as services.

- [ ] A contract is not governed by CISG if buyer provides a substantial part of the value of materials used to make the goods.

- [ ] CISG does not govern contracts for goods bought for "personal, family or household use" unless seller neither knew nor ought to have known of that purpose.

- [ ] Parties may exclude CISG or any of its elements. They may also choose to be governed by CISG even though in the absence of the election, they would not be.

- [ ] CISG does not govern torts suits, though tort damages may be recovered if they result from breach of contract.

- [ ] CISG does not determine title to property, though it does allocate the risk of loss.

- [ ] CISG does not apply to determine the validity of a contract or any of its clauses unless it applies by its terms. This certainly applies to capacity and duress. Whether it applies to other questions of validity, voidability, or enforceability is unclear.

- [ ] CISG does not govern set-offs against the contract of other responsibilities between the parties resulting from other transactions.

- [ ] Where CISG applies in the U.S., it preempts comparable state contract law and tort issues that are essentially breach of contract. The federal courts have federal question jurisdiction without regard to the amount in controversy.

CHAPTER 5 Formation and Re-formation

☐ CISG specifically says a contract is formed by offer and. acceptance. Contracts can also be formed by mutual consent even though identifying an offer and an acceptance would be artificial.

☐ CISG does not result in liability for failure to negotiate a sales contract. The laws of some member states prescribe liability for failure to negotiate in good faith.

☐ An offer is a definable proposal to specific persons indicating an intent to be bound in case of acceptance. The identity of the goods and quantity to be sold must be determinable. The price if not specified or determinable is fair market value if one can be ascertained.

☐ An advertisement is not normally an offer, but it may be an offer if the quantity to be sold is stated to be limited to the first number of people who respond with credit cards.

☐ The dealings of the parties may indicate that one or both parties do not intend to be bound until all points are resolved or until the contract is integrated into a formal writing.

☐ An offer is effective when it reaches the offeree.

☐ An offer is revocable unless it indicates that it is not, or unless the offeree reasonably thinks it is irrevocable and acts to his detriment in reliance on irrevocability.

☐ Express rejection terminates an offer.

☐ Acceptance is effective when received.

☐ Silence does not normally accept an offer, but it may be acceptance of new terms proposed in a confirmation or other communication to which the recipient does not object.

☐ Acceptance can be by conduct, but tribunals should be careful to assure that the conduct unambiguously indicates consent.

☐ Normally, acceptance must be of all the terms of the contract.

☐ Where the contract is executory, a purported acceptance proposing differing terms rejects the original offer and is itself a new offer.

☐ Where the contract has been partially performed, some courts count the performance as acceptance of the last written offer, while others find that the contract consists only of those clauses on which the parties have agreed.

☐ After a contract has been concluded, later communications can only be proposals to amend the contract.

☐ Neither consideration nor a writing is required for most contracts, but a writing may be required when one of the parties has a place of business in a state that has reserved to art. 11.

☐ A contract can be amended by mere agreement in words or conduct unless the contract specifies that it must be amended in writing. Even then, it can be amended by conduct.

☐ Where a contract is amended either orally or by conduct, it may be clear that the amendment has taken place, but unclear what the terms of the amendment might be.

☐ The terms of a contract are the terms to which the parties have agreed.

☐ Terms communicated after the contract has been concluded are not terms of the contract, but proposals to amend the contract.

☐ To be a term of the contract, the non-proposing party needs to know that the term is part of the contract, and what the term is. That person also needs to have a reasonable opportunity to consider the term before being bound.

☐ Standard terms printed on invoices are not part of the contract.

☐ Where parties exchange forms with contradictory standard terms, courts sometimes find that the contract was concluded orally so it does not contain the standard terms of either party.

CHAPTER 6 Seller Delivers, Risk of Loss, Conformity of Goods & Third-Party Claims

☐ Seller's main obligation is to deliver physical possession and the ownership of the goods or documents agreed upon free from known intellectual property claims.

☐ The time and place of delivery are crucial to many aspects of seller's performance. They determine where and when the goods or documents must conform, where and when seller must fulfill other obligations, and where and when buyer must pay.

☐ Seller must deliver the goods or documents where and when the contract provides. Usually, parties will provide the place of delivery and passage of risk of loss by using a recognized trade term.

☐ When the contract does not provide and if carriage of goods is involved, seller delivers by handing the goods to the first carrier. The first carrier is someone other than seller or buyer.

☐ Passage of risk of loss from seller to buyer generally occurs on delivery.

☐ Delivery is often made by delivering documents conferring the right to eventual possession of goods.

☐ Trade terms usually do not include a time for delivery. CISG provides that delivery must be within a reasonable time unless the parties have otherwise provided.

☐ Where trade terms are used that can be derived from more than one source, it is important to specify the source.

☐ Students should know the different responsibilities that go with trade terms fob, cif, and the d terms.

☐ In the European Union, there is generally adjudicatory jurisdiction at the place of performance of a sales contract.

☐ Goods must normally conform to the contract. This means that they must comply with the quantity and quality called for by the contract, and be accompanied by any required documents.

☐ Goods must be fit for the purposes for which such goods are ordinarily used.

☐ In the absence of other specifications, the goods must be marketable.

☐ Seller is liable for failure of the goods to be fit for any unusual purpose known to seller before conclusion of the contract, except where it was unreasonable for buyer to rely on seller's skill.

☐ Where seller provides buyer with a model or sample of the goods sufficient to discover any nonconformity, seller is not liable for failure of the goods to conform in ways that should have been discovered from the model or sample.

☐ Seller is not liable for nonconformity of which buyer was aware when the contract was concluded.

☐ Seller is not liable for nonconformity where it was unreasonable for buyer to rely on seller's skill.

☐ Seller is liable for failure to package the goods adequately for their anticipated transport.

☐ Conformity requirements can be disclaimed by mutual agreement.

☐ Goods must conform at the time and place where risk of loss passes.

☐ Seller is responsible for complying with legal regulations in buyer's country except when the rules are difficult to ascertain and seller has no good commercial reasons for discovering them.

☐ Buyer is obligated to examine the goods in a reasonable manner as soon as practicable and to give specific notice to seller of nonconformity within a reasonable time.

☐ Prompt and specific notice is required in order to give seller opportunity to cure, to provide reliable evidence of the nonconformity and when it occurred, and to limit disputes about conformity to the nonconformities listed in the notice.

☐ The timeliness of the notice depends on the nature of the goods, whether the defect is obvious or hidden, the examination required to discover it, and the status of buyer. Less time is allowed for perishable or seasonal goods. Hidden defects should be reported as soon as a reasonable buyer would have discovered them. A person who does not regularly deal in the goods concerned has longer to report nonconformities than a person in the business.

☐ The notice of nonconformity must relate the symptoms, but does not require buyer to divine the ultimate cause.

☐ Buyer who does not give timely and specific notice of nonconformity cannot rely on any remedies provided for nonconformity unless excused. Buyer is excused if seller could not have been unaware of the defect and did not inform buyer of it. If buyer can show reasonable excuse for failure to give timely and specific notice, buyer retains the remedies of price reduction and damages (but not for lost profits), but not the remedies of specific performance or avoidance.

☐ Seller must deliver the goods free from any unexcepted non-IP right or claim of a third party.

☐ Seller must also deliver goods free from any unexpected right or claim based on intellectual property in buyer's state, or a state where the parties contemplated that the goods would be resold or used, but only if seller could not have been unaware of the right or claim, there was no reason for buyer to be aware of the claim, and the claim did not result from following buyer's instructions.

CHAPTER 7 Buyer Accepts and Pays

☐ Buyer is obligated to accept conforming goods and pay for them.

☐ The only way for buyer to assure inspection before payment is to provide for it in the sales contract or to provide for payment at a later date.

☐ Payment is made in the currency specified. In the absence of specification, it is made in the currency of the place of payment.

☐ Buyer taking delivery of more goods than ordered is obligated to pay for the excess. Buyer can refuse the excess, but must take care to prevent the goods from being exposed to theft or damage.

☐ Buyer can likewise refuse to take delivery of nonconforming goods, but must take care to prevent the goods from being exposed to theft or damage.

CHAPTER 8 Breach

☐ CISG distinguishes between breaches and fundamental breaches.

☐ A fundamental breach entitles the aggrieved party to avoid the contract. With other breaches, the aggrieved party must perform as best he can, and his remedies include damages, price reduction, and specific performance, but not avoidance.

☐ Any failure to adhere to the contract is a breach.

☐ A fundamental breach occurs when the other party is substantially deprived of what he is entitled to expect under the contract, provided this is foreseeable.

☐ The parties can specify in their contract breaches that will constitute a fundamental breach.

☐ Some courts define substantial deprivation as a percentage of completion, but there is no agreement about the percentage needed.

☐ Other courts define substantial deprivation as a situation where the aggrieved party has no reasonable use for what has been promised.

☐ Goods that can be easily and inexpensively repaired are not a fundamental breach.

☐ Goods that can be easily resold are not a fundamental breach if seller regularly does business in such goods.

☐ Failure to deliver seasonal goods by a date early enough for the seasonal market is a fundamental breach.

☐ A defect in documents that would prevent their transfer is likely to be a fundamental breach.

☐ Failure of buyer to pay anything is a fundamental breach.

☐ Buyer may commit a fundamental breach by reselling the goods in a prohibited territory.

☐ The party committing the breach must be able to foresee that it will be fundamental.

CHAPTER 9 Excused Performance

☐ CISG generally requires parties to perform their contractual obligations.

☐ Performance is excused if a party rightfully avoids the contract.

☐ A party may suspend performance temporarily if it becomes apparent that the other party will not perform a substantial part of his obligations as a result of: (a) a serious deficiency in his ability to perform or in his creditworthiness; or (b) his conduct in preparing to perform or in performing the contract. The suspender must immediately give notice of the suspension. If the other party provides reasonable assurance of performance, the suspender must perform.

☐ A party may avoid the contract if it is clear that the other party will commit a fundamental breach (anticipatory fundamental breach). Requirements for this are substantively the same as for suspension, and the result is more to the party's liking.

☐ A fundamental breach of one installment of an installment contract permits the aggrieved party to avoid the contract for that installment.

☐ A fundamental breach of one installment may, under appropriate facts, constitute a fundamental breach of the entire contract.

☐ Liability for damages is temporarily excused if: (1) the failure is due to (2) an impediment that is (3) beyond his control and (4) he could not reasonably have been expected to have taken into account and (5) whose consequences for the contract he could not have avoided or overcome. The party must give prompt notice to avoid damages. All these terms should be interpreted in the context of what is commercially reasonable.

☐ An impediment is not unforeseeable if it is within the party's normal sphere of operation.

☐ The exemption from liability for damages disappears with respect to actions after the impediment is removed or it could be overcome.

☐ Other remedies such as price reduction or avoidance are available to the aggrieved party.

☐ There is no doctrine of excuse for hardship in CISG.

☐ It is unclear what adequate assurance might be. Performing the contract is adequate assurance where the complaint is failure to perform, but a party cannot demand more than the contract requires as adequate assurance. It appears that adequate assurance may be an oral or written statement that the party will perform the contract.

☐ A party is excused from performing if prevented from doing so by the other party.

CHAPTER 10 Non-Judicial Remedies

☐ If seller performs early and buyer notifies seller that the goods or documents are non-conforming, seller may cure the nonconformity up to the time of performance if the cure does not cause buyer unreasonable inconvenience or unreasonable expense.

- ☐ After the time set for performance, seller may still cure subject to the above and also on condition that buyer has not avoided the contract and that buyer is certain of reimbursement for cure expenses that buyer advances.

- ☐ A credible offer to cure makes a fundamental breach non-fundamental.

- ☐ Buyer loses the remedy of price reduction if buyer refuses a cure.

- ☐ Where seller offers to cure, if buyer fails to respond within a reasonable time, seller may perform within the time he has specified.

- ☐ Buyers can call on sellers to repair the goods to make them conform, as long as this is not unreasonable.

- ☐ Repair would be unreasonable if it were more costly than replacement.

- ☐ Buyer can only demand replacement goods if the breach is fundamental.

- ☐ A U.S. court is unlikely to order repair or replacement because it is a form of specific performance.

- ☐ CISG has no provision giving buyer the right to cure defective performance, but one might be implied because most remedies accorded to either buyer or seller are reciprocal.

- ☐ Either party may fix a reasonable additional period for the other party to perform their contractual obligations. This is called *nachfrist*. Granting additional time is strongly advised as a practical matter because it demonstrates reasonableness.

- ☐ Setting a date for performance to which the other party does not timely object raises a presumption that the period is reasonable.

- ☐ It is unclear whether a reasonable time is computed from what is reasonable for buyer, what is reasonable for seller, or what is reasonable for both.

- ☐ In determining whether the time given was reasonable, courts have included the time after the expiration of the time stated but before the contract is declared avoided in determining whether the time was reasonable.

- ☐ Where seller breaches, buyer may reduce the price to an amount that bears the same proportion to the contract price as the value of the goods delivered bears to the value that conforming goods would have had.

☐ Price reduction is a substitute for damages suffered when the value of goods delivered (or not delivered) is less than the value of the goods ordered. Damages may not be collected for that loss, but price reduction can be combined with damages for other losses.

☐ Price reduction may be hard to use in cases where it is difficult to value the goods. A cover transaction is likely to be more persuasive than opinion evidence of value.

☐ Where the contract gives buyer the right to make choices about the goods but buyer refuses to choose, seller may make the choice subject to buyer's objection.

☐ A party can avoid the contract if the other party commits a fundamental breach, or if the other party does not deliver, the injured party grants additional time (*nachfrist*), and the other party does not deliver within the reasonable additional time.

☐ To avoid the contract, one party must send timely notice of avoidance to the other. Courts have construed notices liberally to find that they are notices of avoidance.

☐ When a contract is avoided, buyer returns the goods, seller returns the purchase price, and neither price reduction nor specific performance is a permissible remedy.

☐ Delivering nothing is non-delivery. Delivering the wrong quantity of the goods ordered, or delivering the right quantity of nonconforming goods, or paying only part of the purchase price, is not non-delivery. Whether delivery of entirely different goods than those ordered is non-delivery remains to be seen.

☐ With an installment contract, whether there has been delivery is determined installment by installment.

☐ Buyer may not avoid the contract if buyer cannot return the delivered goods to seller in substantially the same condition in which buyer received them. However, buyer can still avoid the contract if part of the goods have deteriorated as a result of the required examination on arrival; if they have been sold, processed, or transformed in the ordinary course of buyer's business before buyer ought to have discovered the lack of conformity; or if the inability to restore goods to seller is not due to buyer's act or omission.

☐ Seller's return of the purchase price must be accompanied by interest. Courts have used a number of different measures to determine the rate of interest and whether it is simple or compound.

☐ Buyer must account to seller for any value received as a result of having possession of the goods.

☐ Buyer in possession of the goods must preserve them and arrange to convey them to seller. The cost of doing so is likely to be part of the damages suffered.

☐ Goods may be sold if they are likely to spoil before the other party can obtain and dispose of them. All goods may be sold if the other party does not take possession within a reasonable time.

☐ A party who properly elects avoidance after a breach may also collect damages suffered.

CHAPTER 11 Judicial Remedies

☐ No tribunal may grant either buyer or seller extra time to perform the contract. The parties may agree to extra time, and are encouraged to use the *nachfrist* procedure.

☐ Specific performance of the contract is an available remedy. There are few decided cases about it, as aggrieved parties usually prefer avoidance and damages.

☐ Both avoidance and price reduction are inconsistent with specific performance, so an aggrieved party who elects either remedy may not seek specific performance.

☐ Requesting a cure and granting extra time are both consistent with specific performance.

☐ A court need not order specific performance where it would not order it in a similar case under domestic law.

☐ Under U.S. law, specific performance is usually available only when the remedy at law is inadequate, usually because the goods are unique or it would be difficult for the aggrieved person to secure a substitute transaction.

☐ However, a U.S. court is likely to enforce an arbitral decision calling for specific performance.

☐ Damages may be awarded for all losses suffered as a result of contract breach, including lost profits.

☐ Damages are limited to those that the breacher ought to have foreseen as possible when making the contract. They do not include damages that the victim could have avoided by mitigation. Damages only include losses that are reasonably certain.

☐ Damages are intended to put the parties in the economic position they would have occupied had the contract been performed. In easy cases, that might only be the cost to repair the goods to be equal to what was promised, or the difference in value between what was promised and what was delivered.

☐ Damages may include seller's cost of reselling goods buyer has refused; buyer's liability to sub-buyers for malfunction of goods buyer has resold; or loss of buyer's resale profits.

☐ There are two special provisions for damages when the contract is avoided. When the aggrieved party reasonably covers, the aggrieved party may claim damages as the difference between the contract price and the cover price. When there is no cover, it is the difference between the contract price and the fair market value. The aggrieved party is not limited to these measures of damages.

☐ Even where there is no avoidance, parties have successfully used those damages measures.

☐ To be liable for damages, the breaching party must have been able to foresee the type of damages that would result from the breach by the time the contract was concluded. It is less clear that he must foresee the amount of those damages.

☐ Some cases have questioned whether resale of the goods by buyer is foreseeable.

☐ The aggrieved party is charged with mitigation, reducing the amount of damage caused by the breach as much as is commercially reasonable. In a declining market, an aggrieved buyer is charged as though he had found substitute goods within a reasonable time at the then-prevailing market price.

☐ The aggrieved party must even be willing to mitigate with the breacher, or with the aggrieved party's competitor.

☐ Damages for buyer's breach should be paid in the currency called for in the contract. Damages for seller's breach should normally be paid in buyer's currency. Some courts order damages paid in the currency of the court.

☐ Damages include general dispute resolution costs. They do not include attorney's fees. Whether attorney's fees of the prevailing party in the breach of contract action can be recovered depends on the domestic law of the forum. Attorney's fees incurred to defend suits resulting from the breach are included in damages.

☐ Damages include compensation for lost volume of sales.

☐ The parties may limit or modify their liability for damages, or provide for liquidated damages, to the extent that such a provision would be valid under domestic law.

☐ Interest is due on any sum in arrears. Alternatively, interest can be recovered as damages when it can be proven.

☐ Most courts hold that interest on damages begins to accrue at the time of breach, even though the amount of the liability is unknown at the time.

☐ Courts are in disagreement about whether interest is simple or compound and the rate of interest.

☐ Interest is paid in the currency in which the sum on which interest is calculated is paid.

CHAPTER 12 Procedure

☐ The procedure in CISG cases is normally dictated by the law of the forum.

☐ CISG specifically places the burden of proof for excuse from paying damages due to an impediment on the person seeking the excuse.

☐ CISG does not speak specifically to the burden of proof in other situations.

☐ The party seeking recovery under a general rule has the burden of proving its elements, while a party seeking an exception to a general rule needs to prove the elements of the exception.

☐ The burden of proving nonconformity of goods is on the party alleging it.

☐ If the UN Limitations Convention applies, the statute of limitations is four years from delivery of the goods.

☐ If the UN Limitations Convention does not apply, the statute of limitations is determined by the choice of law rule of the forum, which usually points to forum law as procedural.

CHAPTER 13 Letters of Credit

☐ The letter of credit is comparatively inexpensive and responds to seller's principal problem of not being paid, while being flexible enough to accommodate buyer's principal problem of paying but not receiving the goods ordered.

☐ Buyer asks her bank to issue an irrevocable letter of credit for the purchase price. Buyer's bank sends a communication to seller's bank promising to pay a fixed amount on presentation of named documents within a specified period. Seller's bank notifies seller that it has received the letter of credit. For payment, seller presents the specified documents to seller's bank and is paid. Seller's bank presents those documents to buyer's bank and is credited with the amount. Seller's bank pays seller.

☐ Buyer is only protected if one of the required documents is a certificate from a reputable inspector that the goods conform to the contract.

☐ The letter of credit transaction is not governed by CISG, but by domestic law and an international trade custom incorporated in the contract called Uniform Customs and Practices for Documentary Credit (UCP).

☐ The sales contract and the letter of credit are separate contracts. Breach of the sales contract is not a defense to a request for payment under the letter of credit.

☐ To compel payment, documents must strictly comply with the letter of credit. Strict compliance means that a reasonable bank examiner believes that the documents are genuine and refer to the same transaction in the manner called for by the letter of credit.

☐ Banks are usually insulated from liability in letter of credit transactions if they act in good faith.

☐ A court may temporarily enjoin the payment of a letter of credit if a material document is forged, materially fraudulent, or payment of the letter of credit would facilitate a material fraud by the beneficiary on the issuer or the applicant. An injunction will not issue unless the remedy at law is inadequate and buyer is likely to prevail at trial. A court will not enjoin payment to a holder in due course.

CHAPTER 14 U.S. Income Tax Considerations

☐ Income tax considerations may influence whether a sale of goods takes place and is likely to influence its form.

☐ The U.S. taxes the worldwide income of its citizens, residents, and corporations.

☐ To relieve double taxation on foreign income that is taxed abroad, the U.S. grants a foreign tax credit for foreign income taxes paid.

☐ The foreign tax credit is limited to the percentage of U.S. income tax due that taxpayer's foreign source taxable income bears to taxpayer's total taxable income.

☐ Income from the manufacture and sale of goods is sourced at the place of manufacture.

☐ Income from the purchase and sale of goods is sourced at the place where title to the goods passes.

☐ By changing the place where delivery occurs, the parties can change income from the purchase and sale of goods from U.S. source to foreign source, thereby increasing taxpayer's potential foreign tax credit.

☐ Changing the source of income from U.S. source to foreign source may also be advantageous to a nonresident alien or foreign corporation.

☐ Tax treaties allocate taxing rights between the parties who sign the treaty. Generally, source countries may tax business income only if taxpayer has significant economic activity there. Investment income is either exempt or lightly taxed in the source country, reserving most taxing rights to the residence country.

☐ In addition to the above, special rules apply when buyer and seller are related parties, either as parent and subsidiary or as commonly owned entities. The first rule is that related parties will not be recognized as separate entities unless they have substantive business activities and are not lifeless facades.

☐ Sales between related parties must be at arm's length prices. For the sale of goods, an arm's length price may be determined by the most accurate of six methods: comparable uncontrolled price, resale price, cost-plus, comparable profits, profit split, or another reasonably persuasive method.

☐ In addition, certain income of controlled foreign corporations is taxed currently to its U.S. shareholders.

☐ A controlled foreign corporation is a non-U.S. corporation more than 50% of whose stock is owned by no more than five U.S. citizens, residents, or corporations, each of whom owns at least 10% of the corporation's stock.

☐ Foreign base company sales income is one form of a controlled foreign corporation's income that is taxed currently to its shareholders. Foreign base company sales income does not include income from the manufacture of goods by the corporation.

Index

A

Acceptance
  By conduct, 5.04
  Of goods, 7.01, 7.04, 8.04, 9.03, 11.13
  Of offer, 5.04
  Of payment, 7.01
  Of seller's offer to cure. 10.06
  Of standard terms, 5.08
  Refusal to accept, 11.23, 11.28, 11.43
  Time for, 5.04
Amend the Contract, see Modify
Anticipatory breach, 9.02–04, 9.08,
  11.12
Applicability of CISG, 4.01–71
Arbitration, 4.21, 5.04, 6.20, 11.14, 11.30,
  11.42, 12.05
  Or litigation, 1.11–12
Astreint, 11.11
Attorneys' Fees, 11.30
Auction, 4.35
Average quality, See Quality of Goods
Avoidance, 11.12
  Damages on, 11.25, 11.28
  Interest payable, 11.42
  Notice of, see Notice
  Requirements, 3.03, 3.05, 6.51, 8.01,
    8.03, 9.01–03, 9.05–08, 10.41–51

B

Barter, 4.32
Battle of the Forms, 5:08–09
Bill of Lading, 1.05, 6.02, 13.01
Boilerplate, see Standard Terms

Breach, 6.12, 8.01–06
  Anticipatory, see Anticipatory Breach
  Burden of proof for, 12.02–03
  Caused by the other party, 9.09
  Compensation for, 2.05
  Cure of, see Cure
  Delivery, failure to accept, see
    Acceptance
  Excused, see Excused Performance
  Fundamental, see Fundamental
    Breach
  Nondelivery of required documents
    as, 6.11, 8.04, 10.02, 10.42, 10.44
  Of Installment, see Installment
    Contracts
  Of quality of goods, 4.12
  Of sales contract and letter of credit,
    13.02, 13.05
  Of title or intellectual property
    obligations, 6.41–43
  Or tort, 4.62, 4.71
  Partial, see Fundamental Breach
  Payment, failure of, 7.01
  Place of, conferring jurisdiction, 1.12,
    6.01
  Remedies for, 3.05, 10.01–21,
    10.41–51, 11.01–44
Burden of Proof, 2.03, 9.04, 10.21,
  12.01–04
Business, Place of, see Place of Business
Business Reasons for Tax Advantaged
  Structure, 14.14

291